D0982635

King of the Delawares:
TEEDYUSCUNG
1700-1763

by

ANTHONY F. C. WALLACE

SYRACUSE UNIVERSITY PRESS

Syracuse University Press Edition 1990
90 91 92 93 94 95 96   6 5 4 3 2 1

This book is published with the assistance of a grant from the John Ben Snow Foundation.

The paper used in this publication meets the minimum requirements of American National Standard for Information Sciences—Permanence of Paper for Printed Library Materials, ANSI Z39.48-1984. ∞

Library of Congress Cataloging-in-Publication Data

Wallace, Anthony F. C., 1923–
    King of the Delawares: Teedyuscung, 1700–1763/Anthony F. C. Wallace.
        p.   cm. — (The Iroquois and their neighbors)
    Reprint. Originally published: Philadelphia: University of Pennsylvania Press, 1949.
    ISBN 0-8156-2498-0
    1. Teedyuscung, Delaware chief, 1700–1775. 2. Delaware Indians—History. 3. Pennsylvania—History—Colonial period, ca. 1600–1775. I. Title. II. Series
E99.D2T4   1990
974.8′00497302—dc20
[B]   90-44170
                                                            CIP

MANUFACTURED IN THE UNITED STATES OF AMERICA

To

MY MOTHER AND FATHER

This very Ground that is under me was my Land and Inheritance, and is taken from me by Fraud; when I say this Ground, I mean all the Land lying between *Tohiccon Creek* and *Wioming,* on the River *Sasquehannah.*

                                                            TEEDYUSCUNG

Contents

Maps

Preface

In the forty-one years since the first publication of this biography of Teedyuscung, there have appeared a number of excellent books and papers on the history and culture of the Delaware Indians. The reader who wishes to learn more about Delaware culture in the late precontact and colonial periods may profitably consult the monograph by William W. Newcomb, Jr., *The Culture and Acculturation of the Delaware Indians* (Ann Arbor: Museum of Anthropology, University of Michigan, 1956); the book by Herbert C. Kraft, *The Lenape: Archaeology, History, and Ethnography* (Newark: New Jersey Historical Society, 1986); and the article by Ives Goddard, "Delaware," in vol. 15, *Northeast,* of *Handbook of North American Indians,* ed. Bruce G. Trigger, 213–39 (Washington, D.C.: Smithsonian Institution, 1978). For those wanting a more detailed historical chronicle of the Delaware Indians and their migrations in the eighteenth and nineteenth centuries, there are the works of Charles A. Weslager, particularly *The Delaware Indians: A History* (New Brunswick: Rutgers University Press, 1972) and *The Delaware Indian Westward Migration* (Wallingford: Middle Atlantic Press, 1978). Mention should also be made of Francis Jennings's study of the role of James Logan, the Penn family's representative in Pennsylvania, in arranging the infamous Walking Purchase: "The Scandalous Indian Policy of William Penn's Sons: Deeds and

Documents of the Walking Purchase," *Pennsylvania History* 37 (1970): 19–39.

Although the brief ethnographic sketch and the historical account given in my book remain substantially valid and the book is reprinted without revision, some of the newer scholarship has emphasized a somewhat different view of the contact history of the Delaware and other northeastern Indians. This trend promotes an image of the natives not merely as subordinate imitators in the acculturation process but also as active and innovative agents in their own adaptation to the European presence. Noteworthy here are the scholarly articles and dissertations of such younger scholars as Marshall Becker and Robert Grumet.

It has been a number of years since I have done research on Delaware Indian ethnohistory. After completing the Teedyuscung biography during the course of graduate work and later publishing a companion piece, "New Religions among the Delaware Indians, 1600–1900" (*Southwestern Journal of Anthropology* 12 [1956]: 1–21), my attention turned to their northern neighbors, the Iroquois, and their famous religious prophet, Handsome Lake. But I did come back to Delaware subjects again in the 1950s and 1960s, when I was retained by Felix Cohen's Joint Efforts Group as principal researcher and expert witness on behalf of the Delaware and other American Indian communities whose ancestors once owned lands north of the Ohio and east of the Missouri rivers. In this work I was assisted by my fellow anthropologist Michal Lowenfels Kane. At that time many tribal groups were bringing suit before the Indian Claims Commission for fair financial compensation for lands sold to the United States in the eighteenth and nineteenth centuries. My own research and testimony on Delaware claims particularly involved lands they occupied in Ohio and Indiana, after emigrating from New Jersey and Pennsylvania.

Teedyuscung, who so strenuously objected to the Walking Purchase, would have been pleased to see his descendants receive at least some recompense for some of their lands, lost so long ago.

A. F. C. W.

Rockdale
January 1990

Preface to the First Edition

This book tells the story of Teedyuscung, a Delaware Indian. It is not simply an historical treatise, or an ethnographical one; it is also, and primarily, a biography. As such it deals in discussions of emotions, motives, and states of mind —intangible matters, indeed, but the stuff of which a life is made—which would lie outside the province of the pure historian or ethnographer. Inference about such things is no enemy to fact, however. I have tried to avoid jumping to conclusions for which there was no evidence; and fortunately Teedyuscung is unique among eighteenth-century Indians for the wealth of material to be found about him in the printed and manuscript archives. Because of his demands for settlement of Delaware land grievances, probably no other Indian in Pennsylvania's colonial history, not even the legendary Tammany or Tamanend, has attracted so much notoriety, or so many casual chroniclers.

Although I have tried to write in idiomatic English rather than in psychological jargon, I have been guided largely by the "culture-and-personality" approach of anthropology. I hope that the book will be of interest not only to historians of the colonial period but also to those anthropologists and psychologists who are studying the effects upon personality of contact between European and "primitive" cultures. The materials in this biography, with its emphasis on drawing (as fully as somewhat meager data permit) a sketch of Teedyus-

cung as a man, constitute one of the few adequately docu-
mented case histories available from the era of colonization.
It is of especial significance, it seems to me, that Teedyuscung
played a prominent role in determining the actual course of
historical events affecting both the Delawares and the Europeans in America. It is the case history of an important man.

For the sake of simplicity in the text certain liberties have
been taken with the standard orthography of Indian names.
The name *Teedyuscung* itself is spelled *Tedyuscung* in the
Handbook of American Indians North of Mexico; I have preferred to use the double *e* because nearly all of the official
colonial records employ this spelling. In the matter of Indian
plurals, I have deliberately Anglicized them with the suffixes
s and *es,* although the *Handbook* in many cases recommends
using the same form for both single and plural (as, *a Shawnee*
and *the Shawnee*).

In direct quotations the archaisms and errors of spelling
and punctuation have been preserved.

A word about the calendar is needed. Before 1752, the
official colonial records for Pennsylvania were dated after the
Julian system, according to which the new calendar year
began on March 25. The Moravian records, however, were
already being kept according to the Gregorian system, which
introduced the new year on January 1. In 1752 Great Britain
and her colonies adopted the Gregorian calendar, dropping
eleven days from the month of September so as to make up
the Julian deficit, and celebrating the new year of 1753 on
January 1, 1752/53. The official dates prior to 1753 have
been corrected to conform with the Gregorian calendar,
which we use today, in so far as the yearly reckoning is concerned; but the daily reckonings before 1752 have been
allowed to keep the old Julian numbering.

The encouragement and assistance of a number of persons
have contributed largely to the merits of the book.

The late Charles B. Montgomery of Philadelphia first suggested to me the fitness of Teedyuscung as a subject for biography. Upon his extraordinary knowledge of the manuscript sources, and his discerning familiarity with almost every character in pre-Revolutionary Pennsylvania, I have leaned very heavily, both in the gathering of the materials and in the impressions of men and events.

I wish to make special acknowledgment to Dr. Frank G. Speck, Dr. A. I. Hallowell, and Dr. Loren C. Eiseley, anthropologists at the University of Pennsylvania, for illuminating suggestion and encouragement. To my father, Dr. Paul A. W. Wallace, I owe thanks for assistance in reaching source materials and for a careful criticism of the manuscript. Mr. Edmund S. Carpenter, who also read the manuscript, gave me much appreciated advice on the choice of a title. My thanks are also due to Dr. Julian P. Boyd; to Mr. Howard H. Brinton, Custodian, and Mrs. Eleanor Melson, Secretary to the Custodian, of the Department of Records of the Yearly Meeting of the Religious Society of Friends of Philadelphia and Vicinity; to Mr. M. H. Deardorff; to Dr. Leonidas Dodson; to Dr. William N. Fenton; to the Genealogical Society of Pennsylvania; to Mr. William A. Hunter, Senior Archivist, Pennsylvania Historical Commission; to Dr. William E. Lingelbach, Librarian of the American Philosophical Society, and Miss Duncan and Miss Hess of the Library staff; to Mrs. Greta Mullin, Curator of the Dauphin County Historical Society; to Miss Helen E. Myers, Librarian at Lebanon Valley College; to Dr. Claude E. Schaeffer; to Col. Henry W. Shoemaker, formerly State Archivist of Pennsylvania, and Miss Albert and Mrs. Davenport of his staff; to Dr. St. George L. Sioussat, Chief of the Division of Manuscripts, Library of Congress; to Mr. David Wallace; to Mr. C. A. Weslager; to Mr. R. Norris Williams II, Librarian of the Historical Society of Pennsylvania, and to Miss Catherine H. Miller, Miss Sarah Bond, and Mr. Harry Givens of the Manuscript Department; and to Mr. John Witthoft.

And last but not least, to my wife I owe many stimulating suggestions about the personality of Teedyuscung and the style of the book.

A. F. C. W.

Tuscarora
July 1949.

King of the Delawares

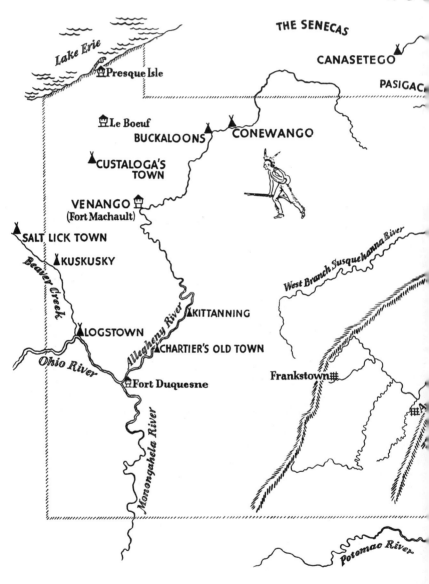

TEEDYUSCUNG'S

170(

THE SENECAS

CANASETEGO

PASIGAC

Lake Erie

⛩Presque Isle

⛩Le Boeuf

▲ BUCKALOONS ▲ CONEWANGO

▲ CUSTALOGA'S
TOWN

VENANGO ⛩
(Fort Machault)

West Branch Susquehanna River

▲ SALT LICK TOWN

▲ KUSKUSKY

Beaver Creek

▲ KITTANNING

▲ LOGSTOWN

Allegheny River

▲ CHARTIER'S OLD TOWN

Ohio River

Frankstown ▦

⛩ Fort Duquesne

▦ A

Monongahela River

Potomac River

𝔛 - Indian Camps and Villages   **⛩ - Forts**

PENNSYLVANIA
1763

ASSINISINK

Chemung R.

OWEGO

OTSENINGO

OQUAGA

TIOGA

North Branch Susquehanna River

WYALUSING

CUSHIETUNK

TUNKHANNOCK

Lackawaxen Cr.

ADJOUQUAY

THE MINISINKS

MINISINK TOWN

ONWACKIN

WYOMING

LACKAWACKA

IG ISLAND

NESCOPECK

POCOPOCO

Hess and Weeser Plantations

Penn's Cr.

SHAMOKIN
(Fort Augusta)

GNADENHÜTTEN
(Fort Allen)

HOCIUNDOQUEN

Bethlehem

WECHQUETANK

MENIOLAGOMEKA

WELAGAMEKA

NAIN

Easton

River

Lehigh River

Durham Furnace

NOCKAMIXON

Tohicon Cr.

Reading

Neshaminy Cr.

John Harris'

Trenton

arlisle

Schuylkill River

Pennsbury

Lancaster

Philadelphia

Susquehanna River

Delaware River

⊞ - Whites' Towns   🏠 - Whites' Settlements

◆{ I }◆

The Delawares
1700-1730

The Indian stands, tall and portly, with a belt of black and white wampum held before him in his outstretched hands. Behind him sprawl his followers, his warriors and councilors, seated in a rough half-moon in the dust, gaudy in the sunlight with white English shirts and brown skin and bright red paint on their faces. He faces the stiff English officers and gentlemen, and the plump, grave Quakers, and he pleads for himself and his people: pleads for peace, for teachers to instruct his children in the white man's ways, for a place to live. "We desire you will look upon us with eyes of mercy!" he cries. "We are a very poor people, our wives and children are almost naked, we are void of understanding and destitute of the necessaries of life. Pity us!"

The speaker is Teedyuscung. He can talk English, although at the moment he is speaking in the Delaware language, which the Indian interpreter at his side renders into the white man's tongue. He wears tall riding boots, for he has come down on horseback from his log cabin in the wilderness, and he wears an English gentleman's suit of clothes tailored in Philadelphia, complete to vest and a row of buttons. He has been baptized a Christian—and can drink a gallon of rum in a day without getting drunk. "I am a *Man!*" he is wont to say.

Think of Teedyuscung and remember him well: he is a man who tried to bridge in one lifetime the cleft between two

1

worlds—the white man's world and the Indian's world; and he died an alien to both.

*   *   *

Teedyuscung was born about the year 1700, east of Trenton, in New Jersey.[1] His father was Old Captain Harris, "a noted man among the Indians," and well enough able to speak the English language.[2] His half-brothers (whether by the same father or mother is not known) were Captain John, Young Captain Harris, and Tom, Joe, and Sam Evans—"a family of high-spirited sons who were not in good repute with their white neighbors."[3] They all eked out a mendicant existence on the shabby fringes of the white settlements, simultaneously dependent upon and resentful of the whites. In Teedyuscung that strange mixture of love and hatred for Europeans which he learned in New Jersey made him notorious as both the enemy and the friend of the white man; and the conflict in his nature between this love and this hatred was the leitmotif of his political career.

The vicinity of Trenton was a difficult place for a growing Indian lad in the early decades of the eighteenth century. Two kinds of people were trying to work out their separate ways of life on the same land, and the friction was rubbing the Delaware culture threadbare.

Contact between Europeans and the Indians inhabiting the Delaware River Valley had been firmly established by 1625. It is reported that the Dutch made an abortive attempt to establish a fort and trading post on the lower Delaware as early as 1598. The first Dutch settlements on Manhattan Island were made in 1609, and in 1614 Fort Nassau was built near the future site of the town of Albany, on the Hudson River; traders from these places soon entered into indirect commercial relations with the Indians in the neighborhood of Minisink, across the mountains on the upper Delaware. In 1614 Captain Hendrickson, from the Dutch colony of

New Netherlands, made a successful trading expedition up the Delaware and Schuylkill rivers. His trip led to the formation of the Dutch West India Company in 1621. In 1623 a Dutch trading post and fort was built on Delaware Bay, and thereafter the Indians of the lower Delaware River Valley remained in intimate contact with the Dutch and their Swedish and English successors.

About 1641 some Englishmen, apparently from New Haven, built a short-lived trading post on the Schuylkill which was almost immediately destroyed by the Dutch, jealous of their trade monopoly. In 1643 the Swedes of the Swedish South Company built Fort Elsenborgh close to the Dutch post of Fort Nassau, the original Dutch settlement of 1623. By 1682, when the first colonists under William Penn's charter reached Pennsylvania, the Indians of the valley had for two generations been subject to continuous and powerful acculturating influences from the whites in New York, New Jersey, Maryland, and the Philadelphia area.

The objective of all this competitive activity on the part of Europeans along the lower Delaware River was the lucrative trade in furs and peltries, together with the raising of tobacco. Two vessels leaving the Delaware River in 1644 carried with them 2,127 beaver skins—a respectable quantity for one trade center, although proportionately not as great as that furnished by the more northerly Indians around the Great Lakes to the Dutch and English at Albany. The writer is not sufficiently acquainted with the economic history of the period to be able to say with certainty how much and precisely what sort of goods were paid to the Indians of the lower Delaware, the Schuylkill, and the Susquehanna rivers for beaver and other furs and skins, but interesting food for speculation is afforded by the report of barter-prices at Albany in 1689. There, for one beaver skin, an Indian could take his choice of eight pounds of powder, forty pounds of lead, a red blanket, a white blanket, four shirts, or six pairs of stockings; and for two beavers he could get a gun. A Swedish engineer who visited

New Sweden from 1654 to 1656 accused the English in Virginia of selling guns to the Delawares at ten to twenty beavers apiece. If the modest average quantity of two thousand beavers, together with quantities of otter, mink, deer, fox, and other skins, had been traded annually on the lower Delaware for the thirty years since 1623, when the trade began in earnest, then a considerable quantity of European goods, in the form of red and blue cloth, arms and ammunition, axes, knives, hatchets, copper and brass kettles, hoes, spades, shovels, glass beads, awls, bodkins, scissors, mirrors, needles, and so forth, must have begun to circulate among the Delawares by the middle of the seventeenth century, even admitting that the Delawares were less active in trade than the Susquehannocks of the Susquehanna. And the population along the Delaware was not much over two or three thousand persons.

By 1650 the Dutch along the lower Delaware were expanding their trading posts to take up good farming country, and in 1655 the Delaware Indians of the neighborhood were sufficiently sophisticated—and alarmed—to demand changes in the barter prices, insisting that two deerskins were worth one piece of cloth. By 1657 the Dutch were being annoyed by drunken Indians. Men, women, and children alike were becoming intoxicated on beer supplied by unscrupulous traders. And by 1660 the Dutch were beginning to have serious trouble with the lower river Delawares, although here matters did not come to open war, as they did at Manhattan. Murders and reprisals, thefts and threats, kept the infant white communities continually in a stew. The impression is inescapable that by 1660 the Indians of the lower Delaware, at least in the vicinity of the settlements, were thoroughly demoralized and no longer capable of maintaining the integrity of the old tribal life.[4]

The settlement of New Jersey commenced in earnest about 1670; and in 1682 Penn's first colonists arrived at the mouth of the Delaware River. In the generation from 1670 to 1700 the great exodus began, the Delawares of the lower reaches of the Bay, southern New Jersey, the neighborhood of New York, and the lower part of the Delaware River itself, selling their lands for trade goods and recoiling upon the less influenced communities in the back country, which as yet had not been directly entered by white settlers and traders. As they moved, they carried with them the sentiments and values of trader Indians, thus infecting the more or less aboriginal communities with the virus of European tastes.

Since about 1679 white settlements had been made in the neighborhood of Teedyuscung's birthplace near Trenton, and by 1710 arrogant and contemptuous white men claimed title to most of the arable land by virtue of "Indian purchases." Smallpox, syphilis, and other white-borne plagues had been gnawing out the core of the Delaware population there since about 1600; and rum, offered in exchange for peltries and furs, was poisoning the minds of the survivors, blotting out the memory of the old culture. Rum gave momentary relief from anxiety; but in order to buy rum, the Delaware had to hunt. Game was scarce now, and to find it the Jersey Indian had to stay out in the hinterlands for longer and longer periods of time, leaving his women and children to be debauched in his absence. Too often on his return he and his family and friends engaged in an orgy of drunkenness, and in the hours of intoxication pent-up jealousies, grudges, and fears were let loose in a frenzy of mayhem and murder. The old arts were dying in Jersey. Pottery, stone cutting and pounding tools, leather garments, the bow, utensils of bark and bone, ornaments of shell, were no longer widely used, because the Delaware depended on the white man to supply him with guns and ammunition, copper kettles, steel knives, hatchets and hoes, stroud blankets, and the rest of the long list of trader's goods. And all of these things had to be paid for with land or with skins and furs. Hence the atmosphere, which when the whites first landed had been one of mutual tolerance and respect, was now electric with suspicion. The Jersey Delaware could not live without the white man's goods, yet he suspected that the white man was scheming to steal his land. The white man needed the Indian's peltries in order to make his profit, but the heathen native's presence in and about white settlements was a perpetual offense to the ambitious Christian.

Every year there were more and more whites and fewer and fewer Delawares in the region around Trenton. During the first three decades of the eighteenth century many of the New Jersey Indians moved, as their corn lands and hunting territories were submerged under the flood of European immigrants, out into the wilderness lands of the upper Delaware River Valley. Here, in what is now northern New Jersey and east-central Pennsylvania, remained some still unshattered Indian communities. The trek north and west entailed new miseries, however, for although these emigrés were now on better hunting grounds, the migration and the now exaggerated emphasis on the chase were making breaches in the continuity of the old social system.

*   *   *

The term "Delaware Indians" refers to those natives of North America who, at the time when they were first met by white people, inhabited the Atlantic Coast from Delaware Bay to Manhattan Island; the lands drained by the Delaware River and its tributaries; and the west bank of the Hudson River as far north as Kingston, New York. This territory includes Pennsylvania east of the Susquehanna drainage basin, the coast of Delaware north of Cape Henlopen, the whole of New Jersey, and a small portion of southeastern New York. In this stretch of country there is a variety of climates and of ecological zones: the bare and windswept seacoasts, rich in fish and shell-fish; the flat, swampy lowlands of New Jersey and Delaware; the undulating woodlands of southeastern Pennsylvania; the cool, forested mountains among which the northern Delaware flowed. The many communities, collectively called Delaware, who lived in this general area were never a political unit; there were differences in dialect; there were differences in culture—particularly in the economic adjustment to differing habitats. But they recognized themselves as a common group; and we do not know enough confidently to essay a finer analysis, which indeed might obscure their own consciousness of a common society.

These Indians were named after the river which ran through the heart of their country; this river in turn had been named for the English Lord De La Warr. Their name for themselves was "Lenni Lenape," signifying, like so many aboriginal names, "the real" or "the original people." Both titles have been used widely in the literature. At the present time the descendants of these Delawares are living on reservations in Oklahoma and Ontario.

It is impossible in a few pages to describe adequately the way of life of a people who through unnumbered generations have devised a well-integrated system of techniques for satisfying all of the needs of life; but it is necessary to make some effort here to characterize Teedyuscung's people. It is just as impossible to evaluate such a culture as "higher" or "lower" than our own; it was just different. We do not know enough to say honestly whether ignorance of cities, of metals, of the wheel, of firearms, and of domesticated animals is a measure of inferiority. At any rate, none of these dubious criteria of "higher culture" (excepting firearms) were first invented by the ancestors of those white people who found, and pitied, the "uncivilized" Delaware Indians in the early years of the seventeenth century. A few hundred years before, these Europeans too had, like the Delawares, been getting along happily enough with stone, leather, wood, and bone.

Before the white man came, these eight thousand (more or less) Algonkian-speaking Delawares had been sedentary village-dwelling people who lived rather by agriculture and large-scale fishing than by hunting and trapping, although the latter were important adjuncts to their economy. They normally spent their summers in community settlements of two or three hundred persons, along the rivers in the case of the inland farmers, or, in the case of the coastal fishers and shell-gatherers, near the shore. In winter the communities broke up, family bands traveling up the rivers to their hunting territories in the interior. Each hunting territory, whose clearly definable boundaries were natural landmarks such as streams and mountain ridges, seems to have been owned collectively by the members of a family. Some of the territories were large, as much as two hundred square miles in area.

It is not clear to us now just what the family groups were like which exploited the hunting territories. The territory may have been passed on from father to son, or to other relatives, in the paternal line primarily; or it may have been "owned" by the members of a maternal lineage. Certain it is that the maternal lineages were the most conspicuous mechanisms of descent and family affiliation among the Delawares.

A maternal lineage, comprising all the persons who recognized themselves as having common descent through the female line from an actual female ancestor, might number fifty or more men, women, and children. The various households of the lineage normally tended to live in a rectangular bark "longhouse" whose length depended on the size of the lineage, and the number of members of other lineages who were living there with wives or husbands. The women, under the leadership of the matron or "chief-maker," cultivated the land and prepared the food. The male sachem, who gained office from appointment by his lineage's chief-maker, represented the lineage in masculine affairs, such as treaties and sales of land, and warfare. Members of the lineage were theoretically supposed to avenge the death of one of their number, or, in case of a kinsman's forfeiting his right to live through the murder of a member of another lineage, to buy back his life by the payment of blood-money.

Several lineages normally were banded together to form a community, represented by a titular chief sachem (whose real power was slight). We find traces of these autonomous communities in references to the Delaware "nations" which appear with bewildering variety in the provincial records of New York, Pennsylvania, and New Jersey: the Chikahocki, the Schuylkill, the Raritan, the Minisink, the Cohansey, the Navesink, the Mantas, the Eriwonec. . . . These communities seem generally to have been composed of one or several villages located on a riverside alluvial plain, or along the shores of a bay or inlet. The community assumed ultimate jurisdiction over the lands of its constituent lineages, and in the summer its members gathered in one or two villages to farm, to enjoy social intercourse, and to settle civil and political problems. In 1600, on the eve of the European invasion, there were probably thirty or forty of these Delaware communities, distributed over what is now the entire state of New Jersey and adjacent parts of New York, Pennsylvania, and Delaware. Each community was autonomous, at one juncture entering into a military alliance with its neighbors, and at another pursuing its own way independently.

The public affairs of the community were decided by a council of the older and spiritually powerful men—the sachems, representing the lineages, together with private men of distinction. The function of the chief sachem of the community was primarily ceremonial and coördinative: the determination of policy lay in the hands of the community council. In conferences with the whites, the chief sachem sat in the middle of a half-moon of councilors; behind the councilors in a second half-circle sat the "younger fry." The sachem controlled the course of debate by signaling to the various speakers that their time to deliver the (pre-arranged) speeches had come. The chief sachem directed the communal hunting drive in the spring at the opening of the new hunting year. The village or villages were fully occupied during the horticultural activities of the summertime, and on the occasions of the Big House Ceremony, which was the focus of the Delawares' religious system, and was signalized by the recitation of the visions by which men and women had first been introduced to their guardian spirits.

The sib system cut across these geographically and economically anchored communities. There were three sibs: Turtle, Turkey, and Wolf. Each lineage belonged to one of the three. Since sib affiliation, like lineage affiliation, followed the female line, all the members of any one lineage were members of the same sib. No one might marry a person of his own lineage or sib. Inasmuch as these three sibs were known throughout the Delaware country, it was likely that in any community there would be several score representatives of each of the sibs (although of course a community might be characterized as a "Wolf town," for instance, from the predominance of members of that sib living there). In the absence of any overall political organization, the sib system acted as a sort of social cement, binding together, by ties of more or less obligatory friendship, sib members in widely scattered communities, and providing a measure for social classification in intercommunal religious and political meetings. A Delaware traveling far from home could usually find shelter and aid in the lodge of a fellow sib member, even though he might personally be a complete stranger.

The Moravian missionary and historian Heckewelder mistakenly confused these three sibs with three obscure geographical divisions: the Unami, the Munsee, and the Unalachtigo. (To the classical scholars who studied them, the Delawares, like all Gaul, had to be divided into three parts.) According to Heckewelder, the Unami were the Turtle, the Munsee were the Wolf, and the Unalachtigo were the Turkey. Heckewelder seems to have been in error all around. Not only were the three sibs more or less evenly distributed throughout the whole area occupied by the Delawares: the tripartite geographical division itself was largely a myth. There is no evidence whatsoever in the literature *prior to*

1763, when the Delawares renounced their claims to the last of their lands, of the existence or functioning of a triple geographical and political division of the Delaware Indians.

The origin of this erroneous ascription of political and territorial values to the sib system can be traced to certain historical events. Let us examine the "Unami" first. The Unami, or Schuylkill Indians, were one of the thirty or forty autonomous Delaware communities. Until 1732, when they sold their land, they occupied an area of about twelve hundred square miles on the upper Schuylkill River in Pennsylvania, between the South Mountains and the Blue or Kittatinny Mountains. Following the sale, they migrated with their chief, Alumapees, to Shamokin on the Susquehanna River, and thence some of them proceeded to the Ohio country. At Philadelphia on August 30, 1757, the Delaware chief Teedyuscung, representing the Shawnees, Mahicans, and Unamis living in the Ohio, reported that these Indians were inclined to peace with the English. "Being asked who the Unamies were he said they were a distinct Tribe of Delaware Indians, and that Alomipies was formerly the King of that Tribe." As we have seen, Alumapees was only the chief sachem of the Schuylkill Indians, and had no other authority.

The "Munsees" indeed appear as a distinct group—of miscellaneous composition—in 1756. By then the Indians of New Jersey had evacuated almost all of their lands, and the erstwhile aborigines of the northern part of the state, and of the west bank of the lower Hudson, had moved into the mountainous region between the upper Delaware River and the North Branch of the Susquehanna. Apparently the various community remnants had coalesced around the Minisink community, and the name "Munsee" gradually came to be used to distinguish the coalition from the core, the Minisink *per se.*

The same thing, of course, had happened with the Unamis. In the Ohio Valley, the fragments of many communities, settling about the core of Schuylkill Indians (Unami proper), who had migrated with Alumapees' three nephews, acquired the common name of Unami. And on the Cowanesque (a tributary of the North Branch of the Susquehanna) a similar event took place. Quetekund, a Unami from the Schuylkill, was chief of one town of heterogeneous population, and Lapachpitton, also a Schuylkill Unami, was chief of another.

The Unalachtigos have never really been found anywhere but in the pages of Zeisberger, Heckewelder, and their copyists. Brinton suggested that they might be the Nanticokes (Unechtigo). He also quoted a Delaware of Moraviantown, Ontario, who used the word "Wonalatoko" for the name of a dialect which was "half Unami and half another language." Trowbridge gave "Woonalautekoa" as one of four subdivisions of the Wolf sib, suggesting that they were a lineage. Speck has suggested that the Unalachtigo were the Naraticon, a community who lived in southern New Jersey. Mr. Edmund S. Carpenter, on etymological grounds, has proposed to the writer that the word "Unalachtigo" might refer to an indefinite way to any Indians—Delawares or otherwise—who lived in southern New Jersey along the shore.

What evidently happened was that Heckewelder observed the three sibs among the Delawares and, being unfamiliar with the sib concept, assumed from his European background that there must be some geographical and political division to correspond to the large social division. Out of the various community ("tribal"), village, and lineage names in his experience, he chose the three which seemed to him and Zeisberger, who were out in the Ohio in the latter decades of the eighteenth century, to be most prominent.[5]

*   *   *

The role of women in Delaware society was a dignified one, and curiously, to our view, correlated with a particular style of architecture. Many Indian dwellings in the early contact period were long, gable-roofed structures of wood and bark or mats, rectangular in ground plan, and similar in general design to the famous Iroquois longhouse. Several families, related through descent in the female line, and hence members of the same lineage, often occupied one lodge. Each of these families (which consisted essentially of two parents and their children) had their own apartment and their own fire, partitioned off from the rest, with neat wooden sleeping bunks covered with rushes or woven mats, and their own household furnishings—wooden mortars with stone pestles for grinding corn, wooden spoons, woven baskets, turtle-shell dishes, and so on. Smaller editions of the rectangular lodges, and dome-shaped wigwams, circular in ground plan, were sometimes built as temporary habitations for single households, and these smaller household dwellings seem to have been preferred by the dispossessed communities who migrated westward and who depended more on hunting for their livelihood. The eldest capable woman of the lineage (the "chiefmaker") regulated the household economy of the larger lodges and, with due attention to the general consensus, appointed (or dismissed) the sachem, who "ruled" his lineage only as long and as far as his advice was acceptable to the rank and file. The high status of Delaware women arose perhaps from the fact that it was they who assumed responsibility for the cornfields and for the ordering of daily domestic affairs, while the men hunted, fished, trapped, engaged in trade, defended their lineages and communities in war, and spoke for them in peace.

In the old days the Indians dressed in clothes made of well-prepared skins. In summer the men wore moccasins and deerskin breech-clouts; they shaved the head, in some communities leaving only a ridge of hair running fore and aft on the crown. Women wore moccasins and skirts. In winter a variety of skin clothes were added: buckskin leggings, bear- and beaver-skin robes thrown over the left shoulder, a special sleeve for the right arm, thick shoepacks. Cosmetics of face paint and bear's oil were used to ornament face and hair.

With the coming of European trade goods, the skin robes were replaced by "matchcoats"—small blankets worn over the left shoulder—or else by "strouds"—two-yard pieces of red, blue, or black cloth thrown over the shoulder like the match-coat. Leggings were now made out of stroud cloth, and shirts were an added luxury. Both men and women found in Euro-pean goods new opportunities for ornament: strings of glass beads or wampum, silver buckles and clasps, red, yellow, or black silk ribbons, bracelets. Moccasins, however, continued to be worn; in fact, it was the whites who usually took over the Indian footwear on the frontiers.[6]

*   *   *

The normal personality in the undamaged, aboriginal Delaware society seems, like that of most Indians of the north-eastern woodlands, to have been remarkable for equanimity in the face of physical misfortune and for superficial equa-bility in face-to-face social relationships. This throttling of overt signs of dissatisfaction and hostility stood in striking contrast to the bumptious, rough-and-ready aggressiveness of the invading whites.

The formation of this type of equable personality can be traced to the treatment and education of the child. Eighteenth-century observers agree that punishment of any kind was avoided. The children, said Zeisberger, "follow their own inclinations, do what they like and no one prevents them, except it be that they do harm to others; but even in that case they are not punished, being only reproved with gentle words. Parents had rather make good the damage than punish the children, for the reason that they think the chil-dren might remember it against them and avenge themselves when they have attained to maturity."[7] Heckewelder agreed that the instruction of the young was never "done in an authoritative or forbidding tone, but, on the contrary, in the gentlest and most persuasive manner; nor is the parent's authority ever supported by harsh or compulsive means; no whips, no punishments, no threats are ever used to enforce commands or compel obedience."[8]

The attitudes thus described do not suggest an intense feeling of emotional interdependence among the members of the family, so much as a discreet care not to antagonize one another. Under such conditions, it seems that the individual would not be likely to develop the sort of punishing conscience demanded by European society. Social coöperation would be achieved by an individual's calculating avoidance of antagonizing his associates, rather than by any powerful inner sanctions of conscience.[9]

This attitude of wary politeness was generalized by the Delawares into a *Weltanschauung* that included the world of animals as well as of men. Toward the brute creation the Delawares preserved a respectful mien; animals valued for their flesh or skins, like the bear, were not treated with casual brutality but were killed with ceremony and in some cases addressed by the hunter as noble enemies. Heckewelder was struck by

. . . the curious connexion which appears to subsist in the mind of an Indian between man and the brute creation, and found much matter in it for curious observation. Although they consider themselves superior to all other animals and are very proud of that superiority; although they believe that the beasts of the forest, the birds of the air, and the fishes of the waters, were created by the Almighty Being for the use of man; yet it seems as if they ascribe the difference between themselves and the brute kind, and the dominion which they have over them, more to their superior bodily strength and dexterity than to their immortal souls. All beings endowed by the Creator with the power of volition and self-motion, they view in a manner as a great society of which they are the head, whom they are appointed, indeed, to govern, but between whom and themselves intimate ties of connexion and relationship may exist, or at least did exist in the beginning of time. They are, in fact, according to their opinions, only the first among equals, the legitimate hereditary sovereigns of the whole animated race, of which they are themselves a constituent part. Hence, in their languages, those inflections of their nouns which we call *genders,* are not, as with us, descriptive of the *masculine* and *feminine* species, but of the *animate* and *inanimate* kinds. Indeed, they go so far as to include trees, and plants within the first of these descriptions. All animated nature, in whatever degree, is in their eyes a great whole, from which they have not yet ventured to separate themselves. They do not exclude other animals from their world of spirits, the place to which they expect to go after death.[10]

Among a people who did not have much experience of punishment in childhood, there was little opportunity for the development of the concept of a Jehovah-like god who dispenses favors to the good and chastises the wicked. There was, certainly, a Great Spirit who was the creator and maintainer of the natural system of the world. But the individual Delaware reckoned not with him but with a personal guardian, who was usually an animal spirit, like the Bear, who watched over and helped the Indian in the manifold crises of life. This Guardian Spirit revealed himself to the Indian youth in a dream or vision; and to him the Indian sang a sacred song describing the vision. The various ceremonies of the annual calendar consisted largely of the recitations of these visions.

For those, like the Harrises, who remained in the Delaware homeland, it was impossible to preserve the ancient cultural heritage. Most of the good land had been sold; and with the exodus of the game there was little chance for hunting and trapping. Rum and disease harried the unfortunates who clung desperately to their patches of corn and beans. And the incredibly prosperous white man (by Delaware material standards) was always present to cheat, to preach, to brawl, to seduce, and to bully. In consequence, not only did the Jersey Delawares try to approximate the whites in goods and manners; some of them were beginning to swing from the pole of native equability to the pole of European aggressiveness.

The reasons for this personality change in the Jersey Delawares are sufficiently obscure to make explanations, however alluring, speculative. But it seems to the writer possible that something of the following sort may have been going on. The individual Indian was finding that the equable and polite way of life, which had worked so well in the old days, was not rewarding when he dealt with Europeans, who regarded this equability merely as a fortunate lubricant for their own commercial machinery. The old techniques of social behavior were thus useless, and the Indian felt tricked and resentful, confused and bitter. In his uncertainty, with the whites before him as examples of successful brigands and also as punishing "fathers" or "brothers" (as they were collectively termed), he began to display "white" personality characters —aggressiveness and ingratiation—which he acquired partly by conscious imitation and partly by the more subtle process of identifying himself with these punishing father-figures.

Teedyuscung is a classic example of the results of this metamorphosis. Throughout his recorded life, as we shall see, he was often pushing, aggressive, competitive; and then again, submissive and ingratiating. Sometimes he tried to solve his problems by noisy verbal and physical attack, and sometimes (as in his affairs with the Quakers) by equally noisy maneuvers of ingratiation. He was anything but equable; but he was also anything but conscientious, except by fits and starts when under the influence of white men. Fundamentally Delaware in personality structure, his dependent, almost childlike relation to the whites gradually entailed changes in his personality: equability was replaced by aggressiveness; self-confidence by ingratiation; and the germ of a "conscience" (in the European sense of the word) was derived from his acceptance of white values, which were pounded into him by white evangelists, white innkeepers, white land sharks, white bureaucrats, white soldiers, and white traders, all of whom were accustomed to the idea that punishment was the mainstay of not only the natural but even of the supernatural order.

⋅⟨ II ⟩⋅

The Walking Purchase
1730-1737

Thus Teedyuscung lived out the first thirty years of his life as a poor Delaware Indian among the comparatively wealthy whites of New Jersey. Although he learned to speak English "pretty well," in addition to his native Delaware, he himself confessed that he was not able to read.[1] In his mature years he freely admitted the sense of inferiority he felt on this account in relation to educated white men. On one occasion he said to Governor Denny of Pennsylvania, "I must confess, to my Shame, I have not made such Improvements of the Power given me as I ought . . . I look on you to be more highly favoured from above than I am."[2] Sir William Johnson he regarded as "a wiser Man than I, and of greater Abilities."[3] It is significant that these two men were particularly difficult for him to get along with amicably. And yet there is no question but that he was of intelligence higher than that of the average white man. The comments of white acquaintances, and his genius for rhetoric, testify consistently to his acuteness of intellect.

To make a living in New Jersey he picked up the craft of basket and broom maker.[4] This trade was already a common one among the detached and dispossessed Delaware families who, like gypsies, wandered from place to place along the river of their name, manufacturing baskets, brooms, wooden spoons, dishes, and the like, and selling them to the white people for food and clothes. These articles were presumably

18

of traditional Delaware design, and no doubt similar to the ones still made by, among others, some of Teedyuscung's own descendants on the Six Nations Reserve in Ontario.[5]

Of the ancient ceremonial forms and observances of the Delawares, Teedyuscung learned practically nothing. In after years it was remarked by Pennsylvania's veteran Indian agents that "he neither understood nor observed" the ancient treaty protocol,[6] that he knew "nothing of Business,"[7] and that even his interpreters were "none of the best; for they [were] Natives of the West Jersey, [had] lived there from their Infancy, and [were] intirely unacquainted with foreign Indians and their Customs."[8]

But in company with nearly all of these natives whose linkage with their people's past was broken, he learned that compensating taste for strong liquor which sits like an incubus on the shoulders of so many Indians who must live in a white man's world.

Whether it was in esteem or in derision (and perhaps it was both), the young Teedyuscung was given the name of "Honest John" by the whites whom he mingled with so much.[9]

* * *

The family of Old Captain Harris did not get along well with their white neighbors in New Jersey. They resented the continuing expropriation of Indian lands and were not afraid to say so. By about 1730 they could no longer live comfortably in the settled parts around Trenton.

As many other Delaware families were doing at the same time, they crossed the Delaware River and entered the province of Pennsylvania in the neighborhood of the Lehigh River.[10] This country, reaching north from Tohiccon Creek to the Kittatinny Mountains, was already the home of a community of Delawares. Here the lineages of the sachems Menakihikon, Tishecunk, Lappawinzoe, and Nutimus, and of

Nutimus' wife, had lived from times beyond the memory of man. No Europeans, excepting a few traders and the white operators of newly built Durham Furnace, had seen these rolling wooded hills and green valleys. The Jersey Delawares settled down as guests of the aboriginal Delaware community, Old Captain Harris becoming chief man in the village of Pocopoco in the Lehigh Gap, and Captain John establishing himself at Welagameka, near the present town of Nazareth.[11] Where Teedyuscung and his wife and infant son stayed is not known. Probably it was at Pocopoco or Welagameka. The Harrises' little plantations soon became the nuclei of larger settlements; other immigrant villages sprang up in the valleys. At Welagameka, cornfields and a peach orchard were planted (and the Forks is still famous for its orchards) . The Tattamy family moved down from the Munsee country of northern New Jersey and Pennsylvania into the Forks of Delaware (as the land between the Lehigh River and the Delaware was called) .

And then white settlers began to trickle into the Forks, as they had trickled into New Jersey—slowly, surely, resolutely. The Indian owners of the land complained to the government in Philadelphia. In deference to their complaints, in 1734 the Indians from the west bank of the Delaware were summoned by the government to Durham, a few miles south of the Lehigh. There they met the young proprietors of Pennsylvania, John and Thomas Penn, sons of revered old William Penn. Teedyuscung was present with the delegation from the Forks.[12] Nutimus and Tishecunk formally lodged their protest with the proprietors, alluding particularly to one white man who had settled north of the Lehigh on the pretense that the Penns had given him permission. This, said the Indians, they could not allow; they had not sold the land.

The young Penns evaded the issue. They replied that no one knew what were the exact bounds of the old purchases. The Indians, they advised, should not grumble. The proprietors would be fair. And in order to come to an agreement about the question, there ought to be a general treaty at which all the chief men of the Indians could be present.

Nutimus and Tishecunk politely answered that they did not remember their ancestors having sold the land, but that if it appeared that this country had been purchased by the Penns, why then "they must be honest and content with the bounds and Limits."[13]

Next May (1735) the same Indians (again including Teedyuscung)[14] traveled down to Pennsbury for the general treaty. This time James Logan, chief justice of the Supreme Court, and *de facto* superintendent of Indian affairs in Pennsylvania, produced a copy of an old deed executed in 1686 which, he said, conveyed to the Penns all the Delawares' lands on the west bank of the Delaware River, *including the Forks*. Some white men were brought in to swear that they had seen the deed signed.[15]

The Forks Indians were shocked. They acknowledged the existence of the deed of 1686, but denied that their land had been included in its provisions of sale. Nutimus protested that he certainly had not sold *his* land, nor had his grandfather, from whom he ultimately inherited it.[16]

Logan locked horns with his Indian antagonist. He asked Nutimus point-blank "how he came to know what the Bargain was or how much land was sold as he was very Young at the time [and] as the Indians had no Writings."

Nutimus' reply was withering and put the Philadelphia lawyer in his place.

He had it from his Father. Besides from the Indian way of selling Land he could not but know. For the Indians who possess Land had it bounded by Rivers Creeks & Mountains & when they sold, the Chief always with the Leave of the others undertook to sell & when he had agreed he called together the heads of the families who had any Right in the Land sold & divided among them the goods he got for the Land telling them for what they rcd those Goods; then the Heads of the families again divide their portion among the Young people of the Family & inform them of the Sale & thus every individual, who have any right must be fully acquainted with the Matter. Besides Whenever a Sale is made, the Chief who sells calls the Chiefs of the Neighbouring Tribes who are his friends but have no right, in order to be Witnesses of the Sale & to make them remember it he gives them a Share of the Goods. So that no Land can be sold without all the Indians round being made acquainted with the Matter. & this we think a Way to have it better known than You take, for when You have gott a Writing from us you lock it up in ye Chest & no body knows what you have Bought or what you paid for it, and after a while by Selling our Land out in small parcels for a great deal of money you are able to build . . . houses as high as ye Sky while we beg having so little for ourselves & dividing that among our friends must live in Wigwams—yet we never claim any Land we have ever fairly sold, we know we have no Right.

Logan next unwisely asked Nutimus how he came to have any right on the west side of the river, since it was known that he had been born on the east side, in the Jerseys. Nutimus said:

His Mother came from this side the River, & by her he had a Right here as he likewise had to some Lands in the Jerseys which his Father left him, & besides the Indians did not consider the River as any boundary for those of the same Nation lived on both Sides of it. — As Nutimus thought this a trifling Question he in banter asked [Logan] how he came to have a Right here as he was not born in this Country?[17]

To an Indian, the whole proceeding was ridiculous. How could the white men say that the Forks were included in the 1686 sale, since it was widely known that the rights of the Indian signers of that deed "extended no farther up the [Delaware] River [than Tohiccon Creek] so that the Land beyond sd. Creek belonged to the Unalimi or up River Indians . . . of which he [Nutimus] was [a] chief?"[18]

In Logan's words, "Nutimus made himself very troublesome."[19]

But Logan refused to admit that the "weak and too often knavish" Nutimus, who had been born in New Jersey, could

inherit land in Pennsylvania. Perhaps he honestly believed
that the land had been bought in 1686. At any rate, unable
to argue the case further, he descended (according to Indian
tradition) to threats of force. In a scene which remained so
deeply burned in Teedyuscung's memory that he remembered it nearly thirty years later, Logan warned Nutimus to
evacuate his land and to cease interfering with the affairs of
the righteous. If he did not do as he was told, threatened
Logan, big logs and trees and great rocks and stones would
tumble down into the Indians' path to Philadelphia. And,
added Logan, he did not value Nutimus, but looked upon
him as no bigger than a little finger of his left hand, whereas
he, Logan, was "a great, big man." And Logan stretched his
arms out wide.[20]

Nutimus ("weak and too often knavish") tried to fight
back. Realizing that the great League of the Iroquois was
influential even in Philadelphia, he resolved to apply to the
Six Nations for protection.[21] Such an appeal would have been
legitimate, since the Delawares were "props" (allies) of the
League. But Logan forestalled his rival. Conrad Weiser, the
provincial interpreter, acting on specific instructions from
James Logan, in 1736 persuaded ten Iroquois chiefs to affirm
(in the absence of Delaware spokesmen, who might have
objected) that their cousins the Delawares had sold all of
their lands in Pennsylvania south of the Kittatinny Mountains.[22] Nutimus' land, Captain John's village of Welagameka,
Tishecunk and Lappawinzoe's home at Hociundoquen along
the Lehigh, lay in the area thus resigned to the Penns for
outright seizure. Pocopoco, Meniolagomeka, and other Delaware settlements north of the mountains were on land which
the Six Nations themselves claimed.

The motives of James Logan in this series of transactions
do not appear to have been altogether ingenuous. A Quaker,
he had come to Pennsylvania with William Penn, and had
remained to amass an estate at Stenton, just outside the city

of Philadelphia, which was (and is) one of the show pieces of
the province. He was reputed to have made his fortune in
land investments and trade with the Indians, and he and his
partner Edward Shippen were the biggest fur traders in the
province. A man of scholarly habits, his library was the finest
in the infant metropolis. Since 1702 he had been a member
of the Governor's Council; since 1731 he had been Chief
Justice of the Supreme Court. Logan had a private financial
interest in Nutimus' land. The Durham ironworks and settlement, just south of the Lehigh, was situated on a tract of
land four miles square, which Nutimus, Tishecunk, and
some others had sold to Logan and his partners about 1726,
and whose sale Logan had taken the trouble to confirm at
Pennsbury in 1735 by a second deed. (These transactions
would remain illegal until the Indians could be persuaded
to admit that the land had already been sold to Thomas
Penn, since by royal charter only the Penns had the right
to buy Indian territory.) The smelting furnace (among whose
owners Logan again was prominent) had gone into operation
in 1727, and the refinery forges then or shortly thereafter. Furnace and forges used up charcoal in enormous quantities,
the furnace alone even at minimum operation requiring the
cutting every year of over half a square mile of timber of
twenty to twenty-five years' growth. By 1737 Logan's Durham
ironworks was probably beginning to run out of timber;
and Nutimus, who lived at Nockamixon, along the river a
few miles south of the furnace, owned the forests surrounding
the Durham tract.[23]

Logan's motives appear even more equivocal when one
considers that he was at that very time working to lay the
foundations of a permanent alliance between Pennsylvania
and the powerful Six Nations. By alienating the Delawares,
who until now had been allies of the Iroquois confederacy,
from both the Six Nations and Pennsylvania, he was threatening to do his province a double disservice.

*   *   *

Having pried loose the Delawares from their protectors, Logan proceeded swiftly to dispatch the unpleasant business. On August 24, 1737, at Philadelphia, he showed the Delawares a map which purported to illustrate the extent of the land which had been purchased in 1686, but which as yet had never been surveyed.[24] This map represented a river, labeled in English "West Branch River Dellaware," joining the main branch of the Delaware at about the same latitude as the confluence of the main and west branches of Neshaminy Creek.[25] The Lehigh River was then generally called the West Branch of Delaware; but it is Tohiccon Creek—some twenty miles south of the Lehigh—which is at about the same latitude as the forks of the Neshaminy. The map did not show the country north of the "West Branch River Dellaware." Thus the illiterate Indian owners of the lands north of Tohiccon Creek *saw* a map of the country south of Tohiccon; but the map's lettering *read* north of Tohiccon. After some hesitation the Indians agreed to confirm the deed of 1686 as it was thus graphically represented. On August 25, 1737, Menakihikon, Lappawinzoe, Tishecunk, and Nutimus signed the famous Walking Purchase deed.[26] This deed (actually it was only a confirmation of the earlier deed of 1686) affirmed that "Mayhkeerickkishsho, Sayhoppy and Taughhaughsey, the Chiefs or Kings of the Northern Indians on Delaware," had in 1686 sold to William Penn a tract of land north of the first Penn purchase of 1682 and west of the Delaware River. The western boundary was to be Neshaminy Creek, and apparently the northward extension of the tract was to be measured by a day and a half's walk along the Delaware, although certain suspicious gaps in the copy left the direction of the walk uncertain.[27] This journey, however, was clearly supposed by the Delawares to terminate at Tohiccon Creek. They expected the walkers to "follow the Course of the [Delaware] River till they came to Tohiccon Creek & then to follow the Course of said Creek till they finish'd their Journey."[28] They were merely confirming the earlier sale of a tract whose northern boundary was Tohiccon Creek, the southern limit of their own lands. Their confirmation of a walking measure did not mean that they or the signers of the deed of 1686 had been indifferent to the exact boundary; it meant simply that they were accustomed among themselves to describe this distance as being a day and a half's walk. As a matter of fact, the distance as the crow flies from the southern end of the Walking Purchase lands to the most northerly elbow of Tohiccon Creek is about twenty miles, and overland it would of course be considerably more.

James Logan had already decided, however, that the purchase would include Nutimus' lands, which surrounded Durham Furnace and extended from Tohiccon Creek to the Lehigh. The general route had been walked in a preliminary way in 1735, and in the summer of 1737 it was surveyed and a path cleared in readiness for the final walk.[29] At dawn on September 19, 1737, three young woodsmen, paced by horses carrying provisions and accompanied by two Indian observers and various interested white men, began to walk northward on the main highway to Durham.[30] When they bedded down that night in the woods near Hociundoquen, the home of Tishecunk and Lappawinzoe, they were already well to the north of Nutimus' land. Entrance to the town was denied because a "cantico" (religious ceremony) was being held. The "shouting" disturbed their rest.[31]

Next morning Nicholas Scull and Benjamin Chew called on Lappawinzoe to ask him to appoint two more Indian observers, the first two having quit the day before in disgust. Lappawinzoe was furious. He told them that they had already "got all the best of the land, and they might go to the Devil for the bad, and that he would send no Indians with them. . . ."[32] By noon the party (minus two of the walkers who had dropped out, exhausted) had reached a point some twenty miles north of the Kittatinny Mountains. A total of fifty-five miles, embracing some twelve hundred square miles, had been covered in the watch-measured eighteen hours.[33]

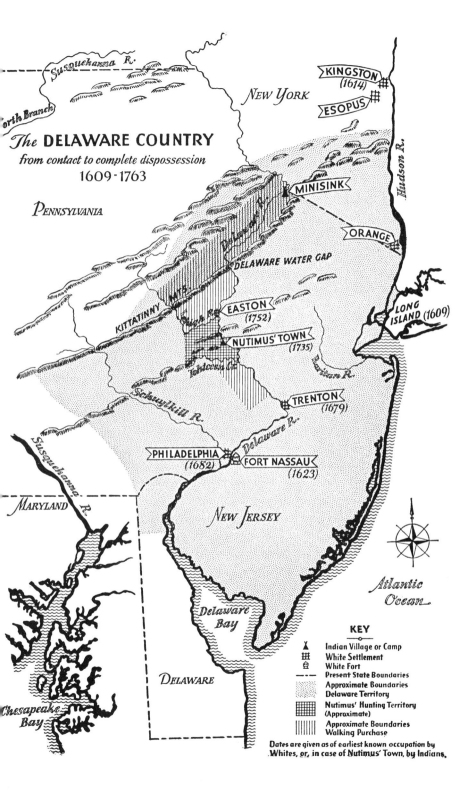

The **DELAWARE COUNTRY**
from contact to complete dispossession
1609-1763

Susquehanna R.

North Branch

New York

KINGSTON
(1614)

ESOPUS

Hudson R.

Pennsylvania

MINISINK

ORANGE

DELAWARE WATER GAP

LONG ISLAND (1609)

KITTATINNY MTS

EASTON
(1752)

NUTIMUS' TOWN
(1735)

Tohiccon Cr.

Schuylkill R.

Raritan R.

TRENTON
(1679)

PHILADELPHIA
(1682)

FORT NASSAU
(1623)

Delaware R.

Susquehanna R.

MARYLAND

New Jersey

Atlantic Ocean

Delaware Bay

Chesapeake Bay

DELAWARE

KEY

⚔ Indian Village or Camp
⌗ White Settlement
⛪ White Fort
--- Present State Boundaries
∴ Approximate Boundaries Delaware Territory
▦ Nutimus' Hunting Territory (Approximate)
▥ Approximate Boundaries Walking Purchase

Dates are given as of earliest known occupation by Whites, or, in case of Nutimus' Town, by Indians.

Logan was prepared to be generous now. Beyond the Kittatinnies lay a rocky, mountainous wilderness, claimed by the
Six Nations and occupied by a few straggling families of
Delawares. So Logan arbitrarily squared off the boundary at
the Kittatinnies themselves, running the line northeast along
the mountain ridges almost to Lackawaxen Creek.[34] His re-
linquishing of the lands to the north hardly helped Nutimus,
Tishecunk, Lappawinzoe, Menakihikon, Captain John, Tattamy, and their families, however, because they lived south
of the mountains, and therefore a reservation of ten square
miles (smaller by six square miles than the Durham tract)
was granted to the Indians of the Forks.[35]

Teedyuscung's father was among the first to denounce the
walk. The path of the walkers north of the mountains on
the second day chanced to lie through Pocopoco, Old Captain
Harris' town. Whether Teedyuscung was there at the time
we do not know. Probably he was not; he was very likely
attending the ceremonies being held at Hociundoquen. But
at any rate, when the walkers and their party returned to
Pocopoco after completing their eighteen hours, they found
Captain Harris in an angry mood. Harris, who could speak
English, entered into an argument with Nicholas Scull, a
surveyor who was accompanying the walkers. In regard to
the rapid walking of the woodsmen, he "seemed as well from
his countenance as his discourse to be greatly dissatisfied."[36]
Harris was not alone in his disapproval. The Indian witnesses
who had been invited to accompany the walkers had left the
party in disgust shortly after they crossed the Lehigh the day
before, saying, "You Run, thats not fair, you was to Walk."[37]
And Alexander Brown, a white man who went along out of
curiosity, said later, "Marshall & Yeats who were tall light
slim men, well formed for walking, walk'd as fast as they
could in a general way to avoid running & kept a horse in a
middling Journey's pace."[38]

Next day the white men returned through Hociundoquen.
Here too the Indians "as well from their Countenances as

discourse appeared much dissatisfied."[39] In fact, before the whites reached the town they were met by an Indian with a gun in his hand, who took a firing position behind a log that lay by the trail, and covered them as they entered the village. Thomas Furniss, another casual member of the party, remembered being surprised,

thro a Consciousness that the Indians were disatisfied with the Walk: a thing the whole Company seem'd to me to be Sensible of, And upon the Way in our Return Home, frequently Express't themselves To that Purpose. And Indeed, the Unfairness practised in the Walk, both in Regard to the way, Where, and Manner how, it was performed, and the Dissatisfaction of the Indians Concerning it were the Common Subjects of Conversation in Our Neighborhood for some Considerable Time After it was over.[40]

There was, indeed, real hostility now against the English among the Forks Delawares. Eight weeks after the walk Edward Marshall, the only one of the woodsmen who had finished the fifty-five miles, visited Hociundoquen and met Lappawinzoe and Tishecunk. Lappawinzoe's resentment had not cooled. Next spring, he said, all of the Forks Indians would go down to Philadelphia, each with a buckskin, to repay the Penns and to take their lands back. The walk, said Lappawinzoe, had not been fairly performed. The woodsmen "should have walkt along by the River Delaware or the next Indian path to it. . . . the Walkers should have walkt for a few Miles and then have sat down and smoakt a Pipe, and now and then have shot a Squirrel, and not have kept upon the Run, Run all Day."[41] Within a short while one Lappakoo, who "against the Minds of the Indians in general" had consented to the walk, was poisoned to death.[42]

Edward Marshall's subsequent history was clouded by that fateful walk. Some time after it was completed, he was summoned to Philadelphia by the Penns to testify concerning the affair. While he was in town, he was strictly cautioned to "hold his peace and converse with no one about it"; and to ensure his discretion, a grenadier was detailed to follow him about "like his shadow." When he had talked himself out, he was "allowed" to go home, carrying with him the "present of several pounds . . . given him by James Logan."[43] During the French and Indian wars his wife and son were killed, and his daughter wounded; and Marshall himself died old and unhappy, complaining that Thomas Penn had not paid him for his services in the famous Indian Walk.[44]

"*Gideon*"

1737-1750

Thirty-seven-year-old Teedyuscung, who had fled from New Jersey about seven years before, now waited for the second coming of the white men. But the flood of European immigration had temporarily set toward the valley of the upper Schuylkill River, to the west. For the first two or three years after the Walking Purchase not many whites entered the Forks. The Indians there stayed on their plantations and girded themselves to resist the expected invasion. Meanwhile angry protests against the purchase were being made to the government in Philadelphia. By 1740, however, over one hundred white families had settled in the Purchase. On November 21, 1740, therefore, the Forks Delawares addressed a petition to the Justices of the Peace of Bucks County, admitting that they had sold bits of land here and there (as at Durham), but denying that they had ever intended to sell the lands above Tohiccon. Thomas Penn, they said, "Wearies us Out of Our Lives."[1] They added that intruders would be met with force. This threat was not idle talk. When that same year a white man tried to settle in the Forks, a Mahican from Esopus (who, like the Delawares from New Jersey, had been dispossessed of his lands) attacked and nearly killed him.[2]

In 1740 white encroachment began in earnest. The Land Office in Philadelphia gave out a lot of warrants to purchasers of land in the Forks, and one of the agents of the evangelist

George Whitefield bought a five-thousand-acre tract which included the plantation of Captain John, Teedyuscung's half-brother. The Whitefield group planned to build a college for Negroes on the tract, and during the summer and fall some Moravian laborers employed by him actually set up two log huts near Captain John's home. But the scheme was abandoned in 1741 and the land was resold to the *Unitas Fratrum* (Moravians) for the establishment of a colony.[3] In December 1741 the Moravians' patron extraordinary, Nikolaus Ludwig, Count von Zinzendorf of Herrnhut, Saxony, arrived in Philadelphia to take over the cares of their incipient community in the Forks of the Delaware, where many Brethren from unsympathetic North Carolina (including those who had come up to work for Whitefield) had found asylum. On December 24 he gave the name "Bethlehem" to the first Moravian settlement, along the north shore of the Lehigh. And in June 1742 he traveled again from Philadelphia to Bethlehem on his way to make a tour of the Indian country preparatory to organizing the mission field.[4]

These Moravians, with whom Teedyuscung's life was henceforth to be indissolubly linked, were a group of Protestant pietists notable for their indifference to sectarian dogmatism and political commitments. Their doctrine emphasized the spiritual awakening (rebirth) and the new life; they lived lives of communal simplicity. Inspired by the writings of John Huss and John Wycliffe, the earliest Moravians had seceded from the Roman Church as early as 1467. Bloody persecution had followed them, at the hands of Catholics and Protestants alike, throughout the Thirty Years' War and after. Of necessity they had become evasive in their attitude toward the Caesars of this world; but the enthusiasm which they hid from the Philistines burst forth in an intense missionary zeal among Indians.

The communal life of the Moravians at Bethlehem was regulated by a severe if unselfish discipline. The products of labor on the church-owned lands were contributed to the common stock; the people ate at common tables and slept in common dormitories, "great numbers together"—an arrangement which facilitated the spread of disease during the frequent epidemics of smallpox. Sacred music was carefully cultivated, and the Bethlehem services soon became famous, as they still are, for their use of organ, trombones, violins, flutes, clarinets, and oboes, playing music chosen with excellent taste. The sermons were not preached to mixed congregations of men, women, and children: instead, separate meetings were held for the married men, the married women, the young men, the young women, and the children. Benjamin Franklin in 1755 attended a children's service. The youngsters were placed in rows on benches, the boys conducted by a young man, their tutor, and the girls by a young woman. The discourse was mild and familiar, "coaxing them, as it were, to be good." "They behaved very orderly," said Franklin, "but looked pale and unhealthy, which made me suspect they were kept too much within doors, or not allow'd sufficient exercise." This last was understandable enough under the circumstances, for that winter the town was being kept virtually under siege by hostile Indians. Franklin learned that the rumor that all Moravian marriages were arranged by lot was exaggerated. Generally a young man was free to choose his mate, subject to the approval of the elders of his class and of hers. But in case several young women were considered to be equally proper for the young man, the lot was resorted to. Franklin objected that, if the matches were not made by the mutual choice of the parties concerned, the spouses might be very unhappy. "And so they may," answered his informant, "if you let the parties chuse for themselves."[5]

The Moravians did not know that, in the eyes of the Forks Delawares, they were trespassers. On June 24, 1742, the Count and a cavalcade of Brethren traveled ten miles north from Bethlehem to build the new Christian settlement of Nazareth on Captain John's property. Here they paused for a day. On the twenty-sixth the Count and nine companions set forth once more. During the day they passed through Moses Tattamy's plantation, a three-hundred-acre tract which he was farming "in a small way." Tattamy, who professed Presbyterianism, received the white men and by way of conversation gave his visitors an account of the mode of sacrifice practiced by his heathen brethren. This fascinating recital, which the Count unhappily did not bother to write down, "afforded Zander an opportunity of speaking to him of the great sacrifice of the Lamb of God, made for the remission of sins." At Clistowackin, another Delaware settlement five miles above Tattamy's, they found further occasion for good words. "In the lodge of an Indian medicine-man lay his grandchild sick unto death." The Count prayed for the dying infant, commending him to the keeping of his Creator and Redeemer, while Zander preached to the villagers who had assembled about the lodge, explaining God's purposes in Christ for the remission of sin and the eternal life.

That evening, soaked by a summer shower, they arrived at a third Delaware village. The sachem invited them to enter his lodge, dry their clothes, and pass the night with him.

Next evening they tented in Pocopoco, Captain Harris' village, and possibly the home of Teedyuscung. It is said that Teedyuscung first heard the Moravians preach in 1742.[6] If that is so, it was very likely now, when the imperious Count, his queenly daughter Benigna, and their solemn retainers took up quarters beside the "medicine man" of Pocopoco.[7]

Teedyuscung's half-brother, Captain John of Welagameka, did not appreciate the honor implicit in the suggestion that his plantation be appropriated for the use of the *Unitas Fratrum*. He and Tattamy protested vigorously to Brother Onas, as the Indians called the government of Pennsylvania.[8] Unscrupulous white trader-settlers, who had nothing to gain from the nearness of a religious community, and whose livelihood depended on the Indians' desire for rum, are said to have egged on Captain John and Tattamy.[9] Nutimus and

Sassoonan (an old Delaware chief who had once lived in the Schuylkill Valley and now was a guest of the Six Nations at Shamokin) likewise revived the charges of fraud in connection with the Walking Purchase.[10]

But the Forks Delawares had lost their case before it was tried. While Zinzendorf was surveying his new mission field, the government of Pennsylvania was taking steps to evict the stubborn Forks Delawares once for all. From July 2 to 12, 1742, a treaty was held in Philadelphia between Pennsylvania and the Six Nations. The primary purpose of the meeting was to concert measures against the French, who were beginning to extend feelers into the lush Ohio Valley, where there were vast hunting lands, exploited by the Iroquois and their tributary allies, and coveted by the English. Canasetego, the Iroquois speaker, formally agreed to a defensive alliance with Pennsylvania. A minor desideratum was to enlist Six Nations aid in removing the Delawares. Toward the end of the treaty Canasetego, on behalf of the Six Nations, was requested by the Governor to cause Nutimus, Captain John, Tattamy, and their friends and families "to remove from the Lands in the Forks of Delaware, and not give any further Disturbance to the Persons who are now in Possession." Canasetego had just finished scolding Brother Onas for allowing white people to settle on the Susquehanna between Harris' Ferry and Shamokin, and on the Juniata, where "they do great Damage to our Cousins the Delawares." He now obligingly (and perhaps with his eye on Onas' purse) scolded the Delawares on behalf of Pennsylvania. His speech, a masterpiece of rhetorical vituperation, charged the refractory Delawares to remove instantly from the Forks and to settle at Wyoming or Shamokin.

Let this Belt of Wampum serve to chastise you. You ought to be taken by the Hair of the Head and shaked severely, till you recover your Senses and become sober. You don't know what Ground you stand on, nor what you are doing. Our Brother *Onas's* Cause is very just and plain, and his Intentions to preserve

Friendship. On the other Hand, Your Cause is bad; your Heart far from being upright; and you are maliciously bent to break the Chain of Friendship with our Brother *Onas* and his People. We have seen with our Eyes a Deed sign'd by nine of your Ancestors above *Fifty* Years ago for this very Land, and a Release sign'd, not many Years since, by some of yourselves and Chiefs now living, to the Number of fifteen or upwards.

But how came you to take upon you to sell Land at all: We conquered you; we made Women of you; you know you are Women, and can no more sell Land than Women; nor is it fit you should have the Power of selling Lands, since you would abuse it. This Land that you claim is gone through your Guts; you have been furnish'd with Cloaths, Meat and Drink, by the Goods paid you for it, and now you want it again, like Children as you are.

But what makes you sell Land in the Dark. Did you ever tell us that you had sold this Land. Did we ever receive any Part, even the Value of a Pipe-Shank, from you for it. You have told us a blind Story, that you sent a Messenger to us to inform us of the Sale, but he never came amongst us, nor we never heard any thing about it. This is acting in the Dark, and very different from the Conduct our *Six* Nations observe in their Sales of Land; on such Occasions they give publick Notice, and invite all the *Indians* of their united Nations, and give them all a Share of the Present they receive for their Lands. This is the Behaviour of the wise united Nations.

But we find you are none of our Blood: You act a dishonest Part, not only in this but in other Matters: Your Ears are ever open to slanderous Reports about our Brethren; you receive them with as much Greediness as lewd Women receive the Embraces of bad Men.

And for all these Reasons we charge you to remove instantly; we don't give you the Liberty to think about it. You are Women. Take the Advice of a wise Man, and remove immediately. You may return to the other Side of *Delaware* where you came from: But we do not know whether, considering how you have demean'd yourselves, you will be permitted to live there; or whether you have not swallowed that Land down your Throats as well as the Land on this Side. We therefore assign you two Places to go, either to *Wyomen* or *Shamokin*. You may go to either of these Places, and then we shall have you more under our Eye, and shall see how you behave. Don't deliberate; but remove away, and take this Belt of Wampum. . . .

Take Notice of what we have further to say to you. This String of Wampum serves to forbid you, your Children and Grand-Children, to the latest Posterity forever, medling in Land-Affairs; neither you nor any who shall descend from you, are ever here-after to presume to sell any Land; For which Purpose, you are to preserve this String, in Memory of what your Uncles have this Day given you in Charge.

We have some other Business to transact with our Brethren, and therefore depart the Council, and consider what has been said to you.[11]

Canasetego, of course, had no legal right to order any Delaware off Delaware lands. The Six Nations laid no claim to the country south of the Kittatinnies (or east of the Delaware River); all he could do was assert his belief that the Delawares had already sold these lands. His manner of doing so was highly impolitic. But Canasetego thought he had might on his side, and a moral ascendancy. Many Delawares (at Shamokin, for instance) were tenants on Six Nations land; and furthermore the Delawares were collectively entitled "women." Hitherto the Delawares, as "cousins" of the Six Nations, had been allies of the Confederacy; they had agreed to follow a policy of peace; they had been autonomous and self-respecting. Their status as women specifically implied only the symbolic obligation to entertain visiting confederate lords in their wigwams, and to feed them "Corn-bread, and Corn-soup with Bear's meat in it."[12] Now Canasetego, draw-ing attention to their "effeminacy," their irresponsibility, and their present weakness, took them by the hair and in a fit of Iroquoian self-importance symbolically dragged them out of the council house. This unexpected and unparalleled insult precipitated a tradition of more or less restrained hos-tility between the domineering Six Nations and the proud but proletarian Delawares which has continued to the present day.

Captain John, Tattamy, Nutimus, and the rest of the soon-to-be-evicted Forks Indians tried one more gambit. They presented a petition to the Governor's Council, representing that, "having embraced the Christian Religion and attained some small Degree of Knowledge therein, they are desirous of living under the same Laws with the English." They asked the whites to *permit* them to remain on the land. Governor Thomas called Captain John and Tattamy into audience before his Council and catechized them. The catechism revealed the Indians to be deficient in knowledge of the Christian religion; they were accordingly ordered to leave as the treaty specified—unless the Six Nations deigned to give them permission to stay.[13]

Richard Peters, the secretary of the Council, wrote indignantly to his employer Thomas Penn about the incident, suggesting that their conversion was a pretense, and waxing wroth at their presumption in signing a letter to the Governor, "Your Honour's brethren in the Lord Jesus."[14] Thomas Penn replied, "I hope the Governor has given such an answer to the Fork Indians as you say he intended, their assurance is indeed astonishing, you have not informed me how they came [to be] converted to Calvinism and I suppose they are not acquainted with much of their doctrines."[15]

There was no more to be done. Although Tattamy, in consideration of his services to the proprietors as messenger and interpreter, was eventually allowed to remain in possession of his three hundred acres in the Forks (where he later became interpreter and preacher for David Brainerd), Captain John had to move. On December 26, 1742, negotiations were completed between the Count and the Captain. Captain John was to be paid for his huts, for the peach orchard, and for a little field of winter wheat; he was also to be permitted to return at will for his crop of Indian corn, which was stored in a sod-covered crib. The agreement was put into the hands of Tattamy, and the luckless family of Captain John departed before the end of the year.[16] They did not go alone. Other Delaware communities picked up their belongings and went away too, some to Shamokin, others to the Ohio, and a few to Wyoming where, with the Shawnees and Mahicans, they planted and hunted, and carried on a large trade in skins and furs with the Pennsylvanians.[17]

Those of the Delawares who lived north of the Walking Purchase line, including Old Captain Harris and Teedyuscung, were momentarily left alone. But in 1749 the Six Nations, presuming on their seventeenth-century conquest of the Susquehannocks, sold the Penns a vast and barren tract north of the mountains which included the last remaining Delaware lands (although from the Iroquois viewpoint these were Delaware only by squatter's right).[18] Two Delawares attended the treaty and confirmed the sale (Nutimus, who had a hunting lodge over the mountains,[19] and Qualpaghach); and part of the purchase money was turned over to them. Nutimus received forty-four dollars as his share, and Teedyuscung later acknowledged that he himself received some cash.[20] But this pitiful compensation was only a sop to Delaware pride.

The end came quickly now. Frederick Hoeth and his family moved into the valley of Pocopoco in the fall of 1750 and built houses, barns, a grist mill, a sawmill, and a blacksmith shop.[21] The remaining Indian inhabitants of Meniolagomeka, Teedyuscung's town southward over the ridge, were forced to evacuate. And so, about to find himself homeless once again, Teedyuscung seems to have decided to throw in his lot with the white people. Late in 1749 or in the spring of 1750, he moved to Gnadenhütten ("The Huts of Grace") where, around their little turreted chapel in the wilderness, the pious Moravians had established a mission to the heathen Indians of North America.[22]

* * *

For Teedyuscung, baptism was the consummation of a long desire. For months he loitered about the mission station, but his reception into the congregation of Moravian Indians was put off again and again because of his "wavering disposition." He was reputed to be "unstable as water and like a reed shaken before the wind."[23] But once, after observing the ceremony being performed for another, he said to one of the white Brethren, "I am distrest, that the time is not yet come, that I shall be baptized and cleansed in the blood of Christ." Asked how he had felt watching the ritual, he replied, "I cannot describe it, but I wept and trembled." Then, moved to confess himself, he poured out his troubles to the missionaries, saying that he had been a very bad man all his life and had no power to resist evil, but that never before had he been so desirous of being saved from sin and of sharing in the Lord's grace. He cried, "O that I were baptized and cleansed in his Blood!" And his baptism was not long withheld after this.[24]

The ceremony itself followed the solemn Moravian ritual for adult baptism. Robed in white, the Indian candidate knelt to receive the sacrament; and when he rose, he rose reborn. As a symbol of this spiritual requickening, the fifty-year-old Teedyuscung was even given a new name: Gideon. After the ceremony the Moravian bishop wrote in the mission journal, "March 12 [1750]. Today I baptized *Tatiuskundt*, the chief among sinners."[25]

Thus the celebrated Teedyuscung, warrior and statesman, began his public career by meekly becoming a Christian.

For Teedyuscung, Christianity meant living with Christians. Until recently he had been living at Meniolagomeka, where his mother-in-law and her three children, and his son-in-law and three children also lived.[26] Meniolagomeka was a small Delaware village of about ten dwelling houses and a "Big House" for ceremonies, nestled away in a nook of the mountains some ten miles east of the mission. After conversion Teedyuscung made his permanent residence at Gnadenhütten.[27] His own family came with him, too. His Munsee wife was baptized as Elisabeth on March 19, a week after her

husband;[28] and nine months later, on December 14, 1751,
his eldest son, twenty-two-year-old Tachgokanhelle, and his
wife Pingtis (a Jersey Delaware whose sister was married to
the distinguished Moravian missionary, Christian Frederick
Post), were baptized as Amos and Justina.[29]

Gnadenhütten was a little sylvan utopia. At the foot of the
hill, on the west bank of the creek, stood the chapel and the
barns and farmhouses of the white Brethren; on the east side
were the log huts of the Indians, spread in a half-moon, part
way up the hillside. Above them lay an orchard, and on the
top of the hill was the graveyard.[30] Here at Gnadenhütten
were gathered together homeless Mahicans and Wampanoags
from New England—landless waifs driven before the flood of
white settlements; earnest missionaries from Germany; Delawares from Meniolagomeka, Pocopoco, and other nearby villages; and zealous English converts.[31] This polyglot population had since 1746 been maintaining an economy curiously
blended of European and native elements. A grist- and sawmill had been erected, and lumber was regularly floated
down the Lehigh River to Bethlehem, the mother settlement.
Each of the various families had its separate garden for growing corn, squash, and beans. In the surrounding forests the
men added to the larder by hunting and fishing. Religious
services, calculated to renew and support the fires of faith,
were conducted by the white Brethren in the chapel. And
in the near-by cemetery were laid to rest the worn-out bodies
of the Indian congregation.[32]

The Christian Indians quickly took on even a personal
appearance that distinguished them from the "wild" ones.
The wild Indians generally wore only a shirt, moccasins, and
breechcloth, whereas the tame Indians "are always cloathed
with something." Wild Indians generally were resplendent
in face paint, a feather, and various ornaments; the mission
Indians soberly denied themselves such barbaric finery and
instead wore "Hats or Caps." The wild Indians got their
heads shaved; Christian ones let their hair grow long. And,

interestingly enough, although the wild Indians carried their guns under their robes (especially in wartime), the Christian ones marched boldly along with gun over shoulder, the barrel pointing upwards.[32a]

There were good reasons for a materialistic "savage" to join the Christian congregation on the Mahoning in 1750. Famine and epidemics of smallpox were disintegrating the Indian society along the Susquehanna. Political pressure from Pennsylvania and the Six Nations was forcing the Delawares out of their villages in the territory of last year's land purchase (which included Pocopoco and Meniolagomeka); white settlers were filtering into the vacated valleys. But the conception of the Indian as a callous materialist is fallacious, ignoring as it does the rich and often, even in a Christian sense, beautiful supernaturalism of native cultures. And anyway, we have no right to assume a priori that Teedyuscung himself was attracted primarily by the obvious material advantages of Gnadenhütten mission life.

*   *   *

The story we have told so far has been poor in concrete details about the first forty-five years of Teedyuscung's life. But we can make some inferences about his motives in becoming a Christian.

At no time does it appear that Teedyuscung enjoyed much security. His very family history suggests instability. He and his brothers were only half-brothers; and between them and Captain Harris was no great love, for it is said that they left their father to starve to death in his old age.[33] Insecurity is the constant theme of Teedyuscung's wanderings from Trenton to the Forks of Delaware and thence to Gnadenhütten; and all his friends were similarly being harried from pillar to post by incessant white encroachments. Uncertainty as to what cultural values he should accept is to be inferred from the disorganized condition of Delaware society, and appears directly in his mixed cultural affiliations, which were half Indian and half white. Against this background stood, to his eyes in high relief, the successes and luxuries of the aggressive, self-confident Europeans. Teedyuscung's life had been built on the shifting sands of a shattered culture and a disinherited society; for him to try to identify himself with the victorious white man, when religious conversion presented an opportunity, was no break with his past, but rather a necessary development of his emotional life.

It would oversimplify the picture, however, to suggest that mere social and economic expediency prompted him to a religious identification with the white people. The essential tenets of Delaware morality were little different from many of those preached with such fervor by the evangelists. As among Europeans, so with the Delawares, such attitudes as respect for the aged, reverence for the Great Spirit, hospitality, marital fidelity, honesty, generosity, courtesy, kindness, loyalty, truthfulness, were valued. The concept of the inner light or spiritual rebirth, so prominent in European religious thought (including that of the Moravians) of the time, had for ages been the very root of Delaware religion. Studies of their ceremonies by both modern ethnologists and colonial missionaries have shown that the consummatory event in the religious life of every Delaware was the experiencing of a vision ("dream"). By methods comparable to those used by Christian mystics—loneliness, fasting, purging, general mortification of the flesh—the pubescent Delaware youth, who was being temporarily rejected by his family, endeavored to persuade the Great Spirit out of pity to manifest himself in the form of some animal or natural force. The guardian spirit thus revealed—be it thunder, or a duck, or a great bear—was the constant protector of the Delaware and was his intercessor before the Great Spirit. The Delaware guardian spirit concept thus recognized the "religious experience" in much the same psychological form as did Protestant doctrine.[34]

Both men and women among the Delawares were considered to be eligible for visions, but not everyone was fortunate enough to receive the dream which revealed a supernatural comrade. It was a great personal misfortune not to have had a vision. Zeisberger, the great Moravian missionary to the Delawares, said, "If an Indian has no *Manitto* [guardian spirit] to be his friend he considers himself forsaken, has nothing upon which he may lean, has no hope of any assistance and is small in his own eyes. On the other hand those who have been thus favored possess a high and proud spirit."[35] It seems probable that Teedyuscung never was one of the happy ones to whom a guardian spirit had been vouchsafed; in later years he complained of feeling, when he was alone, "very little in my Self." If this is true, to Teedyuscung's already formidable social and economic insecurity must have been added the burden of spiritual uncertainty.

Thus conversion seems to have represented to Teedyuscung an effort at identification with the whites, who appeared to him to be the most secure, powerful, and prosperous of mankind; and perhaps also it meant the filling in of a gap in his religious life by the adoption of the white man's manitto, Jesus Christ (the Lamb of God), as his guardian spirit.

❧ IV ❧

Flight from Grace
1750-1754

Teedyuscung was honest in his efforts to comprehend Moravian pietism and to accept a Christian cosmogony. He "exulted" in being called a Moravian, and in later years, when he had left the Huts of Grace (Gnadenhütten), he would "frequently, when in conversation with the Brethren, revert to his baptism, and feelingly deplore the loss of the peace of mind he had once enjoyed."[1] His public rhetoric, at treaties from 1756 to 1762, was interlarded with pious exhortations, such as: "We are all children of the Most High," "I believe there is a future State besides this Flesh," "Let us implore the Assistance of the Most High to bring the Peace to Perfection."[2] These allusions may, of course, in some cases very well have been grounded in the aboriginal Delaware religion, which, like Christianity, postulated a supreme deity, a life after death, and the efficacy of prayer. But Teedyuscung was unique among Indian spokesmen of the period for repetitious appeals to the most high God.

Although, as we shall see, Teedyuscung broke with the Moravians soon after his baptism, his short association with them gave a permanent moralizing cast to his thought. Often enough accused of immorality by white men, and often enough immoral by the standards of his own people, Teedyuscung nevertheless was no moral anarchist. Justice, fairness, honesty, truth, charity were principles which remained in the forefront of his consciousness; and if he used these ideals to justify his ambitions, he cannot be said to have ignored them.

A story is told of Teedyuscung discussing the Golden Rule. The unknown author of the tale begins with a cozy scene. "One evening Teedyuscung was sober." He was sitting by the fireside of a Friend, and both of them were silently looking at the fire, indulging in their own reflections and "desiring each other's improvement." It was at the time of a treaty, in Philadelphia, when Teedyuscung was charging that the Penns had driven certain Indians off their lands without paying for them, and the Quaker was turning over in his mind an accusation of Teedyuscung's. "The words of the governor come only from the outside of his teeth," Teedyuscung had said, and then he had added, "I will talk so too."

At last the silence was broken by the Friend. "I will tell thee what I have been thinking of," he said. "I have been thinking of a rule delivered by the founder of the Christian religion, which, from its excellence, we call the Golden Rule."

"Stop!" cried Teedyuscung. "Don't praise it to me, but rather tell me what it is and let me think for myself. I do not wish you to tell me of its excellence—tell me what it is."

"It is for one man to do to another as he would the other should do to him."

"That's impossible—it cannot be done," Teedyuscung replied. He lit his pipe and walked about the room.

In about a quarter of an hour he came up to his friend, smiling, and said, "Brother, I have been thoughtful of what you told me. If the Great Spirit that made man would give him a new heart, he could do as you say; but not else.

"Now, Brother," he went on, "it is no harm to tell you what *I* was thinking of before you spoke. I thought that the Great Spirit who made the land never intended one man should have so much of it as never to see it all, and another not to have so much as to plant corn for his children. I think the Great Spirit never meant it should be so."[3]

*   *   *

The Moravians at Gnadenhütten had received Teedyuscung, "the chief of sinners," into their flock with reluctance. He soon proved, "by his whole behavior," that the doubts of the missionaries about his steadiness were but too well founded. "He was like a reed, shaken with the wind."[4] In 1754 he lived up to their worst expectations by leaving Gnadenhütten, along with a large party of weeping apostates, for Wyoming on the Susquehanna.[5] The disappointed evangelists laid the blame for this exodus on Teedyuscung, his Mahican comrade Abraham, and the satanic Iroquois.

Actually, however, the Moravians themselves had precipitated the whole migration by promising the Iroquois to settle a band of Indian converts at Wyoming. Since 1742 Zinzendorf had dreamed of establishing a Christian community, to be called Gnadenstadt, on the great flats of Scehantowano, as the Iroquois called Wyoming.[6] In 1745 the Moravian mission at Shecomeco, Connecticut, was threatened with destruction by angry whites, who had been alarmed by French and Indian attacks during the early stages of King George's War. Accordingly Count Zinzendorf, Gottlieb Spangenberg, Conrad Weiser, and the Mahican convert Abraham had traveled to Onondaga to ask the Great Council of the Six Nations for permission to settle the Shecomeco refugees at Wyoming. The Onondaga Council agreed, but the refugees themselves unexpectedly refused, partly because Wyoming lay on the warpath between the Iroquois and the Catawba country, and partly because it was "a country abounding in savages where the women were so wanton as to seduce the men."[7] The consequence of this refusal of the Shecomeco Mahicans to go to Wyoming was the founding of Gnadenhütten. Nevertheless, there was constant intercourse between the Christian Indians at Gnadenhütten and the then-pagan Wyoming Indians, who were a motley population of Nanticokes, Delawares, and Mahicans occupying several small villages along the valley. In the spring hungry heathens would come down expecting to be fed by the Moravians at the mission.[8] These visits were a source of irritation to the property-conscious white men, who did not understand that the basic postulate of the aboriginal economy was the principle of sharing.

The great flats of Wyoming, and the hunting lands beyond the hills, were a crucial area in the geopolity of the Six Nations. Whoever controlled Wyoming at once blocked white expansion northward from Pennsylvania into the Iroquois country and controlled the war and diplomatic trails from Shamokin to Onondaga. The Six Nations had claimed Wyoming, by right of conquest from the Susquehannocks, since 1675, and Shickellamy at Shamokin had acted as their viceroy in the Susquehanna Valley until his death in 1748. The Iroquois policy was to invite homeless tribes, dispossessed by population shifts, to occupy these lands in their name. Christian Frederick Post, in a preface to his second journal of 1758, described the technique:

They settle these New Allies on the Frontiers of the White People and give them this as their Instruction. "Be Watchful that nobody of the White People may come to settle near you. You must appear to them as frightful Men, & if notwithstanding they come too near, give them a Push. We will secure and defend you against them." And if one of these Petty Nations, e.g. Delawares or Shawonese declaring War, it is certainly by the consent and approbation of all the Five Nations, who send or permit their young people to follow such Nations in their War: and in a company of 20 such Warriors I met but 6 Delawares, the rest were of the Five Nations. . . . The Chain of Union between the several Indian Nations is of that nature, that if we have war with one of them, we also have war with them all.[9]

The proposal made in 1745 by Zinzendorf was particularly opportune from the Iroquois point of view because by that year most of the Shawnees—a contingent of whom had been living at Wyoming since 1701—had left for the Ohio. As late as 1742 the Shawnee town on the west side of the river had comprised some thirty or forty houses, and the noise from the settlement was said by travelers to be audible for three miles. In 1744 only six or seven Shawnee cabins remained standing, the others having fallen to pieces; and in April of the same year a forest fire burned over a large area. There were still some Delawares left at Wyoming, ordered thither by Canasetego in 1742, and some Munsees (Delawares from the region of northern New Jersey) on the Lackawanna nearby who had settled there about 1728. But it was obviously to the advantage of the Iroquois to invite the peaceable, stable Mahicans to replace the Shawnees.[10]

The refusal of the Shecomeco Mahicans did not end the matter. Apparently the Onondaga Council took the legalistic stand that, since Zinzendorf on behalf of these Indians had asked for the right to settle at Wyoming, and since the Council had agreed, there existed a sort of contract obliging the Christian Indians to plant themselves down there. Next year the Six Nations sent a message to Gnadenhütten, letting both the Delawares and Mahicans know that "they all were expected to settle at Wyoming." But the Moravian Indians again refused.[11]

In 1748, apparently despairing of the Gnadenhütten band, the Iroquois invited the Nanticokes from the western shore of the Delmarva Peninsula to settle at Wyoming. The Nanticokes came and seated themselves at the southern end of the valley. But in 1753 the Six Nations persuaded them to move again, farther up the Susquehanna to Otseningo, where they would be close to the Iroquois country.[12]

Before the Nanticokes moved away in the spring of 1753, a body of over a hundred of them came down the Warrior's Path from Wyoming to Gnadenhütten, to renew, they said, their old league of friendship with the Delawares and Mahicans.[13] They were in great need of provisions to support them on the trail, they claimed, and would like to ask the missionaries for flour. Sixty bushels were given them.[14] And then they came to the point: they renewed the Six Nations' demand that the five hundred Gnadenhütten Indians come to Wyoming to live. The invitation itself was a mixture of threats and enticements. If the Gnadenhütten Indians obeyed, said the Nanticokes, they would find a fire already kindled for them, and they might plant corn and think of God. But if they remained where they were, the white people (just *which* white people, they did not say) would kill them all.[15]

The mission Indians were in a quandary. There was no advantage in a removal to Wyoming, where they would have to get along in far less comfortable physical circumstances and far less secure spiritual ones. The missionaries seem to have realized what was at issue and to have left the decision entirely up to the congregation, neither opposing nor advocating the move.[16] The question of religion was not directly involved: it was assumed that whether they stayed or went, they would remain Christians. Eventually the congregation replied to the Nanticokes, "No one here is required to stay; whoever wants to go, we will not restrain him."[17]

The original interest of the Iroquois in having the Gnadenhütten converts resettled at Wyoming may have been simply an aversion to seeing Indians being seduced by white missionaries. But their concern quickly became political; for it was discovered, in the winter of 1753-54, that white men were casting covetous eyes on the Wyoming Valley. On July 18, 1753, at Windham, Connecticut, the newly organized Susquehanna Company had appointed a journeying committee to go to Wyoming to view the land, purchase it from the Indians, and survey it.[18] In the fall of 1753 the Indians at Shamokin and Wyoming had seen three "gentlemen-like men" making maps of the land and rivers. The leader of the party had told some of the white settlers southeast of the valley that they would return in the spring with a thousand men.[19] In the following January the sons of old Shikellamy at Shamokin sent a mysterious message to the governor of Pennsylvania, by express.[20]

The Six Nations were suddenly afraid that their land was going to be snatched from under their noses; and not only their land at Wyoming, but also in the Ohio country, where the French, enemies of the Iroquois, were already winning Shawnee and Delaware converts, and were advancing on the Forks of the Ohio, where Pittsburgh now stands.

Pennsylvania also was concerned over the Connecticut threat to the Wyoming lands, and combined with the Six Nations to put pressure on the Gnadenhütten Indians to remove. Penn's charter from King Charles included the latitude of the Wyoming Valley, and although the Penns had not purchased the land from its Indian owners, they considered (as the Six Nations themselves admitted) that they had an option on its eventual purchase. Accordingly, on February 6, 1754, Conrad Weiser, Pennsylvania's veteran Indian agent, was ordered "to get some Peaceable Persons to live on Weyomick, to take Possession in the Name of the Proprietors of Pensilvania."[21] Weiser (perhaps knowing of Zinzendorf's earlier plan) suggested that the Moravians would be suitable persons, and wrote to them about it. The Moravians in reply intimated that they would be agreeable to the idea, provided that "the affair should first be made right with the Onondagas so that white people dare live there."[22]

It also occurred now to the Pennsylvanians that the few Wyoming Indians remaining after the departure of the Nanticokes might not discriminate in their resentment, in case of an illegal settlement, between Quakers and Yankees. So in April 1754 Weiser and his son Sammy went up the Susquehanna to Shamokin, and Sammy carried a message on to the Wyoming Indians, exhorting them to stay true to Brother Onas. "Something has been intimated to me as if you had cause of Complaint against some of our Inhabitants," said Sammy; and he went on to assure them of Onas' esteem and to regret that they had not come to Philadelphia for "these many Years."[23] The Wyoming Indians had, indeed, something to complain about. During the winter a crowd of them had gone up the river to the Mohawks and demanded to know what was happening. The Mohawks denied that the Connecticut men had any right to the Wyoming country.[24]

The schism in the Gnadenhütten community persisted without solution for a year. Some of the Indians, who were attached to the Christian way of life, vehemently opposed the move; and others, perhaps attracted by the freedom and the opportunities for trade that seemed to be waiting for them at Wyoming, just as vehemently advocated it.

Teedyuscung was one of those who wanted to go. There is no reason for thinking that he was prompted by any altruistic desire to preserve Wyoming inviolate to the Iroquois, although the prospect of resisting another white encroachment on Indian lands may have appealed to him. For a long while he had been chafing under the restraints of the severe Moravian discipline, resisting "the influence of the Good Spirit that sought to dispossess him of the resentment that burned in his soul when he remembered how his countrymen were being injured by the whites."[25] Under the circumstances, a real adjustment to the other-worldly austerity of the Moravians was not feasible for him. Teedyuscung was of two minds, as far as white people were concerned, and what satisfied the one offended the other. He was driven to identify himself with the Europeans by an acute sense of his insecurity and inferiority as a member of the broken Delaware society. But this same anxious sense of shame produced a belligerent, resentful, stubborn denial of the authority of the very people he admired. There is a persistent tradition that he was promised a chieftainship among the Delawares at Wyoming.[26] This seems improbable, since as far as is known he had no hereditary claim and was almost completely ignorant of Delaware ceremonial protocol, according to the testimony of white Indian agents who were in a position to know. But he did have an aggressive personality, physical courage, and a gift of speech, and so may conceivably have been offered a place as speaker for the Wyoming Delawares. As a speaker he would have a prominent but not decisive role to play at treaties and councils. But his real motive for leaving can hardly have been simply the desire for a speaker's career. It was impossible for him any longer to play the humiliating part of pupil, follower, and dependent: hence his defection.

Teedyuscung joined forces with the Mahican patriarch Abraham, once of Shecomeco and the first Moravian convert in America, to organize the exodus from the Huts of Grace. Abraham had been with Zinzendorf at Onondaga in 1745, when they asked permission of the Six Nations for the Christian Indians to settle at Wyoming, and now, in his new position of authority as "captain" in the Mahican "nation," he was insisting that having once accepted the invitation, the converts could not refuse to go. Teedyuscung and Abraham tried to raise a party of emigrants. At first they had little success, but they stirred up a good deal of discussion, and there was "contention between husbands and wives, parents and their children." In the end they were able to bring together sixty-five Indians (later joined by five more), who, on April 24, 1754, set off for Wyoming "without a missionary" (as the pious Moravian chronicler Loskiel darkly put it). The moment of leave-taking was painful. Many of the departing Indians burst into tears, promising that they would cleave unto the Lord Jesus and remain faithful.[27]

* * *

Wyoming was a flat green plain, walled in by blue hills, through which the Susquehanna meandered southward to the sea. The grass grew so high on the Great Meadows, it was said, that it overtopped a man on horseback. It was a bright green oasis in the forest that stretched interminably northward to the arctic tundra and westward to the plains.

But in June 1754 the Wyoming Indians were in a critical condition. Sammy Weiser, with his message exhorting them to be true to Brother Onas and to resist the Connecticut people, had arrived about April 24.[28] (The increment from Gnadenhütten had then been on its way.) A spring flood had destroyed the corn and beans which the new arrivals had planted by their homes on the east side of the river.[29] On June 19 Stephen Gardner, the Connecticut traveler who had visited the valley the winter before, came down the river along with a surveyor. They took notes on the suitability of various spots for white settlement. ("Good large Meadows on both Sides. . . . Much Grass. . . . About 4 Miles to the East Mount. & 3 to the West. . . ."[30]) The Indians watched and wondered.

Martin Mack, a missionary sent up from Gnadenhütten to see how the daughter colony was getting along, arrived at Wyoming on the twenty-eighth. He was horrified by the situation he found. In his journal he noted tersely that the Connecticut men laid claim to Wyoming by right of royal charter, and that the Penns, who also had a royal charter, wanted the Indians to reserve the land to them. Thus the Indians were on the horns of a dilemma. The Pennsylvanians were urging them to resist the Connecticut people, but the New Englanders threatened to shoot the horses and cows of the Indians if they did not "sell" the land. The Indians, said Mack, "know there will be a war, as the New Englanders are a people who refuse to regard the Indians as lords of the soil, and who will subjugate them if they refuse to evacuate the Valley."[31]

The Iroquois tried to force the rest of the Gnadenhütten Indians to go to Wyoming. The Onondaga Council day by day was becoming more and more concerned over the crumbling of its dominion in the Ohio. The French, traditional enemies of the League, were on the march and already had occupied several important posts: Presque Isle, Fort Duquesne, Venango (Fort Machault), Le Boeuf, Niagara.

The scattered Indians between Niagara and Fort Duquesne were joining them. Wyoming was beginning to look like a strategic outpost for the protection of the Susquehanna against the French.

In the summer of 1754 three Iroquois ambassadors arrived at Wyoming with a message intended for those Indians who were still at Gnadenhütten. Paxinosa (a Shawnee and the chief man at Wyoming), Teedyuscung, and twenty-two other Shawnees, Delawares, and Mahicans accompanied the ambassadors down to the Moravian mission. The message, delivered by Paxinosa, who spoke Delaware, was a peremptory demand that the Christian Indians join their comrades at Wyoming. When the converts saucily rejected the request, Paxinosa delivered the terrible ultimatum:

The great head, that is, the council of the Iroquois in Onondago, speak the truth, and lie not: they rejoice that some of the believing Indians have moved to Wajomick; but now they lift up the remaining Mahikans and Delawares, and set them also down in Wajomick; for there a fire is kindled for them, and there they may plant and think on God: but if they will not hear, the great head, or council, will come and clean their ears with a red-hot iron![32]

Paxinosa then turned to the missionaries and "earnestly" asked them not to hinder the congregation from moving to Wyoming. The missionaries, he said, would be free to visit their flock whenever and for as long as they wished. But the Moravian Indians in the end said only that they would lay the matter before their "great council" at Bethlehem; in other words, they would not go to Wyoming.[33]

Their refusal to leave the Huts of Grace broke the thin thread of sentiment joining the two settlements. When the Wyoming Indians, behind Paxinosa and Teedyuscung, returned over the dark mountain trail to their sunny island in the forest, they returned knowing that they were black sheep, renegades, and apostates in the eyes of the pious and comfortable Gnadenhütten congregation.

A High Wind Rising
1754-1755

When Teedyuscung ("Gideon") attended the Albany Congress in July 1754 along with the delegation of Wyoming Indians, he figured only (even at the age of fifty-four) as one of the "Young Men"[1]—those "burnt knives" who hung about the fringes of a conference, gathering wisdom and perhaps exercising a check on the councilors, whose decisions could only be effected by the voluntary concurrence of the warriors. Although he had gained some prestige among the emigrants from the Huts of Grace from having promoted their removal, he seemingly did not rank as a sachem. Sachems were the heads of their maternal lineages, appointed by the female chief-makers from among their male relatives. Teedyuscung apparently never did become a sachem in this proper sense. It would seem probable, however, that the officially "young" Teedyuscung was at this time being groomed for a place as council speaker.

The speaker at Delaware and Iroquois councils and treaties was not the chief sachem of his community and did not have to be a sachem at all. Ignorance of this fact has led more than one man of affairs, as well as most historians, into the error of supposing that the Indian who talked the most was the most important. Actually, the chief men seldom spoke in public. Special orators, qualified for the job by long familiarity with council procedure and by intercourse with the sachems, pronounced the words placed in their mouths by

56

the policy makers of the assembly. This was not a humble function, however, for Delaware and Iroquois council procedure was highly formalized. First of all, there was a series of ceremonial introductory remarks to be delivered, welcoming the delegates and putting them in the spirit of free and frank discussion. With strings of wampum in his hands, the speaker symbolically wiped the dust from their eyes so that they could see the truth, cleansed their throats so that they could speak, bored open their ears so that they could hear, and opened a passage from their hearts to their mouths. The speaker was required to know, and to review in detail, pertinent historical events; and it is a matter of record that these recitations were generally correct, even in the matter of dates, after as many as twenty or thirty years had elapsed. (Where the speaker's "minutes" can be compared with verified documentary evidence from other sources, it is usually found that the two statements agree.) Then the speaker had to introduce and discuss the issues under consideration, in proper order, without error or omission. And he had to do all this gracefully, with a combination of frankness and courtesy which should at once bring the real issues into play and persuade the hearers. Small wonder, then, that although in their formally defined capacity the speakers were straw men, mere mouthpieces, they were, as the ambassadors, the Indians with whom the Europeans usually became most familiar; and small wonder that they were reputed among the Indians themselves to be, if not the wisest, at least the "smartest" men.[2]

At Albany Teedyuscung had some opportunity to speak in private Indian councils; but to judge from the story which Philadelphia's whimsical chronicler Watson tells—citing Governor Dickinson as the eyewitness—his efforts were not very impressive. It seems that on one occasion, being somewhat drunk, Teedyuscung was making an ill-timed harangue before a Delaware council. His wife (or perhaps a "chief-maker"), who was present, suddenly interrupted him. Speaking in the Delaware language in a quiet melodious voice, while she modestly looked at the ground, she completely abashed the man. The white visitors demanded to know what she had said. Teedyuscung answered uncomfortably, "Ho! She's nothing but a poor weak woman! She has just told me it was unworthy the dignity and the reputation of a great king like me to show myself drunken before the council of the nation!"[3]

There is nothing to suggest that Teedyuscung played a significant role at Albany or that he even knew what were the issues under deliberation. If we may draw a parallel from his conduct at some succeeding treaties, in which his part was an equally ignoble one, we may guess that Albany to him was one vast grogshop. But whether or not at this time he understood the current of affairs, decisions were being made which within the next few years would determine the course of his life. It will be necessary, therefore, to examine what was going on at Albany more carefully than, in all likelihood, Teedyuscung did.

In the spring of 1754, while the Wyoming Delawares were hunting and fishing, cultivating their gardens, and carrying on "a considerable Indian Trade" with Pennsylvania,[4] shots were being exchanged by the French and English in the ancient forests of the Ohio. The French, pressing south from the Great Lakes, had built forts at Presque Isle and Le Boeuf in 1753. In April 1754 Ensign Ward had surrendered the Ohio Company's stockade at the forks of the Ohio, and Contrecoeur had begun the building of Fort Duquesne. And early in July George Washington capitulated at Fort Necessity.

Fort Necessity, in a tactical sense only a minor skirmish, was a strategic disaster for both the English and the Six Nations. Tanacharison and Scaroyady, the Six Nations' viceroys in the Ohio, had encouraged Washington to resist the French and had summoned the Ohio Shawnees and Delawares (nominal allies of the League) to assist him. Thus the defeat at the Great Meadows not only wiped out English prestige in the Ohio; it shook the authority of the Iroquois over the Shawnees and Delawares. The Onondaga Council quickly repudiated the unlucky viceroys, who fled to Pennsylvania, and instructed the Ohio tribes to remain neutral. But the Ohio Indians, living near the center of the maelstrom, were now inevitably being sucked into the orbit of French power politics. It was not that the Delawares were simply jealous of their "uncles" the Iroquois. Beaver, spokesman for the Ohio Delawares, appealed at Aughwick to the Six Nations for protection. "A high Wind is rising," he said. "We desire You, therefore, Uncle, to have your Eyes open and be Watchful over Us, your Cousins, as you have always been heretofore."[5] Nor was it primarily that the Delawares had old scores to settle with the English. The Ohio Delawares were turning to the French because, as eighteenth-century Indians, they were completely dependent upon white traders for guns, ammunition, cloth, kettles, hoes, knives, and all the other essential tools for living; and after Washington's defeat at Fort Necessity, the only traders in the Ohio country were French.

In July, therefore, the English colonies convened at Albany with their Indian allies, the Six Nations, to concert measures for the common defense. The Albany Congress of 1754 was the occasion of the abortive Albany Plan of Union, promoted by Benjamin Franklin and agreed upon by the commissioners, only to be disapproved by the home government in England and left unimplemented by the particularistic provincial legislatures. The Congress also went through the familiar ritual of brightening the chain of friendship with the Six Nations and their allies. But these prudent resolutions glossed over a radical disunity in immediate policies. Pennsylvania had come to Albany with the intention of buying the whole Ohio country from the Six Nations, as far as the bounds of the Penn charter, and perhaps the Wyoming Valley as well.[6] Connecticut men had come specifically to buy

Wyoming. Both provinces seem to have been motivated by a land hunger peculiarly inappropriate in the critical state of Indian affairs; both provinces succeeded in making purchases; and the Six Nations later repudiated both purchases in whole or in part. Since these purchases gave the Delawares, already being forced into French alliances, a moral excuse for their betrayal of the old chain of friendship, it will be useful for us to consider them, if only briefly.

Conrad Weiser, Pennsylvania's veteran Indian agent, was charged with the task of persuading the Six Nations to sell the Penns the vast territory west of the Susquehanna. Weiser admitted that he was confused by the sudden deterioration of the Indian situation. His policy had rested frankly on the premise that Pennsylvania's security was conditional upon the supremacy of a friendly Six Nations among the Indian tribes in the eastern woodlands. Now, in the high wind from the Ohio, the great Longhouse at Onondaga was rattling and shaking like an empty shanty. "I am perplects with Indian affairs," he said, "and Can not say such or such is best."[7] In his uncertainty, he agreed with the proprietary argument that the intrusion of the French within the charter limits of Pennsylvania could best be met legally by showing the world a valid deed to the land. Perhaps also such a purchase, by legalizing existent white settlements west of the Susquehanna, would allay the perennial Indian complaints against squatters. And of course the opening up of millions of fertile acres to exploitation by the Penns and the merchants of Philadelphia was an alluring opportunity. He avoided considering the effects of the purchase on the Six Nations themselves. Weiser, following the conventional method of arranging a purchase, proceeded to bribe the Shikellamy brothers to influence the Iroquois chiefs in favor of a sale.[8] His efforts were successful. On July 6, 1754, while Washington was marching unhappily back to Virginia, certain Iroquois chiefs representing the Great Council signed the deed conveying to

Brother Onas a vast unexplored territory west of the Susquehanna River.[9]

The Six Nations, however, specifically reserved certain areas. "As to Wyomink and Shamokin and the Land contiguous thereto on Sasquehannah, We reserve them for our hunting Ground and for the Residence of Such as in this time of War shall remove from the French and chuse to live there, and We have appointed John Shick Calamy to take care of them."[10] John Shickellamy, son of the famous old Shickellamy who had died, was a Cayuga, and as such peculiarly fit for the task, since the Cayugas (and Oneidas) claimed particular responsibility for the lands on the Susquehanna.[11] John had orders to let no white man, from either Pennsylvania or Connecticut, settle at Wyoming. If anyone tried to settle there and Brother Onas did not chase him off, the Six Nations would. "No body," said the Six Nations, "shall have this Land."[12]

It would seem strange, therefore, that five days later, on July 11, certain of the same Six Nations chiefs secretly signed a deed conveying to the Susquehanna Company of Connecticut a tract between the Delaware and the Susquehanna which included the Wyoming Valley.[13] The strangeness of this second transaction grows more piquant with investigation. John Henry Lydius, who personally secured the signatures, was an Albany trader of ill repute who had been accused of espionage by both French and English.[14] Lydius had been engaged to secure a deed for the Susquehanna Company by the Reverend Timothy Woodbridge, of Stockbridge, Connecticut; apparently the Reverend Cideon Hawley of Oquaga mission was also concerned in thus promoting the temporal welfare of Christians.[15] The signatures, obtained one by one then and thereafter by Lydius, at the expense of rum and Spanish dollars, were hardly legal evidence of sale, inasmuch as the signatories were not acting as representatives of the Onondaga Council, and since they included not one of the Cayugas, who exercised principal authority over the Susquehanna lands. Perhaps the Indians were drunk or bribed; or perhaps they thought that, in the phrase of latter-day confidence men, they were merely selling the Yankees the Brooklyn Bridge. History, after revealing the machinations of Woodbridge and Lydius, quietly draws the veil over the motives of the Indians.

Onondaga Council members were quick to disavow the deed. One Oneida sachem at a conference at Sir William Johnson's said, pointing to Lydius, "That man sitting there is a devil, and has stole our Lands, he takes the Indians slyly by the Blanket, one at a time, and when they are drunk, puts money into their bosoms, & persuades them to sign Deeds for our lands upon the Susquehanna, which we will not ratify, nor suffer to be settled by any means."[16] Nevertheless, the deed now existed, and the signatures were on it. Conrad Weiser, when he heard about the Connecticut "purchase," did not waste time speculating on whether a court of equity would support it. He saw that its significance lay in what the Connecticut people would now do on the strength of it. He said ominously:

I should be Sorry If the Connectt. people Should Countenance the deed that lydias So feloniously got. If they do and Setle upon the land there will Certainly be blood Shet, for the Indians Allways Said they Would never Suffer any white people to Setle Woyamock or higher up, and If an Indian or French warr Should break out the Consequence of the Conecticut people Setling there, would be bad on the English side, because the Indian would then be oblidge to move away, and to where Can they move too. Only to Ohio and there they would be under the Influence of the french and in their Interest, as the Sinickers and Onontagers now are, and perhaps the rest of the Six Nation dont think themselve Safe without Creeping under the wings of their father Onontio [the French].[17]

After the Albany Congress Teedyuscung and the rest of the Wyoming Indians came back to their valley, blissfully ignorant of Lydius' deed. On July 24 two missionaries from Bethlehem arrived at the Shawnee town on the west bank. Next day Teedyuscung and one of his sons crossed the river to welcome them on behalf of the Delawares. In his best mission manner "Gideon" said that the visit of the Brethren pleased him very much and that he wished that the Brethren might live amongst them.[18]

The condition of Wyoming was peaceful, those few summer days when the missionaries were there: it was the last afterglow of an eon of Indian occupation. The population was living tolerably well, in spite of flood and rumors of war. They kept horses and cattle and hogs; fish swam in the rivers and game hid in the forests; the gardens, probably replanted after the spring flood, were green with young corn. Naked children sprawled in the dust around the bark-covered houses which made up the villages—on the east bank of the river, midway up the valley, the Delaware town, and on the west bank, opposite, the Shawnee and Mahican towns. And now and then the breeze brushed over the meadows, bending the tall grass in waves like the waves of the sea.

The Moravians' four-day visit was a happy one. They were greeted cordially by Paxinosa's wife, a baptized Moravian, who had just returned from Albany with her sons. Nutimus' son, Isaac of Nescopeck (where old Nutimus was living now), politely told one of the missionaries that he too had been baptized at Gnadenhütten. The man of God countered with a sermon. Abraham, the renegade patriarch, organized a prayer meeting for the Brothers on the west bank; and the Brothers pleased the youngest son of Paxinosa, and another Shawnee lad, by playing hymns on the violins which the Indian youngsters owned. They baptized Marie, "the old Mohican mother," and complained that the roofs leaked in the rain. It is a charming scene they paint, of peaceful villages drowsing in the valley under the luminous summer moon; a tragic dream, too close to waking ever to come true.[19]

*   *   *

By fall the news of the Connecticut purchase had reached Philadelphia, and Brother Onas, anxious lest an invasion from Connecticut should simultaneously alienate both land and Indians, looked about for means of forestalling his rivals. Conrad Weiser proposed to send immediately for Hendrick Peters, the Mohawk chief, and to convene the council chiefs of the Six Nations in the spring to disavow the deed. In the meantime some of the Indian traders, many of whom were unemployed since the Ohio country was now closed to the English, should be encouraged "to go to Wayomack and under Colour of Trade take Possession of the Lands and build Houses."[20] A lodge, twenty-five by sixteen feet in ground plan, taking six hired hands sixteen days to erect, was built by Weiser's direction at Shamokin for the Shickellamies, who represented the Six Nations on the Susquehanna and must be conciliated.[21]

By the end of October the Wyoming Indians had learned that the Connecticut people now claimed to have bought their land from the Six Nations at Albany. They sent an imploring message to the Gnadenhütten Indians, entreating them to come to Wyoming, "in order thereby . . . to hold back the New Englanders, so that they should *not settle* there."[22] But the reply of the Gnadenhütten Indians was again discouragingly evasive: "We will talk with the Six Nations about the matter."[23]

In December some of the Connecticut purchasers came to Wyoming to take a look at the lands which Lydius had bought for them. This move alarmed John Shickellamy, and he lodged a formal complaint with Brother Onas. The Connecticut people, he said, were "coming like Flocks of Birds to disturb me and settle those lands."[24] They had threatened to settle the Wyoming lands by force.[25] Having notified the people of Pennsylvania, John traveled up to Wyoming and ordered the Delawares, Shawnees, and Mahicans there not to sell their rights to the New England men, but to prepare a remonstrance to the Six Nations Council at Onondaga.[26]

Meanwhile Brother Onas was busy too. Hendrick was invited down[27] and the Governor gave Shickellamy's complaint to Scaroyady to carry to Onondaga, asking for an explanation of the reports about a Connecticut purchase.[28] Scaroyady left Philadelphia on December 25, promising that the Onondaga Council would set Lydius' deed aside. It was something of an anticlimax when Scaroyady himself signed the deed two months later.

In January 1755 Hendrick came down to Philadelphia with the interpreter Daniel Claus and eleven retainers, by way of Esopus and the Minisinks. When the party reached Bethlehem some of the bearded Brethren approached to look at the heavy old silverheaded chief and his entourage. The Indians, who had never seen long-bearded men before, were terrified and took to their heels "like frightened children." Hendrick spent two weeks in Philadelphia, and during that time repeatedly denounced the Connecticut purchase as invalid, fraudulent, and of no effect, although he himself had signed it. He promised that on his return he would lay the whole business before the Great Council and have the deed withdrawn by decree of the entire body. Hendrick, unfortunately, was killed in the battle at Lake George in September 1755, before laying the case before the Six Nations, but between the conference at Philadelphia and Hendrick's death nine months later, hope ran high in Brother Onas' breast.[29]

The Susquehanna Indians were less hopeful of a peaceful issue. John Shickellamy in March 1755 bluntly informed Brother Onas that if any white men presumed to settle at or near Wyoming, the Indians would kill, first the cattle, and then the people.[30] In the same month he made a special trip to the Cayuga country.[31] And in April 1755 the Wyoming Indians, uneasy between the French on the west and the Connecticut men on the east, finally decided to come down to Philadelphia to cement relations with their nearest neighbor, Brother Onas.

The visit was unexpected. Governor Morris was on the point of going off to meet the newly arrived General Braddock at Alexandria when he was informed that a crowd of

Susquehanna Indians, on unknown business to Philadelphia, were expected daily at Bethlehem.[32] The Indians, arriving at the Moravian town on April 11, were told that the Governor was away from Philadelphia, but they decided to go on. They arrived in the city on the fourteenth and were received, in the Governor's absence, by an embarrassed Council.

Paxinosa was the "king" or head man of the delegation; Teedyuscung, now dignified as "a Sachem of the Delawares," acted as speaker; other Indians present included old Mahican Abraham, Jo Peepy (a Presbyterian convert and the interpreter), Tapescawen, and Scharooniaty. Teedyuscung, on the first day, delivered a suave speech of introduction. The Indians had not come down for any particular business, he said; they just wanted to renew the old covenant of friendship with Brother Onas. Next day Teedyuscung, on behalf of his colleagues and himself, affirmed his loyalty to Brother Onas and also to his "uncles" the Six Nations. He offered a pipe and gave Onas some deerskins to make a pair of gloves.[33] In return the Indians were invited to various Quaker homes in the city, were visited by Quakers at their lodgings, and were given a quantity of presents.[34] But all this was just making polite conversation until Governor Morris returned.

On April 22 Morris was able to attend. He introduced the Indians to the great Governor Shirley of Massachusetts, and feasted them at a "handsome Entertainment." Next day Morris presented belts on behalf of Governor Shirley and William Johnson, who only a week ago had been appointed superintendent of Indian Affairs for the northern colonies. These belts told the Wyoming Indians, in effect, to go home and sit still and wait for orders from Johnson or the Six Nations.[35]

Teedyuscung and the Wyoming Delawares went home and sat tight and waited obediently for orders.

Next fall they were still waiting.

Petticoats, Tomahawks, and Black Wampum

1755-1756

While Teedyuscung at Wyoming waited impatiently for word from Brother Onas and Brother Warraghiagey (William Johnson), the high wind that had been rising in the woods began to fan a little flame. On June 22, 1755, three white persons were killed and scalped at the English fort near Wills Creek.[1] Three weeks later the flame had become a forest fire: on July 9 Braddock's invincible army was cut to pieces by the French and their Indian allies at the Monongahela. This disaster set the seal upon the fate of the Ohio Indians. For them now the only choice was between starvation and taking up the hatchet against the English in return for the guns and ammunition which made life in the forests possible.[2] The decision on similar grounds of the Indians on the Allegheny River and the West Branch of the Susquehanna to follow their Ohio brethren may have been reinforced by a succession of natural misfortunes. That spring two hard frosts had struck the West Branch, killing all the Indian corn in that neighborhood.[3]

Teedyuscung, sitting at Wyoming, was beginning to worry. From the west came word of the victories of the French, and the necessity the Delawares and Shawnees of the region were under, of acquiescing to the hegemony of their Father Onontio. He himself, of course, would not betray the English, with whom he had lived and upon whom he and his friends still depended for trade goods. But all the same, it was strange that Colonel Johnson, in June, had neglected to invite the Wyoming Delawares to the conference at Fort Johnson where the Six Nations, Nanticokes, and more northerly Susquehanna Indians had (albeit lukewarmly) reaffirmed their loyalty to the English.[4] While Tioga and Oquaga Delawares and Hudson Valley Mohawks shared in the glory and loot of the Lake George campaign, which culminated in Johnson's victory over Dieskau in September, Teedyuscung and the Christian Delawares at Wyoming were conspicuously ignored. Their need of encouragement by the English was accentuated by the failure of the crops that summer, the consequence of a protracted drought.[5]

In August the Wyoming Indians took the bull by the horns. Scaroyady, the Iroquois viceroy who had fled from the Ohio following Washington's defeat at Fort Necessity, was passing through the valley on his way to Philadelphia. The Wyoming Delawares gave him a belt to carry to the Governor of Pennsylvania, representing their plight in being "sunk so low among the White People as to be forgot by them," and offering on their own initiative to take up the English hatchet. Privately they told Scaroyady that they wanted to move closer to the Six Nations country up the river. Scaroyady, aware of the strategic importance of the Wyoming band, who served not only to keep out Connecticut settlers but also to protect the line of communications between Onondaga and Philadelphia, said that he would present their case to Onas. He duly delivered the belt and the accompanying proposal to the government in Philadelphia. "One word of Yours," said Scaroyady to the Governor, "will bring the Delawares to join You." But this word was not spoken. Governor Morris temporized, telling the old viceroy that it was the Six Nations' responsibility to order the Delawares to war.[6]

The Iroquois had no desire to see the Wyoming population slide into the French camp through neglect. The Oneidas took what they thought to be Onas' hint and sent a six-foot belt of wampum to the Susquehanna Delawares, calling them and other allies of the Six Nations to the aid of their uncles in a defensive war against the French. Inasmuch as the Delawares were in a quasi-ceremonial way known as "women," the Six Nations "ordered their Cousins the Delawares to lay aside their petticoats and clap on nothing but a Breech Clout."[7]

Now it was up to Brother Onas, Scaroyady warned the government of Pennsylvania in October. Food, clothing, arms, and ammunition for the prosecution of the war could not be supplied by the Six Nations. Unless Pennsylvania supplied the Susquehanna Delawares, they would be absorbed by the French.[8] Already many Susquehanna River Indians had fled to the Ohio and into the arms of the French as a consequence of the ill-advised Albany purchases of 1754.[9] And now the Susquehanna Indians were becoming desperate for provisions and equipment. "We pray Brother Onas & the people of Pennsylvania not to leave us in the lurch, but to supply us with necessaries to enable us to fight the French," they said through their spokesman Scaroyady.[10]

But the Quaker-dominated Assembly was at this moment quarreling, not over how to rationalize subsidies to warriors or how to protect their large investments in the Indian trade, but over who was to pay the bill; and nothing whatever was done. And all the while the French and their Indian allies were organizing for the invasion of Pennsylvania.

The blow came suddenly. About October 12 Andrew Montour, the half-breed interpreter, and old Scaroyady were visiting at French Margaret's Town, on the West Branch of Susquehanna. Word came to them there from the Delaware settlement at Big Island that fifteen hundred French Indians were on the march against Pennsylvania.[11] Montour and Scaroyady hastened to Big Island. There they found six Delaware and four Shawnee warriors, sporting two freshly taken scalps, who said they had been sent hither by Shingas the

Terrible. These warriors said "they had received the Hatchet from the French to destroy the English, which they resolved to make Use of while there remain'd one alive."[12] Scaroyady and Montour, in company with two of the warriors, took this alarming announcement and the two scalps down to Shamokin as fast as they could travel. Scaroyady himself continued on to Philadelphia, stopping only to warn John Harris, while the two warriors delivered their message at Shamokin and then returned to Big Island. Scaroyady was still on the road to Philadelphia when Shingas' envoys, on October 16 and 17, proceeded to kill and scalp some fourteen, and to capture eleven, white settlers in the vicinity of Penn's Creek, between Harris' and Shamokin.[13]

The two scalps meanwhile lay at Shamokin, ominous symbols of the invitation extended to the Susquehanna Delawares to join their Ohio brethren in the war against the English. It was an offer requiring solemn consideration, for almost any response might precipitate conflict with one party or the other. Paxinosa and the Wyoming Delawares, those from Nescopeck, and the Six Nations Indians in the neighborhood were summoned to a council at Shamokin about October 21 to decide what was to be done about the scalps. As yet no news of the Penn's Creek massacre had reached Shamokin. A French Mohawk repeated the rumor that fifteen hundred French and Indians were on the march (actually there were never more than three hundred at any one time on the frontiers of Pennsylvania). But the Susquehanna Delawares, including those at Wyoming, still believing that at the eleventh hour the English would come to their rescue with arms and ammunition, stood firm, and taking their lives in their hands told the representatives of the French Indians: "Come not thro' our Land."[14]

But the hope of the Susquehanna Indians for the good will and support of the English was suddenly smashed. On October 24, while the conference was in progress, John Harris, the white trader, led a party of forty-nine frontiersmen up the river to Shamokin to reconnoiter. He brought with him the bloody story of the Penn's Creek massacre, and learned in return the rumor about the fifteen hundred invaders. Shamokin, on that dark Friday, was alive with undercurrents of intrigue; canoes came and went; both strange and friendly Indians were "all painted Black." And so, when Montour advised Harris and his party to return by way of the rocky east side of the river, Harris, suspecting a trap, decided to go down the west bank. His caution was misguided. Next day, returning by the forbidden west side, he was ambushed at Penn's Creek by 120 French Indians headed by Pisquitomen. Pisquitomen was a nephew of Sassoonan and had lived on the Schuylkill; hitherto he had been a firm friend of the English. Three white men were killed in a running gun fight through the woods; five more drowned as they tried to escape across the river.[15]

The news of this fiasco, when brought to Shamokin a few days later, meant to the Indians the end of their alliance with Brother Onas. They thought they understood now why the English had not supplied them with arms and ammunition to fight the French: obviously the English suspected them of complicity in the liaison between Dumas at Fort Duquesne and the Ohio Delawares under Shingas and Beaver. If the English had trusted the Shamokin Indians, they argued, Harris would have gone down the east bank as friendly Indians had advised. English blood had now been shed on two occasions at Penn's Creek (which was not far from Shamokin); in revenge, they concluded, the English would massacre whatever Indians they could reach.

In a panic the Indians at Shamokin fled up the river to Nescopeck. John Shickellamy, the Iroquois viceroy, and his two brothers wanted to go down among the whites, but the Delawares, who probably felt that John's presence would be a guarantee of security from attack by the Ohio tribes, forced him to accompany the emigrés. A belt was sent out, warning all the Delawares to move away from the English and collect up the east branch of the Susquehanna.[16] By the end of October John Harris was of the opinion that a large proportion of the Susquehanna Indians were actually in the French interest.[17] The French, it was rumored in Philadelphia, were promising to restore the Susquehanna Delawares to their ancestral lands and to release them from their obligations to the Six Nations, provided that they permitted the fortification of Shamokin and assisted in the attacks on the settlements.[18] In November an Iroquois Indian, a secret agent of the Pennsylvania government, was sent up the river on a reconnaisance mission. He found Shamokin deserted. But at Nescopeck there was a perpetual war dance. War parties were leaving by day and by night to attack the frontiers.[19] This news meant that the French had driven a wedge between the white settlements and Wyoming. Only the Warriors' Path—the difficult mountainous trail from Gnadenhütten—remained open; and even this was hazardous because French Indians were everywhere in the woods.

By November, all along the vast semi-circular frontier of Pennsylvania, in an arc from Maryland to the Delaware Water Gap, houses and barns were burning; men, women, and children were being scalped or led into captivity. One settler, James Wright, on November 6 looked out over the country from his house at Hemford "and saw the whole Country so full of Smoke that we can scarce breathe in it (which we can Attribute to Nothing but the Number of Houses Barns and Grain that are burning as we cannot learn the Woods are anywhere on Fire). . . ."[20]

*   *   *

While all this was going on, Teedyuscung and his comrades at Wyoming were still waiting anxiously for ammunition, for orders, for some word that the English had not forsaken them. When the news of the first Penn's Creek massacre arrived, they told two missionaries, who had come up from

Bethlehem to minister to their spiritual needs, that they were "in great Fear of the French Indians & are also under a great Concern lest the White People Should think that they have had a Hand in the late Disturbances."[21]

On November 8 the representative of the Wyoming Indians, Scaroyady, solemnly addressed the Governor and the House of Assembly sitting in joint session in Philadelphia. Scaroyady said he spoke for the still loyal Indians on the Susquehanna, those at Wyoming and up along the river as far as Tioga, "who were about three hundred fighting men . . . now the only Indians in this part of the Continent besides the Six Nations that remained firm to the English interest."[22] He had been sent, he said, expressly by these Indians to renew their earnest request for the English hatchet, and to ask whether Pennsylvania was going to fight or not. At the close of this formal proposal of an implemented military alliance, Scaroyady added bluntly, "Brethren, I must deal plain wth. you & tell you if you will not fight, with us, we will go somewhere else. We never can, nor ever will put up [with] yt. Affront. If we cannot be safe where we are we will go somewhere else for Protection & take care of our selves."[23]

But the Assembly still refused to appropriate funds to build a fort for the protection of the Susquehanna Indians and to furnish them with the food, clothing, guns, and ammunition needed for a winter campaign. Instead, Scaroyady was instructed by the Governor to distribute wampum among the Susquehanna Delawares.[24] The fatal consequences of this rebuff were not long delayed.

*   *   *

Until this time none of the Wyoming Indians had had a hand in the murders.[25] But there had been only silence from Brother Onas after their last-minute appeals through Scaroyady for aid. No professional traders came among them any more, and their slender trade with the Moravians at Gnadenhütten was inadequate to supply their needs. Their ammunition was almost gone, and they were in serious concern over what would happen if they should be attacked. This winter, furthermore, they would require powder and lead merely to exist, since the corn had failed that summer and they must therefore depend largely on the chase for food. Paxinosa, who still controlled the situation, strictly regulated the hunting: no one left the town without first acquainting him where he intended to go and for how long.[26]

The Wyoming Indians were all afraid that the white people were going to attack them. Any European who was seen in the woods was regarded as a potential enemy. Early in November, for example, two Moravian missionaries set out for Wyoming from Bethlehem to rescue the Moravian gunsmith at Shamokin, who was marooned there by the war. (The roundabout way was necessitated by the French Indians' control of the river above Harris.') The two Brethren met several Wyoming Indians on the path. The first whom they encountered had a bundle of skins on his back and a gun in his hand. As soon as he saw the white men, he cried out in a great fright, "Who are you?" The Moravians answered, "Good friends." The Indian told them that he came from Wyoming and was going to visit his brother at Gnadenhütten. "And when he came near us we Observ'd he trembled with Fear," the Moravians reported.

A few hours later, as they were toiling up a mountain, they saw a bearskin, tied up with a carrying band, hanging on a tree. As they went down the other side of the hill, another Indian overtook them on horseback. He said that the owner of the bearskin was afraid of them and had run back into the woods to hide.

Next day, descending the precipitous Wyoming mountain, they came upon an Indian who carried a bearskin, a deerskin, and some meat on his back, and a gun in his hand. As soon as this man saw them, he walked ahead so fast that the two white men could not overtake him, even though they were on horseback, in two miles' distance. But, finally, seeing that they carried no guns (and probably being exhausted), he rested his burden against a tree and waited for them to come up. "He was a Delaware and looked frightened."[27]

On November 9 occurred an incident which made matters even more critical. Charles Brodhead, a young free-lance trader who had plied the Susquehanna Valley before the war and lived above the Kittatinnies at Danesbury, arrived with a friend, unannounced and uninvited, at Wyoming. With a stupidity matched only by his courage, Brodhead charged the Wyoming Indians to their faces with murdering settlers on the frontiers. Not only that: the English, he said, in revenge were coming to seize the Indians and take them in chains to Philadelphia. If anyone resisted, they would cut his head off. Now, said Brodhead, were the Wyoming Indians going to be "quiet and still; or what were they going to do?"[28]

That, of course, depended on what Brother Onas did; and if Charles Brodhead's abusive conduct was a sample of the treatment they might expect. . . . But nevertheless they received him and his companion quietly, and, at a council near the town that evening, gave him two strings of wampum, with the following message to the Governor of Pennsylvania:

Brother, We all, are glad to see Thee & Thou hast done well, in coming to us so great a Way. We know not, what We shall say unto Thee; Thou seest Us here quiet and still. We allways look upon the great Friendship & Love, wch., as We were acquainted at our being last in Philadelphia, our Grand Father beyond the great Water bears towards Us, how his Hands are strech'd out towards Us as his Children, that if any Evil shd. befall Us, he would inclose Us as his Children in his Arms.

Our Grand Father, who has strech'd out his Hands towards Us, has sent a great Governour to Us into this Country, who shall make known unto Us, whats the Will of our Grand-Father, & what we are to do. As we were last in Philadelphia, We have seen with our Eyes the great Governor Colonel Johnson, & have spoke to him with our Mouth, We have heard his Words and he said unto Us, that We should go home, & sit still by our Fire, and not

meddle with any War-Affairs: he would make it out with our
Oncles the 5 Nations, & then send Us Word, what We should do.
The Governor of Philadelphia said also to Us, that if Colonel
Johnson did not send Us Word, *he* would; We shd. in the mean
Time sit still by our Fire, & since that Time We have heard
nothing neither from the Colonel Johnson, nor from the Gov-
ernor, nor from our Oncles the Five Nations. This makes Us
thoughtfull, that We dont know what to say nor do. We are as
Children here till We hear further Answer what has been made
out with our Oncles, & till We receive Words. We believe, that
We are in great Danger. For We hear the Hatchets fly about our
Ears, & we know not, what will befall Us, and therefore We are
afraid.[29]

Anxious to ensure the safe arrival of their message in Philadelphia, they even offered Brodhead an escort back to the
settlements.

An immediate effect of Brodhead's threats was to alarm
the Wyoming Indians still more. Sentries were posted in the
woods to guard the approaches to the valley.[30] Teedyuscung
himself, although then he was not equal in influence to
Paxinosa, resolved that if a reassuring reply did not come
within a certain time (apparently one month) he would believe that the Governor regarded the Wyoming Indians as
murderers, as Brodhead had said.[31]

But for the time being councils of moderation prevailed.
After a week's impatient waiting for a reply from the Governor, the Wyoming band decided to ask for advice from
the white Brethren at Gnadenhütten. On November 17 they
sent messengers thither with a plea for counsel. "We, being
friends of the English government, are in great fear and dis-
tress," they declared. "We are in danger of being attacked on
all sides by enemies, who are much enraged. We are no less
afraid of the white people, who suspect us of having been
accessary to the murders, committed in various places. We
wish to speak of these matters to the governor of Philadelphia. But we cannot go thither without a proper passport.
We are in danger of being murdered by the white people.

Tell us therefore what to do."[32] The Brethren referred the request to the Northampton County authorities, who made out the desired passports. These passports were then sent up to Wyoming.

On the twentieth another messenger, Jonathan, the son of old Mahican Abraham, came to Gnadenhütten. The tracks of French Indians had been seen along the Susquehanna between Nescopeck and Wyoming, he said; and there was reason to believe that the strangers intended soon to attack the frontier settlements. There had been a meeting at Wyoming to consider this, and Jonathan had been sent down to learn whether the way would still be safe for five or six sachems to come down to see the Governor in Philadelphia. Jonathan was reassured and set off on his return, promising to be back at Gnadenhütten with the ambassadors on the twenty-fifth.[33]

But the sachems were forestalled in their journey. On the evening of November 24, 1755, a squad of French Indians, led by Captain Jachebus, a Munsee from Assinisink, attacked the mission at Gnadenhütten, killing ten of the white Brethren. The Indian Brethren, forewarned of the assault, scattered in the woods at the first shot. When the little army of two hundred white men, raised by the Moravians to ward off the attack at which Jonathan had hinted, arrived at Gnadenhütten, they found the Huts of Grace deserted and partly burned. In and about the smoking embers of the married Brethren's dwelling-house on the west bank of Mahoning Creek lay the bodies of the ten martyrs; the barn and stable, the cook house, the bake house, the single Brethren's dormitory, the commissary, the mill, and the chapel where Teedyuscung had been baptized—all lay in ashes. The huts of the Indian congregation on the east bank stood empty. Most of the Indian Brethren had fled north towards Wyoming, some southward to Bethlehem, where they remained throughout the war, under the protection of the government of Pennsylvania.[34]

Garbled news of the massacre and of the flight of most of the Indian congregation to Bethlehem was first brought to Wyoming by a bewildered old man, who imagined that the whites had "imprisoned" all of the two hundred-odd Gnadenhütten Indians.[35] The error was congenial to the Wyoming Indians, however, who now thought that all hope of an understanding with Brother Onas was at an end. They needed some such grounds for rationalizing the pro-French policy necessitated by their isolation. The "imprisonment" of the Christian Indians became an article of moral justification for taking up the hatchet against the English. It was seized upon and cherished eventually even by persons like Teedyuscung who had once voluntarily become members of that very congregation, and had left it at their pleasure. Soon, the illusion fattening on Brodhead's earlier threats, it was bruited about at Wyoming that the Moravians had decapitated all the Indians who had fallen into their hands, and sent the heads in sacks to Philadelphia. Thousands of Pennsylvanians were supposed to be marching to destroy the Susquehanna Indians. By December the Indians were threatening to avenge these mythical atrocities by attacking and burning first Bethlehem, then Easton, then Nazareth, and then all other white settlements in the Forks of Delaware, and massacring all the inhabitants.[36]

But Teedyuscung, although in later months he charged the Moravians with enslaving the Christian Indians, in November was still one of the thirty or so warriors at Wyoming who were reluctant to break irrevocably with the English. On one occasion he and Paxinosa together persuaded two hundred warriors to wait "until they had certain assurance of the truth of the charge" before laying waste to Bethlehem.[37]

While economic anxiety and military fear were frothing up into rationalized fury among the Delawares and Mahicans at Wyoming, Charles Brodhead was pursuing his leisurely way down to Philadelphia with their now obsolete message to the Governor. On November 29 twenty full days after he had received it, he delivered their belt, along with an excellent piece of advice, which if tendered earlier might have been useful. When he was at Wyoming, said Brodhead, the warriors were very willing to accept the English hatchet; but if the hatchet were withheld, he did not think they would remain loyal. It was very important to bring these Wyoming Indians over to the English side, because they would then be joined by other undecided groups, and would form the nucleus of a native army which could protect the frontier from the Delaware River to the Susquehanna.[38]

Governor Morris was gratified by this sentiment. He was, he wrote to Sir William Johnson (newly appointed baronet) rather miffed at these savages' complaints of being ignored; but he would pacify them by a well-timed apology. The apology took the form of a polite invitation to the Wyoming Indians to join those from Shamokin (which was, unknown to him, now deserted) and Nescopeck (now the headquarters for 140 French Indians) in a little conference at John Harris' on the first of the new year. There, said Morris, he would assign to them a proper part in military operations. On December 8 Charles Brodhead, Aaron Dupui, and Benjamin Shoemaker were delegated to carry this answer back to Wyoming.[39]

But by then it was too late. By December 11 Brodhead's home was under siege, and Dupui's plantation was attacked soon after. No message could have got to Wyoming even if anyone had wanted to go, for there were hostile war parties ranging through the woods all the way from the Allegheny Mountains to the Delaware Water Gap. And anyway, no one wanted to go. As James Hamilton said at Easton, "Everybody is . . . afraid of stirring a step without a strong Guard."[40]

*   *   *

The attacks on Brodhead's and Dupui's in the Minisink region north of the Forks, and on Hoeth's in the Pocopoco

Valley where a few years earlier had stood the home of the Harrises, were part of a general assault against Northampton County which gained the pro-French Indians some twenty-six prisoners and perhaps double that number of scalps. In this December wave of attacks the Wyoming Delawares for the first time participated.[41] Not all of the Wyoming Indians, however, even yet were taking up the hatchet. Thirty warriors and their families, led by the peaceable Paxinosa and including the few Shawnees, still stood neutral; eighty joined the French.

Up until the time of the Northampton massacres, Teedyuscung seems to have stood neutral, with sympathies tending toward the English. He had, however, resolved to act according to the answer, or failure to answer, to the message sent to the Governor by Brodhead's hand in November. The answer had not come; and it may be significant that it was on December 10, 1755, exactly one month after Brodhead's departure for Philadelphia, that the first attacks by Wyoming Indians occurred. At any rate, about this time Teedyuscung seceded from the peace party and joined the faction which wanted war against the English. He made "an Exceeding large" belt of wampum, which he sent to all the Indians living in the Ohio country, with the following words: "I am in exceeding Great Danger, the English will kill me, come and help me." After sending the war belt, the war party openly took up the hatchet, Teedyuscung along with the rest.[42] Paxinosa, who tried to dissuade them from making war on their old friends the English, was told at last that if he said one word more he would be knocked on the head.[43]

Being the only member of the warrior's party who had substantial council experience, Teedyuscung with the common consent took over the management of their diplomatic affairs. Whether by accident or design, he had chosen the faction which included no prominent men and no recognized speakers. As long as his views were those of the majority, more vigorously expressed, no one questioned his status. The warriors inevitably looked to him to be their spokesman, and he, having no individual superior, began to call himself "king" or "sachem" in the messages which he sent out. He exerted himself primarily to buttress the position of the eighty Wyoming renegades by soliciting the support of the Six Nations and by coördinating the activities of the Susquehanna Delawares, who were all, as prisoners and scalps began to arrive in their towns, cutting themselves adrift from the English.[44]

Teedyuscung's efforts to enlist the aid of the Six Nations were not crowned with success. In November he sent three scalps and some belts to the Senecas by hand of Cutfinger Peter, and a belt to the Oneidas, asking for aid against the English. This last was a naïve request and drew no answer. The Six Nations (including the pro-English Oneidas) had already ordered the Susquehanna Delawares to take up the hatchet against the French. They themselves had accepted the English hatchet, and some of the Mohawks had fought beside Johnson at Lake George. At that very moment the Six Nations were meeting at Onondaga, at Sir William Johnson's instance, to draft a message to the Susquehanna and Ohio Delawares and Shawnees, ordering them to stop killing the English and to present themselves at Onondaga to explain their actions.[45] Only the westernmost of the Six Nations Indians, the Geneseo Senecas, were avowedly in the French interest.

Teedyuscung was annoyed at the silence to his demands. At Tunkhannock, a village north of Wyoming, he showed Scaroyady (who late that December was going up the Susquehanna on a reconnaisance mission on behalf of Pennsylvania) a large belt of black wampum thirteen rows wide. "This," said Teedyuscung, "I am now going to send to the Six Nations, and as this is the third Time, if they send an answer, well and good; if they do not, I shall know what to do."[46]

Scaroyady, who had no one with him but Andrew Montour, presumably eyed Teedyuscung's warriors and said nothing. He had already been threatened with death by the Delawares at Wyoming. There he had been treated with open contempt, although he was known to be a man of authority among the Six Nations and an experienced and eloquent speaker. The Delawares would not so much as touch the belts he laid before them; they threw them aside and gave him ill language. While he was consulting with the elders in the evening, the warriors out-of-doors were heard crying, "Let us kill the Rogue; we will hear of no Mediator, much less of a Master; hold your Tongue and be gone, or you shall live no longer. We will do what we please."[47] And when he attempted to present a belt to stop a war party of eighty men from starting out, they contemptuously shoved the wampum aside with a stick, muttering that they had killed numbers of English already and would sooner or later kill them all.[48]

At Tioga the itinerant Scaroyady met two sets of messengers, one from the Oneidas and Cayugas, the other from the Mohawks, with belts for the Delawares demanding that they lay down the hatchet and repair to Onondaga.[49] The pro-French Tioga Delawares expressed submission and sent two deputies to the Great Council, which reprimanded them "sharply" and told them to put aside their arms. But the "submissive" answer of the Tioga Delawares was made with tongue in cheek. Although they promised to "stop and repent," they also said that two war parties had just gone out, and that the war would continue, as far as they were concerned, until all Indians held captive by the whites were set free.[50] The Six Nations' "allies to the southward"[51] were in no mood to be peaceable; they even threatened to conquer the Iroquois after destroying the whites.[52]

Now that they had at last crossed their Rubicon, the Susquehanna Delawares were having an orgy of aggressiveness; after the tense anxiety of indecision, they were enjoying the thrill of throwing off all restraint.

Teedyuscung himself, immediately after Scaroyady had

gone by, set out with thirty men in quest of scalps, in open defiance of the wishes of his "uncles" the Six Nations.[53]

*   *   *

That scalping raid was pretty much a family affair. Of the thirty warriors in Teedyuscung's party, three were sons of his (including Amos and Jacob), three were half-brothers (Sam Evans, Tom Evans, and Peter, alias Young Captain Harris, who had been baptized by the Moravians), and one was a nephew (Christian, the son of his half-brother Joe Evans). They reached the settlements north of the Kittatinnies, close by the Delaware, on New Year's Eve. No time was wasted. Teedyuscung and his three sons and their comrades quietly surrounded a party of four white men working in the fields of the Weeser plantation. The elder Weeser and Hans Adam Hess were suddenly shot down, and the two young men, Leonard and William Weeser, were seized by the Indians who rushed out of hiding. Amos, Teedyuscung's son, personally captured William and immediately handed him over to his father.[54]

Next morning Teedyuscung, again leading his little band of warriors, descended on two other plantations in the neighborhood. At the farm of Peter Hess they killed Nicholas Burman and another hired hand, and captured Peter Hess and his elder son Henry. At nine o'clock they visited the place of Peter Hess's brother, where they killed Nicholas Coleman and a laborer named Gottlieb, and took prisoner Peter's brother and one other man. After firing the stables, burning the house and a barrack of wheat, and killing the cattle, most of the horses, and the sheep, they led off three horses and the prisoners northward over the Second Mountain. At the Great Swamp they caught up with five of their party who had turned homeward the day before with the Weeser boys.

The Great Swamp was thirty miles from Weeser's, and old

Peter Hess was failing, apparently, after the long walk. Rather than be burdened with a useless old man, they killed him, stabbing him to death, stripping off his clothes, and taking his scalp, while his son looked on helplessly. Then they went on.

At dark they called a halt and, feeling themselves to be safe, kindled a fire. The prisoners they tied to trees with ropes. No watch was set. During the night (which Henry Hess said later was the coldest night of the year) the captives nearly froze to death. Some of the Indians were awake till dawn: it was too cold to sleep.

On January 3 Teedyuscung brought his war party back safe, with prisoners and scalps, to Wyoming. But he found Wyoming had been deserted, from fear of an attack by the English, by all of its inhabitants, who were gone up the river to Tunkhannock. And so on to Tunkhannock they marched, reaching the town next day. Tunkhannock had a war-swelled population of one hundred men, women, and children. They stayed there until the cold spell was over. When the freeze ended, the whole community—Teedyuscung, war party, prisoners, and the hundred Delawares—walked up along the river to Tioga. Teedyuscung remained at Tioga until corn planting time. Then he went up to a village called Pasigachkunk ("Little Shingle" or "Little Passeeca") on the Cowanesque, along with his prisoner, Henry Hess.[55]

Teedyuscung never went out with a war party again. He had amassed sufficient honor from his one successful venture to assure his status as a sachem in fact if not in customary law. But this did not mean that he had laid down the hatchet. His function now was that of coördinator and "boss." His backroom politics extended even to such projects as trying to persuade a runaway Negro to organize a slave rebellion.[56] And his family, followers, and friends continued to go to war. Every few weeks small parties of five or six Delawares set out from Tioga against the white settlements at Allemengle and the Minisinks; and they came back with prisoners and scalps.

It is important, in assessing Teedyuscung's motives in his brief orgy of blood-letting, not to fall into the error of those historians who call the killing of a white man a massacre and the killing of an Indian a battle. Unchivalrous as the Delaware pattern of warfare was, it was not monstrous. It did not transgress the code which was accepted and followed by the eastern woodlands Indians. Indeed, Teedyuscung's own conduct was somewhat more generous than that of many of his comrades. None of his prisoners was ever tortured; those killed were killed in haste. And there is no question that, from a military viewpoint, the tactic of the Delaware attacks, in which Teedyuscung coöperated, was most efficient. One has only to read the story of the panic, the confusion, the complete disintegration of the frontier, to realize that the total war waged by the Delawares and Shawnees was well on the way to destroying the province of Pennsylvania.

The reason why the Delawares did not press the attack, even though they were able to infiltrate and lay waste whatever part of the province they wished, lay in the nature of their military tradition. War, in Delaware society, was not a function of political organization. When tension between families or communities arrived at the breaking point, direct action was taken by whoever desired it. This meant that men with courage, prestige, and ambition gathered around them parties of warriors who agreed to follow these temporary leaders in specific, separate forays. Discipline, strict enough in combat, ended with the dispersal of the band at the close of the raid. Consequently, there was no machinery for mounting a sustained, coördinated offensive. The effectiveness of Delaware war-making was in direct proportion to the number of warriors in the field; if reverses, or hunger, or mere lack of interest in the war suddenly reduced the number of warriors on hand for raids, no discipline was available to maintain the campaign. Tactically, the Delaware captains might show great skill; but of collective strategy there was very little but what a loose understanding among communities could achieve.

Teedyuscung, like other Delawares, was not impelled to fight by simple economic interest. The whites were a symbol of humiliation to him; war gave him an excuse for killing white people. But, he could say (as other Delawares were saying) that his fury arose from the fact that his lands had been stolen from him. He was fighting for justice. He and his countrymen had been cheated of their birthright, and he was rushing to avenge the injury (twenty years later). Leading a successful war party was also a wise move for an Indian with political ambitions, and Teedyuscung does seem about this time to have set himself toward attaining a place of authority. But here too we can see the working of that double motive: that desire at once to emulate and destroy the whites. Gun and scalping knife; power, place, and fame: these were tools with which Teedyuscung labored to convince himself that the white men weren't so important after all.

But, even though war acted as a cathartic in Teedyuscung's emotional economy, it is important to remember that his lifting up the hatchet against the English was only performed in fact, if not in wish, after he had taken all reasonable measures to ally himself and the Wyoming Indians with Brother Onas. The Wyoming Indians had been neglected by the English, and this neglect had not only wounded their vanity, it had put them in a critical economic position, without traders to supply their need for ammunition, and an impossible military one, surrounded on all sides by war parties of French Indians. Teedyuscung would probably never have taken the plunge into open aggression if Brother Onas had not put him into a situation which offered no other alternative. Malice and spite against the English were certainly motives in Teedyuscung's life; but they did not become effective until his motives of identification and admiration were withered by neglect.

Fear

1756

There was fear along the Susquehanna that winter. Fear kept the villages continually in a stir. Fear was epidemic: fear of starvation, fear of the Six Nations, fear of the French, and above all, fear of the English. The entire fighting strength of the Susquehanna Delawares was not much more than two hundred men, although they, in conjunction with the Ohio Delawares, who numbered about seven hundred, had by March killed some two hundred people in Pennsylvania, and captured an equal number. There were English prisoners in almost every one of the Delaware towns from Nescopeck to Pasigachkunk. Having ravaged the white settlements, they now lived in dread of return raids by the better armed and more numerous white men. Their anxiety was augmented by hunger, for the warriors' absence from their families on the continual forays meant a serious decline in the returns from the winter's hunting.

At the end of January the river between Harris' and Tioga was virtually uninhabited. Teedyuscung himself early in the month had taken his followers, prisoners, and scalps up to Tioga, out of range of English revenge, where they lived in a body. These followers of his—"a considerable force"—included Delawares, Mahicans, Shawnees, and Nanticokes from Wyoming, together with a few straggling Six Nations Indians who had turned against the English.[1] The Delawares who left Wyoming just before Teedyuscung reached the town with his prisoners had scattered far and wide. On New Year's day some of them had attacked and put to flight a company of raw militia who, under the direction of Benjamin Franklin, were trying to erect a fort at Gnadenhütten to guard the pass. After routing the soldiers the Indians had completed the work of the November massacre by burning the deserted dwellings of the native congregation at Gnadenhütten East.[2] This blow, they thought, would inevitably draw forth retaliation, and they had fled, some into the Ohio country to the protection of the French at Fort Machault, others to Tioga.[3]

In February, Wyoming was repopulated by Paxinosa and a few pro-English Shawnees and Iroquois, including the kidnapped Shickellamies, and by refugees from Nescopeck. The neutral families lived in a separate town from the warriors' party. Two Six Nations Indian spies, sent up the Susquehanna for intelligence by Conrad Weiser, reported that it would have been as much as their lives were worth to set foot in the "warriors' town."[4]

But by the end of February the second Wyoming population was almost completely without provisions. This meant that they would either have to make peace with the English (which seemed unlikely at the time), or else settle closer to the French. Although Paxinosa opposed this latter alternative, he was afraid to speak, since he had been threatened with death if he did not keep silent. Canoes were built and preparations were made to move to the Ohio by way of Tioga.[5] At the beginning of March a rumor was circulated that the English were coming. The Wyoming population had been living in a condition close to panic for weeks. The inhabitants, about one hundred in all, hid their precious supplies of grain among the rocks and fled into the woods, where they remained in hiding for two weeks. When they finally returned to the town, they found hundreds of Indians were assembling there to make the trip up river to Tioga and the Ohio. Four days later the whole town marched off in a body —men, women, children, and portable possessions. They arrived at Tioga nearly starving. A council was held immediately and it was decided to split into two parties. Over half of the families marched on westward to the Ohio and, they hoped, French supply houses; the rest elected to remain at Canasetego, a village about forty miles west of Tioga on the banks of a tributary of the Susquehanna.[6] Canasetego was not far from Pasigachkunk.

During the winter Tioga had been the rendezvous of some fifty warriors, who continually talked of vengeance for wrongs done them by the English, from time to time went out on forays in bands of a dozen or so, and succeeded in collecting twenty white prisoners.[7] But by the end of March French intelligence was reporting that six hundred warriors were gathered there.[8] These refugees had converged on the town from all directions, and many of them had come from Wyoming.

* * *

Up to now during the war the Six Nations had been unable to play any decisive role in affairs on the Susquehanna. Although nominally the Onondaga Council possessed authority to direct the actions of the guest populations there, the Six Nations had been flouted openly. Their viceroy, John Shickellamy, and his family had been kidnapped and carried to Nescopeck and thence to Wyoming, where John was rescued in February by the two Six Nations Indian spies, and brought down by them into Pennsylvania.[9] The orders sent to the Delawares to take up the hatchet against the French, in the fall of 1755, and the command to cease warring against the English, in December, had been ignored. Scaroyady had been insulted and threatened with death. These affronts had not passed unnoticed in the Iroquois country. In some private councils, independent of the Great Council, it was agreed to cut the Delawares off if they refused to make peace with the English; but this decision did not represent the common policy of the Six Nations.[10] Unable to deal with their nephews, the Six Nations dumped the whole problem in the lap of Pennsylvania, saying, "We always look'd upon the Delawares as the more immediate care of Onas, that they were within the circle of his arms."[11]

The reason for this vacillation—alarming to those like Weiser and Johnson who leaned upon the Six Nations as the English colonies' first line of defense against the French—lay in the defection of some of the Senecas and Cayugas. These tribes, the westernmost of the Six Nations, were really closer to the French than to the English, both geographically and politically. The Senecas had not joined in the December message to the Susquehanna Delawares commanding them to lay down the hatchet.[12] And in February 1756 over a hundred Seneca and Cayuga men, women, and children had visited Niagara to make peace with the French.[13] These Geneseo Senecas and some of the Cayugas constituted an anti-English faction in the councils of the Confederacy, sapping the force of the League and making any sort of unified action impossible. Apparently their position was a coldly realistic one. The French and English, they said, were slowly squeezing the Indians to death between them. Therefore they were offering the Delawares, Shawnees, and Nanticokes full incorporation into the League if they coöperated in driving the English back to the line of the Kittatinny Mountains. After making peace with the English, they would starve the French out of the Ohio. (The French were notoriously unable to maintain self-supporting agricultural settlements.) Negotiations were even afoot with the Cherokees and the Creeks, to the south, to persuade them to come into the alliance and to settle on the Ohio.[14]

But now the pendulum was swinging the other way. Teedyuscung had appealed to these Senecas for aid in the fall of 1755 and had been given the hatchet in reply. But now, as he sat shivering and ill fed in his winter camp at Tioga, watching the starving refugees pouring out westward to an uncertain destiny in the Ohio country, it began to appear that

the English in Pennsylvania must be winning the battle. In
1755 there had been talk of the French building a fort at
Shamokin; now Brother Onas and Scaroyady were planning
for the erection of an English fort there. And by April, when
the government of Pennsylvania declared war, it was becoming increasingly difficult for war parties to make successful
raids, for the English had stretched a string of blockhouses
across the frontiers all the way from the Delaware River to
the Allegheny Mountains.

In March the Mohawks and Oneidas, who were firm in the
English interest, took action at Otseningo. They had been
prompted to it the month before by Sir William Johnson,
who had asked them to stop the Susquehanna Delawares from
fighting the English.[15] The Mohawks and Oneidas sent messengers to Otseningo, the Nanticoke town far up the Susquehanna near the Mohawk country. The Nanticokes obligingly
invited all the Susquehanna Indians to a "great Meeting" at
their town. Although none of the Delaware sachems attended
(perhaps because the great migration north and westward
was under way), over three hundred Delaware warriors assembled, together with chiefs of the Shawnees, Chickasaws,
and Mahicans. There the message of the Mohawks and
Oneidas was delivered. The substance of it was a demand
that the Delawares sober up; their actions were regarded by
the Six Nations as the behavior of drunken men. The Nanticokes, who had remained neutral throughout the war, seconded the Iroquois demand with a belt of their own a fathom
long and twenty-five rows wide asking the Delawares to lay
down the hatchet.

The Shawnees, Chickasaws, and Mahicans readily agreed
to make peace; few of them had done any fighting. But the
Delaware warriors maintained a truculent tone. They looked
upon themselves as men, they said, over whom no other
nation had any authority. "We are Men," they declared, "and
are determined not to be ruled any longer by you as Women;
and we are determined to cut off all the English, except those
that may make their Escape from us in Ships; so say no more

to us on that Head, lest we cut off your private Parts, and make Women of you, as you have done of us."[16] They refused to acknowledge any of the Six Nations as their "uncles" except the Senecas.

This "rash Speech" was answered patiently by the Iroquois deputies, and the Delaware spokesmen were brought at last to give conditional allegiance to the principle of peace. If their chief men were willing, they said, they would put aside the hatchet. They demanded an exchange of prisoners —an odd request, because, according to Governor Morris, only one Delaware was imprisoned in Pennsylvania, and he was "put in Jayle in order to keep him out of harms way" after a mob accused him of burning some plantations, whereas the Delawares themselves had hundreds of white prisoners. They were referring, presumably, to the Christian Indians at Bethlehem. The Delaware delegates promised to send the peace belt to the Ohio tribes, and to attend a formal peace treaty with Sir William Johnson at Onondaga in the spring.[17]

Teedyuscung did not go to Otseningo, but on hearing the news of it he made a trip to the Mohawk country to find out for himself what the sentiments of the Iroquois were. He was told in no uncertain terms that he must stop all warfare and make peace with Pennsylvania. In a long conversation with Canyase, one of the principal councilors of the Mohawks, he was given to understand that as a Delaware he had better do what the Mohawks (under whose "protection" the Delawares then were) told him. The Delawares, said Canyase (echoing Canasetego twelve years earlier), were lowly, effeminate creatures subordinate to the Six Nations; they were only "half-men."[18] Teedyuscung returned to Pasigachkunk indignant at the cold-blooded insults he had received—but no longer sure that the French was the winning side.

*   *   *

In Philadelphia, divided councils were the fashion. On April 14 a declaration of war was published, with a scalp bounty appended to give it emphasis: $130 would be paid for each scalp of a Delaware male over ten years of age, $50 for a woman's scalp, $150 for male prisoners, $130 for women and children.[19] But from April 19 to 23 a conference was held at the home of pacifistic Israel Pemberton, the prominent Quaker merchant, and Scaroyady and Conrad Weiser were persuaded to agree in principle to the suggestion that a peace treaty be held, at Quaker expense, between Pennsylvania and the Delawares.[20] Sir William Johnson, the imperial negotiator with the Six Nations and their allies, was offended by both policies, regarding the declaration of war as prejudicing the negotiations begun at Otseningo, and resenting the treaty of peace (which was eventually held) as infringing on his own prerogatives as sole imperial negotiator with the Six Nations and their allies. Governor Morris, however, with a happy inconsistency dispatched four peace emissaries to the Susquehanna Delawares twelve days after he had declared war against them. Captain Newcastle and Jagrea (both of them Six Nations Indians), William Locquies, and Augustus of Bethlehem were directed to acquaint the Delawares with the news of the Otseningo conference and to invite them to a treaty with Brother Onas.[21]

The ambassadors found the Susquehanna Valley deserted. No one was living at Wyoming and the houses there were all burnt down or fallen to pieces. The Christian Indians, Augustus discovered, had gone off with the enemy Indians to the neighborhood of Tioga.[22]

But at Tioga they found a horde of Delawares and Mahicans, mostly hostile to the English. Captain Newcastle, as an Iroquois, was able to bluff his way into their respect. When the chiefs of the surrounding villages sent word that they wanted Newcastle to visit their towns one by one, Newcastle haughtily refused. "It was Customary," he said, "to transact Matters of Importance and of a public Nature, in

the most public Place. . . . The Meeting should be at Tiao-
gon." The chiefs finally agreed to come to Tioga.

Captain Newcastle was polite, suave, and aggressive. After
announcing that he brought a message from the King of
England, he commiserated with the unhappy Delawares. An
evil spirit, he said, had evidently thrown dust in their eyes,
so that they had become lost and unable to see what they
were doing. This evil spirit had also stopped up their throats
with "some poisonous Stuff or other" so that they could not
speak to their brethren the English, and had plugged their
ears so that they could not hear what was said to them. Newcastle, the Iroquois ambassador, accordingly rubbed their
eyes, cleaned their throats, and bored open their ears with
the customary three strings of wampum, following the
ancient Six Nations protocol for solemn conclave. (The same
"three rare words of requickening" are found also in the
Iroquois Condolence Ceremony.[23]) He then informed them
of the peace agreements recently made at Otseningo, in which
the Tioga Indians' great men had not joined, and proposed
on behalf of Brother Onas that "the old Treaties of Friendship . . . be renewed and good Friendship restored as good
as ever it was." The Tioga Delawares were invited to come
down to Philadelphia to a peace treaty. "I know very well,"
he said, "that you are a foolish People like little Children,
and that it was for want of Understanding that the Evil Spirit
had such a Power over you. I promise you that the Blood
shall be covered with Sand, and we will joyntly pull up a
large Tree by the Root, and there dig a Hole as deep as to
the Waters below the Earth and there we will threw in and
bury our Hatchets and so plant the Tree upon that hole
again so that neither your Posterity or ours will ever be able
to find it."

Then Teedyuscung, the speaker for the Delawares, was
introduced by Paxinosa, who was acting as interpreter
("because Newcastle talks good Shawanese and Paxanosa [a
Shawnee] talks good Delaware"). Teedyuscung rejoiced that

peace was about to be reëstablished between Brother Onas
and the Delawares and Mahicans of the Susquehanna Valley.
The Delawares, he said, subscribed wholeheartedly to the
Otseningo agreements. "We have laid aside our Hatchet and
will never make use of it more against you or your Brethren
the English," he told Newcastle. But, he said, he could not
speak for the Ohio Delawares.

In Weiser's limpid translation, Teedyuscung's speech is
almost poetry. Sincerity, candor, and artifice were so in-
geniously blended in it that the hearer, and probably Teedyuscung himself, could not know where one ended and the
other began.

Brother Onas [he pleaded], We desire you will look upon us with
Eyes of Mercy, we are a very poor People, our Wives and Children
are almost naked, we are void of Understanding and destitute
of the Necessaries of Life. Pity us.
Bretheren, There is a great Number of our People among you
and in a Manner confin'd, we desire you will set them at Liberty,
or rather give them a safe Conduct to Wayomick where we intend
to settle, as on your Fireside there we will joyntly with you kindle
a Council Fire which shall always burn and we will be one
People with you.[24]

Eloquence could do no more to melt the anger of Brother
Onas.

But confusion still beset the English. No sooner had the
cheerful news of peace been brought back by Newcastle to
Pennsylvania than her neighbor New Jersey declared war.
This was on June 2.[25] On June 3 Governor Morris of Pennsylvania proclaimed a thirty-day armistice on the east side
of the Susquehanna, giving as his reasons the Otseningo conference, the Tioga treaty, and the cessation of Indian raids
since Newcastle's return.[26] On June 12, nine days after the
armistice was published, a raiding party of one hundred New
Jersey militia entered Pennsylvania and proceeded to Wyoming, where they fortunately were able to satisfy their valor
with burning four deserted villages.[27] Just before the New

Jersey irregulars set out, however, Newcastle had been directed to go back to Tioga with a formal invitation to treat with Brother Onas, and assurances that the Tioga Delawares were free to attend Johnson's treaty at Onondaga also.[28] When Pennsylvania learned about the New Jersey expedition, Newcastle was recalled, and he was not sent out again until June 26, when the road was clear and safe.[29]

*   *   *

Teedyuscung had to go home to Pasigachkunk early in May to plant corn.[30] His feelings about the political situation remained undecided throughout the spring. In spite of the pressure being brought to bear by the Six Nations and Sir William Johnson, and in spite of the glowing promises of reconciliation offered by Newcastle on behalf of Brother Onas, Teedyuscung was not eager to creep back like a kicked puppy to the feet of the white men and their Iroquoian allies. And there was still good reason to doubt the honesty of the whites. A rumor reached Tioga about the first of May that an English army was on the march against the Susquehanna Delawares.[31] (This "army" was probably Newcastle and his three companions.) Other rumors had it that the proposed English fort at Shamokin was intended not only to resist the French but also to secure unpurchased lands along the river.[32] Had Teedyuscung known (if he did not know) that Brother Onas was also planning to build a fort (never actually constructed) at the upper end of the Wyoming Valley,[33] his uneasiness would have been even more acute. As it was, he decided to see what the French had to offer him.

After planting his corn, and leaving his wife to take care of things at home, Teedyuscung and a group of the Delaware warriors began a march northward to visit the French post at Niagara. Their path lay through Seneca country. At Geneseo they were unexpectedly stopped by the hitherto pro-French Senecas and advised not to go on to Niagara. But the

Delawares were defiant. They had been made men (i.e., had
been given the hatchet) by the Senecas, they said; now they
intended to use it. It was the Senecas who had encouraged
them to attack the English. "You now want to throw all the
blame on us," said the Delawares, "and make peace, which
we will not hearken to, but will go to our Father [the French]
who will assist us, and protect us."[34]

Teedyuscung and his hungry Delaware cohorts reached
Niagara expecting to find that their Father was as well supplied with bread and gunpowder as ever. The meeting was
a disappointment. The French were hungry themselves, for
the English blockade was cutting off the French settlements
from their supply bases in France. When Teedyuscung asked
for goods and ammunition, he was put off with specious
promises. "If they would come again in two months," said
the French commandant, "they should have everything
aplenty, all what their eyes could see or hearts desire."
Teedyuscung himself was given "a fine dark brown Cloth
Coat laced with Gold." The French commander pounded his
chest, showed them mine tunnels underneath possible avenues
of attack, and displayed a faked letter from King George in
which the English sovereign proposed to his French brother
the extermination of the Indians. But no amount of courtesy
and boastfulness was sufficient to erase the suspicion of poverty. When the Delawares left, they said that in the fall five
hundred of their people from the Susquehanna would move
into the French zone in the Ohio. The Indians could make
specious promises, too.[35]

While Teedyuscung was sounding out the French at Niagara, Sir William Johnson and the Six Nations were waiting
impatiently at Onondaga for the Delawares. On June 13
Johnson dispatched two messengers to hurry them up.[36] Johnson had gone to some trouble in arranging this treaty to
reunite the Susquehanna Delawares firmly with the English
and the Six Nations. He had even, at great expense, brought
thirty Mahicans and Munsees to Onondaga, all well clothed

and well armed, simply to prove to the Delawares how well the English treated even the humblest of their Algonkian allies. These "River Indians," who had recently been given asylum by the Mohawks, were to be Johnson's object lesson in the advantages of an alliance with the English.[37]

The messengers returned to Onondaga on June 27 with a small delegation of twenty-six Susquehanna Indians, mostly Shawnees and Nanticokes; only two young Delaware warriors came with them.[38] The Delawares in and around Tioga were probably holding off until they heard from Teedyuscung whether or not the French would be able to guarantee their security. There was also a council being held among the Indian nations in the Ohio country to plan new attacks on Pennsylvania, an all-out assault by an army of several hundred warriors, and the decisions of this council were daily expected.[39] But shortly following the messengers from Onondaga, news came from Teedyuscung, discouraging too much confidence in the French. Immediately a delegation of Tioga Delawares and Shawnees, who together were the core of the Indian population on the Susquehanna, set off for the meeting at Onondaga. Paxinosa went as head of the Shawnee, Nutimus with three others of his countrymen as representatives of the Delawares. They arrived at Onondaga on July 1.[40]

The treaty at Onondaga, which took place while Teedyuscung was preparing for the treaty with Pennsylvania, officially ended the war between the English colonies and the Susquehanna Delawares. (Paxinosa declared that none of the Susquehanna Shawnees had been involved.) The manner of reconciliation was quaint, however. On July 10 Sir William formally demanded of Nutimus, the Delaware "king," whether he was ready to make peace. Nutimus (with only five or six Indians in his entourage) loftily replied that he would consult his nation. Sir William, in alarm, hurried to the Six Nations, asking them to persuade Nutimus to make terms. What happened when the Iroquois descended on

Nutimus is not known; but he agreed to subscribe to the peace.

Next day Johnson repeated the question: Would the Delawares agree to a peace? He wanted, he said, an immediate and satisfactory reply. Nutimus then delivered a prepared statement. The Delawares, he said, had been seduced by the French and their comrades the Senecas. "Since we have lost our ancient counsellors," he said, "we are ignorant of . . . what passed in the days of our ancestors . . . and our Uncles the Six Nations have not taken due care to refresh our Memories nor to remind us properly of our several engagements." There were elements of special pleading in this appeal, but undoubtedly the displacement of Delaware communities had caused an interruption in the handing down of tradition which confused the whole pattern of intertribal relations. Nutimus then promised to lay down the hatchet and to deliver up the English prisoners, and from henceforth in diplomatic affairs to follow the lead of the Six Nations. The Delaware chief gave Johnson a belt of wampum symbolizing the new covenant and chain of friendship; Johnson reciprocated with a peace belt which Nutimus engaged to transmit to the Ohio Delawares; and the two men shook hands.

Sir William now proceeded to take off the Delaware petticoats; that is, in his honorary capacity as a member of the Onondaga council, he formally relieved the Delawares of the title of "women" which Canyase and Canasetego had used in a derogatory sense. This move, however, was going beyond what the Six Nations had anticipated. Although the title of "women," as applied to the Delawares following their decline after 1737, did have an ignoble connotation, it also symbolized their status as allies and probationary members of the Iroquois Confederacy; other subordinate members of the Confederacy, including the Tuscaroras, Mahicans, and Nanticokes, have also been called "women."[41] And so the Six

Nations delegates politely applauded Johnson's gesture, but said that by themselves they could not authorize such a step. The Onondaga Council would have to ratify the action which Johnson, presuming on his position as honorary counselor of the Six Nations, had taken on his own initiative.

All this was preparatory to Johnson's offering the hatchet to the Susquehanna Indians and to the Senecas. The Senecas first took up the war belt, Paxinosa took it up for the Shawnees, and finally Nutimus for the Delawares. Everyone then sang the war song. Nutimus, "the Delaware King," sang "with remarkable warmth."[42]

*   *   *

While Nutimus was at Onondaga going through his paces to please Sir William Johnson and the Six Nations (a performance for which he was paid "a present in Cloaths, Cash, &ca Amountg. to £36.15.00"),[43] Teedyuscung was celebrating his impending visit to Pennsylvania. At Canasetego lived a daughter of the famous French Margaret. In the early part of July Teedyuscung paid her a visit of a week or two which culminated in a "drunken frolic." When he was drunk Teedyuscung's latent hostility to the English was able to find expression. In the presence of a white man, a prisoner who later escaped and told his story, Teedyuscung said cynically, "The Indians could make Peace and . . . the Indians could also break Peace when made."

When Teedyuscung left French Margaret's daughter (after selling an "English Female Prisoner" to buy a horse) he rode down along the river to Tioga.[44] There forty or fifty Delawares, coming from the treaty in the west, arrived just as he was about to set forth again to treat with Brother Onas. These western Indians asked him to lead them in a raid against the white settlements. But Teedyuscung, whatever his impulses might tell him, was not willing to do this. He was going to see about peace, he said, at the behest of the

Mohawks. The western warriors would be wise to sit still and wait until he came back.[45]

Teedyuscung seems to have been prompted to go to the treaty largely by motives of economic expediency. The French had failed him; the Six Nations and English were asking for his aid; and he and his people were desperately in need of traders' goods. Paxinosa's son and three other Shawnees, sent to Bethlehem early in July by Captain Newcastle, were reported as being out of ammunition and "extreamly Bair in Cloaths."[46] A Susquehanna Delaware sachem told a white prisoner (who also escaped and reported the remark) that the "several" Indians who were going to Pennsylvania were actually going to see whether the English were strong and to get provisions. Food was scarce on the Susquehanna that spring and the French scalp bounty was only one loaf of bread per scalp. To the Delawares, looking at the Six Nations, who were being fed and clothed by the English and were at peace to boot, there seemed to be little profit in starving while they fought French battles.[47]

Teedyuscung and eight retainers arrived at Fort Allen on July 15, 1756,[48] the "King" riding the horse which he had bought with the money he made selling the "English Female Prisoner." They were escorted by Captain Newcastle, who had finally made his second trip to Tioga to bring the Delawares down to the treaty. On the seventeenth Teedyuscung went on to Bethlehem. In the woods behind him he left about twenty-five warriors, camped at various stations between Fort Allen and Wyoming. These warriors were instructed, in the case of their leader being injured, to fall upon the settlements and avenge him.[49]

At Bethlehem, a war-swollen village of eight hundred inhabitants and the headquarters of his one-time Moravian mentors, Teedyuscung's spirit expanded. Once a poor pensioner of the whites, now he was returning to their homes as a great chief, a man of importance, solicited by the powers of the world. He acquired a new pair of shoe buckles to grace his steps.[50] And on the eighteenth he conferred with Timothy Horsfield and Major William Parsons, who had been charged with the entertainment of the Indian guests of the province. He came, he said, as the king of ten nations, and would wait for the Governor of Pennsylvania at Easton.[51] After thus announcing his presence and his importance, he proceeded on to Easton, the place of treaty, with an entourage of 109 Indians, chiefly Senecas.[52]

Captain Newcastle bustled off to Philadelphia to deliver Teedyuscung's announcement. Even that redoubtable Iroquois was impressed. He advised the Governor not to delay. Teedyuscung, the great warrior, was ready to make peace, but the times were dangerous. "Tarry not," said Newcastle, "but Hasten to him."[53]

He Who Makes the Earth Tremble

1756

According to John Pemberton, a Quaker who knew Teedyuscung well, the meaning of his name was *one who makes the earth tremble*. He supposedly received this title from his being "a very large and portly man." John Pemberton may have been misled, however. Dr. Frank G. Speck, an anthropologist long acquainted with the Delaware language, has informed the writer that the name can best be translated *as far as the wood's edge*. Perhaps Teedyuscung used his name to add to his stature.[1]

But when Teedyuscung came to Easton in July 1756 he did not need to depend on etymology for reputation. He was a physically impressive figure in his own right—"a lusty raw-boned man"—and the gauntness which he owed to a winter's semi-starvation must have merely added to his imposing carriage. He nearly overwhelmed Major William Parsons, Penn's sickly agent in the Forks of the Delaware, who had been instructed to entertain the Indians until the Governor arrived. Teedyuscung, said Parsons in awe, was "haughty and very desirous of respect and command he can drink three Quarts or a Gallon of Rum a day without being drunk." Parsons went on to credit his guest with being the man who had first persuaded the Delawares to join the French and attack the frontiers. "He was the man" commanding the

Indians who perpetrated the massacre at Gnadenhütten in November 1755.[2]

This final accretion of notoriety Teedyuscung did not deserve. As a matter of fact, on the road between Bethlehem and Easton he had got into a violent argument with a Shawnee warrior who had been one of the party which massacred the missionaries at the Huts of Grace. Perhaps Teedyuscung cherished a sentimental attachment to his old teachers and the place where he was (temporarily) saved from sin. At any rate, whatever its origin, the dispute ended with the Shawnee dead by the roadside and Teedyuscung riding on to Easton amid awed retainers.[3]

There was something Odyssean in Teedyuscung's return to the Forks. Run out of New Jersey, sneered at by clerks for making baskets, pitied by missionaries, elbowed from the Forks of Delaware, and finally lured off to Wyoming, he was come back, like Ulysses, gaunt and battle-scarred, to claim his own. "Lo, the poor Indian, with untutored mind . . ." Pope could write in England; but in America the unbidden suitors trembled. The wives of his warriors strutted about the streets of Easton in gaudy shirts made out of Dutch tablecloths, looted from the homes of murdered settlers.[4] He himself had killed white men; he had murdered a man by the roadside on his way to this very treaty. What might he not do if he were crossed?

Even Governor Morris was not a big enough man to face down the legend of Teedyuscung. Morris proposed changing the place of meeting to Bethlehem. Teedyuscung wrote back to the Governor of Pennsylvania:

Brother, I am very glad to hear from you. At the Distance of 400 miles from hence I received your Invitation to come and make peace. I understood that you had laid a Junk of Fire here at Easton that I might come and smoke my Pipe by it. Brother, since you sent that Message I am come and will stay here, And I can't understand what you mean by sending me about from place to place like a Child.[5]

The meeting place remained Easton.

It did not take Teedyuscung long to discover the moral advantage he possessed; and when he knew that he was feared, he cast off all restraint, indulging in an orgy of drink and boastfulness. Irresponsibly he called himself "the King of Ten Nations"—a title which stuck to him, at least among Pennsylvanians. He and his "Wild Company" were "very much on the Gascoon and at times abusive to the Inhabitants for they all spoke English more or less." Teedyuscung, said Major Parsons, was full of himself, constantly repeating that whichever side he took must stand, and the other fall. He said insolently several times that he had just come from the French, who had pressed him earnestly to join them against the English, and that when he had decided which side he wished to join, he would publish it aloud to the world. At other times he said that he had not come down to the English for the sake of what presents they would give him (evidently the thought of presents was in his mind), but only to make peace, and that if the English accepted his proferred alliance they would find him a true and useful ally. He also said that if he wanted, he could release most of the English prisoners in Indian camps.[6]

In order to emphasize his new-found dignity, Teedyuscung —significantly—considered it necessary to assemble a wardrobe of European clothes. In his public, official appearances he affected the "fine dark brown cloth Coat very much laced with Gold" which the French had given him at Niagara, a gesture at once of flamboyance and defiance. Instead of moccasins he wore riding boots, or shoes adorned with buckles. He wore European checkered cloth trousers rather than Indian leggings, and below the trousers he sported stockings decorated with scarlet gartering. His shirts were probably the ruffled garlic or tandem popular in the Indian trade. He combed his hair with a trade comb, washed his face with soap, took snuff, drank rum, and ate gingerbread and molasses when he wanted a snack. He played cards to pass the time. And of course, as befitted his status as "King," he never walked where he could ride the horse he had bought with an English female prisoner, and equipped with a new saddle and bridle.[7]

*   *   *

Such was the heroic spectacle which Teedyuscung gave to the inhabitants of Bethlehem and Easton. But his flamboyant behavior seems to have covered up an acute fear of appearing ridiculous to his hosts. Behind the mask of royalty one can see a man who was afraid of white people, ashamed of his race and his culture, torn between the desire to identify himself with the Europeans and the desire to conquer them. When he was drunk he was able to bleed off his anxieties in braggadocio and insult. When he was sober he more often tried to placate, to imitate, and to fall in with white suggestions. But the two sorts of behavior were not confined to intoxication and soberness respectively; they overlapped, and in his most friendly moods spitefulness showed; in his most aggressive, hints of remorse.

Thus the killing of the Shawnee may have satisfied in part a dimly understood desire to make amends for the murders *he* had committed on white people, even though at the time of the murder Teedyuscung was trying to entice away converts from Bethlehem[8] and was browbeating his hosts at Easton. And thus, when Teedyuscung in a relatively jovial mood was chatting with a blacksmith at Stroudsburg, spite crept into his humor. The blacksmith had greeted him familiarly with, "Well, cousin, how do you do?" "Cousin, cousin," repeated Teedyuscung; "how do you make that out?" "Oh, we are all cousins from Adam," said the blacksmith. "Ah," returned Teedyuscung, "then I am glad it is no nearer."[9]

Teedyuscung's arrogance and bombast while he waited at Easton can be regarded as a strenuous effort to bridge a social gap. His official position, that of a speaker, did not authorize any such aggressive assertion of his own consequence; indeed, his gasconade was bad manners by both the Delawares' and the white man's book. As has been suggested in earlier chapters, Teedyuscung was probably not a sachem, since he had never been appointed to the position by the female chief-makers of his lineage. He had merely acted as a speaker for the Delawares on several occasions, and it was as ambassador (i.e., speaker) that he was coming down to Pennsylvania. It was Nutimus, the sachem who in conjunction with Paxinosa enjoyed the highest prestige along the lower Susquehanna, who had attended the definitive treaty of peace with Sir William Johnson at Onondaga. Teedyuscung's visit to Brother Onas was of secondary importance, serving merely to confirm the covenant already subscribed to by the major parties. Teedyuscung furthermore in no way represented the Ohio Delawares, who were several times as numerous as those on the Susquehanna. As a successful warrior and a father he had gathered about him some of his immediate relatives (chiefly his sons and brothers and their households) over whom he exercised a *de facto* sachemship.[10] His commission as an ambassador apparently stemmed from these families; from the general moral pressure of the Six Nations on the Delawares to stop fighting and make peace; and from Nutimus.

The whites, however, did not yet know how slender were the roots of his importance, and for the moment were accepting Teedyuscung at his own valuation. He had said he was the king of ten nations: the Six Nations, the Munsees, the Unamis, the Mahicans, and the Lenapes; and the Pennsylvanians, who were eager to find someone with whom to make peace, were only too glad to agree. They did not question whether he was really the king of the ten nations or merely endorsed by them in his pacific intentions. The whites wanted a king to deal with, and a king they would have. Even Teedyuscung was surprised at the way the white people swallowed all his rant and strident gasconade; he was so surprised, indeed, that he wept.

The occasion of his weeping was a public dinner given by Governor Morris to Teedyuscung and the twenty-three other official Indian delegates (of whom no less than seven were his sons, grandsons, and nephews).[11] The Governor, as anxious to please the terrible barbarian monarch as that monarch was to impress the Governor, tactfully did not segregate the Indians and the whites but mixed them, Indian and English, side by side at the table. The fare was sumptuous, with plenty of meat and plenty of drink, and the cooks were careful to give the Indians the best portions. All this, with pleasantry in conversation and a few compliments from the Governor to the "King," so overcame Teedyuscung that he burst into tears. He had been bad, said Teedyuscung, and had come to Pennsylvania expecting different treatment. In pathetic detail he expressed his sorrow for all the mischief which he had done. But now, being convinced of the openness and goodness of the Governor and his people, he would return to his former love for them and would be a faithful worker for peace.[12]

Much of Teedyuscung's sudden efflorescence of love for the whites can be laid to the Quakers, who had taken the initiative in arranging the treaty and who, true to their engagement, showed up at Easton in numbers, along with a wagon-load of gifts for the Indians and a subscription of £1,200.[13] (The Assembly of Pennsylvania, by comparison, had contributed only £300 to the treaty's expenses.)[14] This entry of the Friendly Association for the Gaining and Preserving Peace with the Indians by Pacific Measures, as a separate body in the arena of forest diplomacy, was a revolutionary departure from precedent. Traditionally the proprietors and their agents had sole authority in Indian affairs. The Quakers were in effect seceding from the established order and were trying to manipulate the proprietaries by manipulating the Indians. Their objectives, other than humanitarian, were to retain the commercial good will of the Indians and to discredit the proprietors.

Teedyuscung had come to Easton in a spirit of curiosity concerning these people, about whom the halo of William Penn still clung, though slightly mildewed by contact with the Walking Purchase. Captain Newcastle, the Six Nations go-between who had effected the meeting of Brother Onas and Teedyuscung, was a firm Friend. (When he died, a few months later, he was buried at his own request in the Friends' Burying Ground.) On the trail down from Tioga, Newcastle had told Teedyuscung about the many virtues of the Friends, and had also told him that the Quakers were not proud like other white people. Teedyuscung would see, said Newcastle: the Quakers would come to meet *him*.

On the twenty-fifth Teedyuscung visited the lodging of Governor Morris to present him with a string of wampum to open his eyes and clear his throat.[15] As he was talking with the Governor, in trooped the Quakers. Teedyuscung was overjoyed. "Now here's Quakers!" he cried. "Now I believe all I have heard to be true!" And at once he announced his regard for and confidence in those excellent people, the Society of Friends.[16]

Later in the day four of the most prominent Friends—Anthony Morris, John Evans, William Brown, and Israel Pemberton—called at Teedyuscung's lodgings to shake hands with him. Probably no white man had ever taken the trouble to solicit the esteem of Teedyuscung (this visit was prior to the tearful dinner party) and Teedyuscung simply soaked up the compliment like a sponge. Their courtesy was a welcome change from the curses and ribald abuse he was receiving at the hands of drunken and bitterly hostile townspeople. He said he was *very* glad to see them, and that Newcastle had told him about the Quakers, and how they would come to meet him. Now that he found it to be true, he was touched to the bottom of his heart, and would not even talk to the Governor unless the Quakers were present.

"To avoid giving offense we did not stay five minutes with him," wrote the diarist of the Quaker party. The offense they feared was not to Teedyuscung but to the Governor; but their caution was unavailing. The Governor, jealous of the Friends, who represented the anti-proprietary assembly, at once proclaimed that no unauthorized persons (meaning the Friends) would henceforth be allowed to speak with the Indians. This embargo was legally justified, since it rested on the royal charter, which defined Indian affairs as the prerogative of the Penns and their personal representatives.

But the Governor's edict, besides being antagonizing, was too late. Teedyuscung had been won over to the Quaker side of the fence. That evening he and many of his friends came uninvited to sup with Pemberton and the Friends at their inn. It was with some difficulty that the Quakers were able to persuade the Indians to return to their lodgings, immediately after supper, without taking a drop of liquor. But the mildness of their exhortations, and their manifest esteem, brought the Indians to promise that they would wholly refrain from drink that night, so that they might be fit for business next day.[17]

*   *   *

Next day, true to their promise, the Delawares appeared at the council sober. The Quakers, also sober, although not invited, were present in force ("by attending at the time and place, and crowding ourselves in, [we] obtained admittance and kept minutes").[18] Although sobriety did not remain the Indians' constant style of behavior, the Quakers continued, with ostentatious modesty and stubborn virtue, to attend the meetings by strong-arm methods.

The course of the treaty was strewn with disillusionments for the Governor and his henchmen. Teedyuscung's opening speech on the twenty-eighth, couched in more modest terms than his previous unofficial pronouncements, was chiefly a presentation of credentials. "I am here," he said, "by the Appointment of ten Nations, among which are my Uncles the Six Nations, authorizing me to treat with you, and what I do they will all confirm." This was all right; and so was his claim to be one of the two "kings" appointed by the ten nations to transact public business. But then he went on to admit, "I am but a Messenger from the United Nations, though I act as a Chief Man for the Delawares"; and he referred to the Six Nations as "uncles."[19] These vague and contradictory pretensions were somewhat confusing, from a monarch who had entered the town like a conquering lion. That night, at the dinner described earlier in this chapter, Teedyuscung gave further evidence of modesty.

On Thursday, the twenty-ninth, Governor Morris spoke. Observing that few Delawares were present, he assured Teedyuscung that the invitation to the treaty had been official. He reminded him that one of the prices of peace was the exchange of prisoners. And then, no doubt hoping to equal the Quakers in flattery, he made Teedyuscung "Agent and Counsellor" for the province of Pennsylvania. "You owe it," he said, "to the Country in which you was born."[20]

Teedyuscung rose to the bait. He stood up and taking a large belt of wampum in his hands, held it up before the Governor. The belt showed the black stick-figures of two men, with outstretched arms, on a white background. Between the two men was a hollow square. This belt, said Teedyuscung, was the Independence Belt by which the Iroquois made men of the Delawares. He, Teedyuscung (i.e., Nutimus, whom he was representing) had been at Onondaga in treaty with the Six Nations when Newcastle came to Tioga on his second journey, and at this treaty the Six Nations had renewed their covenant of friendship with the Delawares. "Formerly we were accounted Women," said Teedyuscung, "and employed only in Womens Business; but now they have made Men of us, and [have given us] this Authority as a Man to make Peace."

The belt, said Teedyuscung, had other meanings too. "This Belt further denotes," he declared, "that whoever will not comply with the Terms of Peace, the ten Nations will join against him and strike him; see the dangerous Circumstances I am in; strong Men on both Sides; Hatchets on both Sides; whoever does incline to Peace, him will I join." He waxed almost lyrical over the prospect of peace. "This is a good Day; whoever will make Peace, let him lay hold of this Belt, and the Nations around shall see and know it. I desire to conduct myself according to your Words, which I will perform to the utmost of my Power. I wish the same good Spirit that possessed the good old Man William Penn, who was a Friend to the Indians, may inspire the People of this Province at this Time."

The Governor, thinking that this was the consummation of peace, began heartily to take up the belt—only to be stopped by Teedyuscung, who explained that there was still one more meaning left in the belt. "You see," he pointed out, "a Square in the Middle, meaning the Lands of the Indians, and at one End the Figure of a Man, indicating the English; and at the other End another, meaning the French; our Uncles told us, that both these coveted our Lands; but let us join together to defend our Lands against both, you shall be Partakers with us of our Lands."

This last construction was somehow ominous. It suggested that peace was contingent upon Pennsylvania's guaranteeing the territorial integrity of the Delawares and Six Nations on the Susquehanna and out in the Ohio. Furthermore, it left clouded the exact status of Teedyuscung in the whole matter. Accordingly, next day the Governor and Conrad Weiser invited Captain Newcastle, who was trusted as an honest messenger, to their lodgings to tell them about the belt. Newcastle was emphatic in his insistence that the belt was very important. It had been sent by the Six Nations to the Delawares, he said, and was "a Belt of great Consequence."[21] But next day Newcastle gave an interpretation of the belt somewhat different in tone from any of Teedyuscung's:

Cousins the Delaware Indians: You will remember that you are our Women, our Fore-fathers made you so, and put a Petty Coat on you, and charged you to be true to us, and lye with no other Man; but of late you have suffer'd the String yt ty'd your Petticoat to be cut loose by the French and you lay with them and so became a common Bawd, in which you did very wrong and deserved Chastisement, but notwithstanding this we have still an Esteem for you and as you have throw'd off your Piece, and become stark naked which is a Shame for a Woman We now give you a little Prick & put it in your private Parts and so let it grow there, till you shall be a compleat man. We advise you not to act as a Man yet but be first instructed by us and do as we bid you and you will become a noted man.
Cousins: The English & French fight for our Land, Let us be strong and lay our hand to it, and defend it. In the meantime turn your Eyes & Ears to us and the English our Brethren & you will live as well as we do.[22]

This new rendering of the "Independence Belt" was both less complimentary to Teedyuscung and less reassuring to Brother Onas.

Newcastle's motives in giving the Governor this reading of the belt were partly those of an angry man. He may have been jealous of Teedyuscung's pretentious behavior. At any rate, the two Indians had quarreled, and Teedyuscung ("in a friendly manner") had warned Newcastle. He had heard, said the Delaware monarch, that Newcastle had not long to live; two Delawares had been overheard plotting to kill him by witchcraft.[23] Newcastle, when he learned of this, went immediately to the Governor and told him all about it, asking that it be put down in writing so that, when he died, the guilty party should be known. While Newcastle was talking, Teedyuscung bolted into the room and loudly scolded him. It was all foolishness, he said, turning to the Governor. "He bewitched! The Governor was too wise to hearken to such silly Stories!" But next morning Newcastle nearly died of a sudden, violent attack of pleurisy.[24]

And on the afternoon when Captain Newcastle, Conrad Weiser, and the Governor were discussing the belt in private, Teedyuscung got wind of their meeting and burst "all of a sudden" into the room, and "with a high Tone of Voice" demanded to know what was going on. "I desire all that I have said, and you have said to one another, may be taken down aright!" he cried. "Some speak in the Dark; do not let us do so; let all be clear and known. What is the Reason the Governor holds Councils so close in his Hands, and by Candle Light? The Five Nations used to make him sit out of Doors like a Woman.—If the Five Nations still make him a Woman, they must; but what is the Reason the Governor makes him a Woman, meaning, Why does he confer with Indians without sending for him, to be present and hear what was said?"

The Governor smoothed the matter over as best he could, saying that nothing secret was going on, that this was no council; that in fact he had just sent for some women, at Newcastle's direction, to make a present of wampum for Teedyuscung.

Teedyuscung went off, muttering, "He that won't make Peace must die."[25]

Three months later, Captain Newcastle did die—of small-pox—in Philadelphia.[26] A coincidence, of course; but did the dying Newcastle think so?

*   *   *

On July 31 the treaty ended in profuse expressions of friendship. Teedyuscung promised to bring down his ten nations to a formal treaty of peace in the fall. The Governor presented him with an armful of half-finished belts and new black wampum (more valuable than the white) to use in persuading the western Delawares to join the peace. Brother Onas also handed over a wagon-load of goods to the "King" to distribute among his people, as a present from the Governor on behalf of the Assembly and the Quakers. (The Quakers, who had contributed the largest proportion, were careful to include with the wagon-load an itemized list of the part given by them.)[27] Thomas Penn in England, on hearing reports of the treaty and of the "very extraordinary . . . different sort of Behaviour of this Chief from first to last," expressed the hope that Teedyuscung would become the chief of all the minor nations along the Susquehanna. Dealing with one man of power (the constant dream of European administrators who did not appreciate the democratic qualities of Indian society) would save the trouble of separate treaties and would also save money because the presents for the various tribes could be lumped together.[28]

Teedyuscung departed very much impressed with the advantages of coöperating with Brother Onas. For one thing, the English had proved themselves to be militarily active: while he was in Easton, the royal declaration of war against France was read; and the long-discussed fort at Shamokin was begun. The show of troops and arms put on in the little town must also have given him pause. But more important, from his standpoint, was the generosity of the English. From the French at Niagara he had got only promises. In Pennsylvania both Governor and Quakers had vied with one another to give him presents in goods and wampum. He had been presented with a horse, feasted and complimented; he had been introduced to the aristocracy of the province, and accepted by them as a peer. He was greatly flattered by the punctilious adherence of the proprietary officials to Indian protocol in the conduct of the treaties (although "he neither understood nor observed them himself" and "knew nothing of Business").[29] His whims had been humored and his desire for display acceded to. For a poor Jersey basket maker, this was triumph beyond his most wistful dreams.

The Mutiny at Fort Allen
1756

After leaving Easton, Teedyuscung returned at once to Fort Allen, escorted by four white soldiers and by his own retinue, who were carrying the presents. When the Indians arrived at the fort, they learned that its commander, Captain Reynolds, was in Philadelphia; the officer in charge was a Lieutenant Miller. Miller was known among his brother officers as "that little impertinent Body,"[1] but to Teedyuscung, who judged white men by their professions of friendship, the Lieutenant appeared to be a good fellow. The goods were cached in the woods eighteen miles beyond the fort. Teedyuscung considered them too heavy to carry all the way up to Tioga and so he sent a messenger to his wife at Pasigachkunk instructing her to send down some help.[2] Then they returned to Fort Allen to wait.

Lieutenant Miller, as temporary commander of the fort, had at his disposal the hogsheads of rum (military stores) which Captain Reynolds had been in the habit of selling to his troops. (Some of them owed him their whole monthly pay and more besides.) With this rum the Lieutenant entertained the Indians, paying especial attention to Teedyuscung. Teedyuscung had in his possession sixteen deerskins, which, he said, were intended for a present to the Governor of Pennsylvania, to make him a pair of gloves, and he asked Miller to give orders that the skins be tied together and laid in a loft in the fort. The Lieutenant wanted the skins for himself, however. When Teedyuscung had spent all his money for rum, the Lieutenant suggested that he sell the skins. One skin, said Miller, was enough to make the Governor his gloves. Young Ben, the private interpreter of the "King," tried to prevent the fraud. Ben told the Lieutenant that he did not understand the Indian way of speaking. Teedyuscung, he said, knew very well that the Governor would not use sixteen deerskins to make a pair of gloves. But it was all to no purpose. The Lieutenant kept teasing Teedyuscung and plying him with rum until "the old man" was off guard and sold the skins for three pounds English money. Ben himself counted out the cash, but what became of it afterward he could not learn. No doubt Teedyuscung spent it for more rum.[3]

The rest of the Indians of Teedyuscung's party were likewise buying rum; nearly all of them were drunk most of the time. Crowded within the little fort, with its tiny barracks surrounded by the fifteen-foot stockade and six-foot firing platform, were soldiers, Indian men, and Indian women. On the night of August 5 Teedyuscung struck the spark which exploded the situation.

Teedyuscung had brought three women into the fort, one of whom he kept as his own; the other two were running about and joking with the Lieutenant and two of the enlisted men. Christian Weirick, a drunken corporal, jealously demanded that the women be turned out of the fort. The Lieutenant refused, alleging that there was no shelter made for them outside. This answer enraged Weirick. He seized "that little impertinent Body" and threw him to the ground. Weirick then went to the women and along with some of his comrades behaved "very indecently with them the whole Night." In the morning, fearful of contracting a venereal disease from their consorts, they washed themselves in a prophylactic mixture of rum and water.

The brawl did not end with Weirick's mayhem on the Lieutenant. While Miller slept off the effects of his beating in the Captain's cabin, Weirick went on to wreck the fort. A soldier named John White started to scold Weirick for striking his lieutenant. Weirick cursed, grappled with White, and "attempted to tear him to pieces." Philip Bortner stepped out of the guard room. Weirick assaulted Bortner and pinned him down on a bench. Bortner screamed for help. Two other soldiers came in. Weirick seized a gun and whirled it about as a club; "he drove about the Fort like a Beast and not like a Man & beat them two down." Weirick then went wholly berserk, breaking heads, shooting guns, smashing windows, benches, and muskets, and even tearing part of the chimney down and throwing the stones through the windows of the guard room. Sergeant Bossing ordered the guard to take Weirick into arrest, but the guard were afraid to stir. Finally Sergeant White and the four soldiers from Reading who had been Teedyuscung's escort ran off to Fort Hamilton, a few miles away, for reinforcements. Lieutenant Miller stood at the door of the fort, howling into the night for them to come back.[4]

By the ninth Teedyuscung had sobered up sufficiently to realize that the riot which he had precipitated was not a recommendation to Brother Onas. So he had a white man write down a little note to Major Parsons at Easton, excusing himself:

Agust ye. 9th. this is to Certify the Indian King is yeat at Fort Allen but he Desireth that Mr. Horsfield [at Bethlehem] nor any of his Frends in Beathlehem, or in Easton, will thinck anything amiss In him for Staying so Long, but he has Sent two Messengers, up to Tehogo, for to tell them that he is very well used by the Inglesh, and that some of them Should come doun and help them up with his Goods which Is the Reason he Stayeth so Long. . . . he has behaved himself very well at the fort and what he said in Easton he Desireth to be forgiven for he was in Drinck, for he was Informed that he Should Say that he Killed Some of the Inglish but he came to make peace and Desireth that it Should be so.
Postscript. The King Desireth that after you have read it, that

you will Send it to major Parsons at Easton to Let him Know how all the affares are with him and he is Going out To-Day up to his Goods and Expecteth more Indians In very Soon, So no mor but the King Remembreth his Love to all his frends in Bethlehem and Eston but more Especiley to Major Parsons.[5]

Parsons, however, had already learned from other sources about the mutiny at Fort Allen and had written orders to the commander there to build a brush shelter outside of the fort for the Indians. The Indians were to be kept out of the stockade by sentries, and their ration of rum was to be a quarter of a pint per day. Parsons was not so much worried about the breaches of discipline, although they were ominous enough. What mattered was that if Teedyuscung did not make haste to report to the Delawares and the Six Nations, and begin to collect the distant tribes, winter would preclude any further treaty this year; thus the "great & Honourable work nothing less than the work of peace" would collapse.

Teedyuscung left Fort Allen on the eleventh, ashamed, it was said, because Parsons had had to order the rum ration reduced to a gill per day. Twelve miles out from the fort, young Ben, his interpreter, left him, saying he saw nothing but want and hunger before him at Tioga. (Ben had been born and bred among the whites in New Jersey.) A few miles farther on, Teedyuscung came to the cache of presents—only to find that they had all been burned! He turned around and came back at once, suspecting that this bit of arson had been committed by enemy Indians. A few days earlier there had been discovered the tracks of about twenty Indians marching eastward toward the Minisinks, and Teedyuscung had assumed that these Indians were hostile because "they marched mostly abreast or aside of one another whereas the Indian manner is when they have no unfriendly or hostile Intentions, always to march one after the other."[6]

Teedyuscung may actually have spoken with the war party and learned their plans; at any rate, when he came back to Fort Allen, he did not remain but continued on to Bethlehem, arriving there on the evening of August 17, with his son and a few associates. His purpose was to persuade the Christian Indians to leave Bethlehem. He told them that a body of Indians was going to attack the town in three weeks, and that if any natives were found living with the whites, the attackers would destroy them too. He made a special effort to draw off his niece Theodora, who was a baptized member of the congregation. As for himself, he said, he was going to Tioga and thence to a nation of Indians "far beyond the French, that were in the French interest." But the Moravian Indians steadfastly refused to leave.[7]

It is probable that Teedyuscung was being sincere in his efforts to bring off the Moravian Indians to a safe place around Tioga, although the Brethren themselves felt that his attempts to seduce the Christians were motivated by mere spite. Certainly he did know of a plan to lay waste the white settlements in the Forks, and was aware that French arms were still able to shed blood on Pennsylvania frontiers. His son Amos had just left on an embassy to the Alleghenies, where French influence was strong. On the fifteenth Oswego had fallen to the French, and advance rumors of its capture may have been circulating in the woods. When the news was confirmed, at any rate, it almost wrecked the English alliance with the Six Nations. The fact that work had just been begun at Shamokin on Fort Augusta was not yet a guarantee of security for pro-English Indians on the upper Susquehanna. His friendly advice was thus given at the risk of antagonizing the war faction among the Delawares, for, although he had asked the Moravian Indians not to reveal his warnings to the whites at Bethlehem, he must have known that they would not keep the secret.

Teedyuscung and his son had also come to Bethlehem for medical aid. In a drunken fit the two of them had been fighting. Teedyuscung's son had hit his father a blow with an axe that cut his chin through to the bone, leaving a gash an inch and a quarter long. Teedyuscung had got in a few blows too: he had crushed his son's chest and the young man was spitting blood. They went together to the Moravian doctor and Teedyuscung received a plaster for his chin; his son was given some medicine.[8]

It is significant that both of them looked to the white man's medicines for aid in addition to or rather than the aboriginal remedies. The system of medical treatment in vogue among the Delawares was not markedly inferior to that of the Europeans of the day. Sweat-baths, blood-letting, cupping, and bone-setting were accepted techniques, and the household pharmacopeia included many harmless and some few useful drugs. In addition to household herbal remedies, there were paid professional medicine men or shamans who magically exorcised disease by a variety of antics which were extremely offensive to the missionaries. The bedside manner of these shamans differed from that of the European doctors; but no doubt it had equally felicitous psychological effects.

Next morning Teedyuscung set off for Fort Allen again, with five retainers carrying five heavy bags of meal—the treaty Indians having consumed all their provisions during their protracted stay at the fort. At the house of John Hays, some sixteen miles south of Fort Allen, and close to the ancient site of Hociundoquen, he stopped off for a drink. While he was there, Major Parsons and Captain Insley from Easton walked in.

Teedyuscung was anxious to create a good impression. He told Parsons that he was glad to see him; that he had been expecting him, in fact, having been told that the Major was on his way to the fort.

Parsons, after inquiring after his health, informed Teedyuscung that he was making this visit on the Governor's orders, to learn why he had not set off for the Indian country according to the terms of the treaty.

Teedyuscung parried the question by telling a cock-and-bull story about how he came by the plaster on his chin. He had been in very good health, he said, until a few days before.

His horse had stumbled over an old tree lying in the path and had thrown him over its head, so that he cut his chin badly when he fell. He and his son, who had some disorder in his chest, had both gone to Bethlehem to see the doctor. (Parsons did not learn the truth until he got to Fort Allen.)

Parsons, Insley, and Teedyuscung rode together the rest of the way to the fort. Teedyuscung was talkative and friendly. Among other things, he told the Major about the affair of the deerskins which he had intended for Governor Morris' pair of gloves. Parsons told him that if he still meant the skins for the Governor, he would take them out of the hands of Lieutenant Miller and send them to Philadelphia. At this Teedyuscung "seemed extremely well pleased"—a natural reaction, for he had already drunk up the money he received for the skins. When they got to the fort, Teedyuscung took down the skins (there were only fourteen of them now), wrapped them up in a bundle, and gave them to Parsons, asking him to take care of them and send them to Governor Morris. Parsons conscientiously fulfilled this request, so that the episode of the Governor's gloves had a happy ending after all.

But this was not all they talked about. Teedyuscung casually remarked as they were riding along that he and his followers had two white male prisoners at Tioga, whom they would bring down to the next treaty. This information affected Parsons, who inquired anxiously about their condition. Teedyuscung reassured him. One of them, he said, was his own, and at that very moment was not more than ten miles from the fort with some of his warriors. The other belonged to Young Captain Harris, his half-brother, and was only forty or fifty miles away, taking care of Harris' wife and children in Harris' absence! (Both of these men had been captured during Teedyuscung's New Year's Eve raid on the Weeser plantation.) Parsons pressed Teedyuscung to send his prisoner to the Governor, offering him "a very handsome Reward" if he would do so. "The King," as Parsons was wont to call him, replied agreeably that he would be glad to deliver him up to Parsons or to anyone else Parsons would send for him.

At noon next day Teedyuscung and his brother, Young Captain Harris, left Fort Allen with great expressions of pleasure and good humor. At parting Teedyuscung desired to be kindly remembered to his brother, the Governor of Pennsylvania, and promised that this time he would not return until he had accomplished everything agreed on at the treaty. Captain Harris told Parsons that when he came down he would bring his prisoner and as many others as he could procure. Parsons, who was still anxious about the captives' welfare, asked Harris to treat the young man well. Harris mildly told the Major that he had adopted the prisoner as his own brother and had treated him kindly ever since he had owned him.[9]

The flurry aroused in Philadelphia by reports of the mutiny inspired, but not instigated, by the "King," died away gradually. Lieutenant Miller, after a brief arrest, was allowed to retain his station at Fort Allen, whence he ran away the next summer "with another Man's Wife," from then on leaving History to her own devices.[10] Captain Reynolds, the commander at Fort Allen, during whose absence the riot had occurred, was transferred to a minor and remote outpost.[11] As for Teedyuscung himself, no one apparently took the trouble to chasten him. War and taxes and drunken Indians (to say nothing of drunken soldiers)—these three, to the frontiersman's mind, were inevitable.

This Land Is My Inheritance
1756

Teedyuscung's wife Elisabeth and her two youngest children came back to Bethlehem from Fort Allen on August 21. They were accompanied by a military escort to protect them from the white people. At Bethlehem, she and the children were given rations and quarters at the Crown Inn (at the expense of the province) while Teedyuscung, now provincial agent, carried invitations to the forthcoming treaty among the tribes.[1]

Elisabeth told the Moravians that her husband, on leaving Fort Allen, had gone to the region of the Minisinks to stop his warriors from making more raids.[2] Probably he had. Doubts, however, of his authority to make peace were beginning to arise in the minds of both proprietary officials and Iroquois statesmen. On the same day that Elisabeth reported Teedyuscung to be busy on behalf of peace, the new governor of Pennsylvania, Colonel William Denny, wrote a report of the Easton treaty to Sir Charles Hardy, governor of New York. (Denny had arrived in Philadelphia only the day before to replace Morris, who had tired of fighting the Quakers, and the sentiments he expressed were undoubtedly those of Richard Peters, veteran secretary of the Governor's Council.) Teedyuscung's conduct at Fort Allen, observed Denny, gave "reason to suspect the sincerity of his Professions and the truth of the declarations about his being appointed to be King by ten nations."[3]

Captain Newcastle, the Six Nations warrior who had been go-between for Governor Morris and Teedyuscung in the spring, was also uneasy about the report of the riot at Fort Allen.[4] He had already offered to go north to Sir William Johnson to discover "the whole truth." Denny now took advantage of the offer and sent Newcastle at once to New York, carrying the letter to Hardy and a black-and-white belt for Johnson, asking about the status of the "King." Johnson replied on the tenth that he was "totally ignorant" of any such king of the Delawares and of any king at all of the Six Nations.[5]

John Shickellamy, who in 1754 had been appointed Six Nations overseer on the Susquehanna, with especial responsibility for the Delawares, was the next to belittle Teedyuscung. He had been to Onondaga and had just returned to Pennsylvania after a lonely and dangerous journey down the river. Toward the end of August, Shickellamy had met the "king" some thirty miles above Wyoming. The meeting, however, was a cold one. Shickellamy hated the sight of Teedyuscung and would not speak to him; he only saw him at a distance.

The Six Nations, said Shickellamy in Philadelphia, were displeased with Teedyuscung. Teedyuscung alone had incited the Delawares to attack the English.[6] His pretensions to be a king were false. It was true that in the preceding winter the Delawares had raised him to chiefhood and that he was now head man at Tioga; but the Delawares had other chiefs besides him.[7] That the Six Nations had chosen him, or anyone else, as king was not true. Teedyuscung had simply been advised by the Six Nations to make his peace with the English and "had no other authority."[8]

These reports damaged the confidence of the Pennsylvania officials in Teedyuscung's sincerity. They were between Scylla and Charybdis, it seemed. Not only would it be useless to treat with an unauthorized representative of the Delawares; it would be positively dangerous to encourage the pretensions of an Indian disliked by the Six Nations. On the other hand, no one wanted to prolong hostilities by examining too closely the credentials of a possible peacemaker.

On October 1 Governor Denny received a letter from Lord Loudoun, commander-in-chief of the British forces in North America, forbidding him on any account to hold a second treaty with the Delawares. Henceforth all Indian affairs would be handled by Sir William Johnson.[9]

That letter decided Denny. As far as he was concerned, there would be no second treaty.

*   *   *

While whites and Iroquois argued about his authority, Teedyuscung was busy strengthening his position as the indispensable man among the Susquehanna Delawares. At a council called at Tioga in September, he and the representatives of the tribes discussed the peace.[10] Teedyuscung's arguments in favor of peace were in the main economic. The Indians needed the white man's wares: powder, lead, guns, knives, cloth. During the war, the Delawares had been forced to sell their skins and furs to the French, who paid poorly. If peace could be made again with Brother Onas, the Indians could trade with the English, who gave better goods and more of them.[11] (The difference in rates was due in part to the French colonial administration's practice of farming out the trading monopolies to entrepreneurs who, freed from competition, were able to charge high prices. Among the numerous English traders, many of them unlicensed, keen competition and a more adequate supply of goods kept prices down.)[12] The council agreed with this reasoning. The speeches to be given at Easton were decided on; Teedyuscung, the speaker, memorized everything.[13] Early in October he and his delegates started back toward the settlements.

The party of nearly a hundred men, women, and children

had not marched far before a lone Indian runner overtook them. He carried a string of wampum and a message from Sir William Johnson, warning them that the Pennsylvanians were planning to massacre the Delawares and had only waited for the second treaty in hopes of killing more Indians. Teedyuscung's head would be cut off; everyone would be killed.

They disregarded the message and went on. A second lone messenger arrived with a larger string and another warning. Teedyuscung ignored this one too. But just before they reached Wyoming, a third runner came up with the same warning and "a very broad and long Belt of Wampum."[14]

Teedyuscung called a halt at Wyoming and sent down a message to the Governor, announcing that he was at Wyoming with his followers and some prisoners, but complaining that he was afraid of coming any farther lest he be killed. With the message he sent ten Christian Indians and four white prisoners, including the Henry Hess whom Teedyuscung himself had captured ten months before.[15] He also requested that his wife and a keg of rum be dispatched to him at Wyoming. Elisabeth again refused to go to her husband: she said she thought it best for her to stay in Bethlehem. The rum was sent without the woman.[16]

Johnson, of course, had not sent the warning messages. He had expressed his willingness to let Denny continue the treaties begun at Easton in July, even though they infringed on his prerogatives. The French, however, had excellent reason to wish to sabotage the negotiations. Whether the warning was sent from a French post, or whether French Senecas or Delawares originated it, is unknown. It may even have been the work of some disaffected members of Teedyuscung's own band, for a Six Nations Indian who met the party on its way down from Tioga reported that some of them expressed hatred of the English.[17] But whatever its particular origin, the warning was a clumsy ruse by French interests to break up the peace negotiations.

Reassured of the province's good faith by the Council's

reply, Teedyuscung and his retinue continued on their way to Fort Allen. There was confusion, however, in Philadelphia. Denny had been out of town when Teedyuscung's string arrived. Without waiting for his return, the Council had sent word express to Wyoming, encouraging the Delawares to continue to Easton.[18] When Denny returned at last, he declined to approve the Council's action and refused to treat with the Delawares.[19] It did not matter that they were already nearing Easton. Lord Loudoun's letter had been explicit: "I do hereby for the future forbid you or your government from conferring or treating with these Indians in any shape or on any account whatsoever." The Council argued. At last Denny agreed to meet the "King"—in Philadelphia.[20]

Meanwhile, Teedyuscung was proceeding on the understanding that the place of meeting was to be Easton. The Indians reached Fort Allen on October 24. Thirty of them camped under the walls of the fort while a hundred more stayed in the woods.[21] A few days later Teedyuscung went on almost alone to Easton. His henchmen were shy of the whites.

At Easton, Teedyuscung discovered that he was under the surveillance of the Six Nations. The doubts sown by Shickellamy and Newcastle were bearing fruit. Newcastle had just returned from his mission to New York, reporting that Teedyuscung had no authority from the Six Nations to treat with Pennsylvania.[22] Probably as a result of the accounts of Teedyuscung given by Shickellamy, Newcastle, and Scaroyady, who had delivered Newcastle's message to Johnson, two Cayuga and two Mohawk warriors had been assigned to watch Teedyuscung's actions. Conrad Weiser, who reached Easton a couple of days after Teedyuscung, observed that the four Iroquois were very sober, in contrast to the Delawares, and were evidently charged "with some particular Business." When news came that the Delawares who remained behind at Fort Allen were unruly and demanding liquor, one of the Mohawks was dispatched north to keep them quiet.[23]

But Teedyuscung was not seriously alarmed. He knew

that the jealousies which his claims aroused at Onondaga were no menace as long as Brother Onas needed him. And Onas obviously needed him now; why else would he invite him to a second treaty? So he demanded winter clothes, refused to travel to Philadelphia to treat with the Governor there, and became royally drunk.

While the "King" lolled over his rum, a rumor spread that the thirty Delawares who remained at Fort Allen, and the hundred Munsees encamped at Trout Creek, just north of the fort, were planning to attack Easton during the treaty. Governor Denny, who had finally set out for Easton, stopped on the road. He refused to go on until he was given assurance that the way was safe again.[24] Had Teedyuscung been sober, he might have saved himself, as well as the Governor, some embarrassment. As it was, it was the Six Nations observers who had to reassure the Governor that this evil rumor was "but the Singing of ugly Birds." They urged him to be brave and to come on. The Delawares, they said, were uneasy at his absence.[25] When the Governor at last reached Easton, Weiser asked Teedyuscung whether it might not be proper to invite the Indians at Fort Allen and Trout Creek to the treaty. Teedyuscung could hardly oppose the suggestion. Accordingly, Moses Tattamy was sent off with the invitation. Honest old Moses came back with the disconcerting answer, "As it was agreed between *Teedyuscung* and them that they should come no farther than the Place where they were, and that the Goods, in case of Success, were to be brought and divided at *Fort-Allen,* they intended to stay whilst the Treaty continued." Moses also revealed the limited sources of his "King's" authority. It was those 150 Indians alone who had chosen Teedyuscung as their representative. But if a peace were concluded by him, "all the Indians at Diahogo [Tioga], and many more different Tribes, or Towns, would be exceedingly pleased with it and would confirm it."[26] This vague assurance could not be taken to mean that Teedyuscung's word was law along the Susquehanna, any more than the

shadowy promises of the Ohio Indians to ratify Teedyuscung's peace meant their allegiance to him. It meant only
that other Indian groups were anxious to see what sort of
terms Teedyuscung could get from the whites.

Moses' report, duly entered in the minutes of the treaty,
added to the growing suspicion that Teedyuscung, the lo-
quacious Jersey basket maker, was not all that he claimed to
be. The province, however, had no one else with whom to
treat. Conrad Weiser, the shrewd provincial interpreter, remarked, "I am apt to think that Teedyuscung's authority,
or influence, is not so great among the Indians as he first
gave out, or was represented to this government, but I take
him to be entirely in our interest, and will do what ever he
can to serve Pennsylvania."27 And, as we shall see, at the
moment when Teedyuscung's stock was falling in the eyes of
the proprietary party, of Johnson, and of the Six Nations,
another faction within the province was reaching him a help-
ing hand. The Quakers wanted to champion an Indian
against both the proprietors and the Six Nations together.

*   *   *

The conference formally opened on November 8, a Monday. In the morning, the Governor sent Weiser to the "King"
with his compliments. He asked whether Teedyuscung intended to speak first. Teedyuscung replied that it was his
duty to speak first, and suggested that the first meeting be
held that same morning. Accordingly, at eleven o'clock the
Governor marched from his lodgings to the place of conference, escorted by a detachment of British regulars and a
company of Weiser's militia. Flags flew, drums beat, music
shrilled.28

There was a considerable number of persons present: some
forty Indians, including Teedyuscung and the Jersey Delawares who were his principal supporters, and several Six

Nations observers; the Governor and his Council; the Commissioners of the Assembly (including Benjamin Franklin); the officers of the troops then in town; and a crowd of citizens of Philadelphia (mostly Quakers) and Easton. The conference must have been held in the open air: no building in Easton at that time was large enough to hold such an assembly, the town having been founded only four years earlier.

Teedyuscung opened the meeting with a short speech in Delaware. (He spoke English well enough for fluent private conversation, but in public he always preferred the dignity of an interpreter.) He reminded the Governor of the first Easton treaty, and testified to his own diligence in spreading the good news of the projected peace. He introduced his comrades as sincere lovers of peace. He opened the Governor's eyes and ears and cleared his throat. With a belt of eight rows of wampum he banished mutual suspicion. "Brother," he concluded, "I have done for the present, and another Time, if God spares Life, I will begin the main Matter I came to do." Everyone understood this "main Matter" to be the formal drafting of peace terms.

The Governor, remembering the late alarm about the Trout Creek Indians, and Newcastle's damaging report, gave a belt to open the "King's" eyes and ears, and also the passage from his heart to his mouth, "that in what you have to say to this Government they may both concur, nor the Mouth utter any Thing but what is first conceived in the Heart . . ."[29]

Colonel Denny's exhortation was well timed if inadequate. Teedyuscung had been commissioned by the Tioga Delawares at the September council to make peace; he had memorized his speeches; but what he said during the next few days was not what he had been told to say. After the treaty, Joseph Tattamy told Conrad Weiser how Teedyuscung had disregarded instructions and betrayed his trust as speaker. "He spoke confused," said Joseph. "Tho' nothing that was wrong or false in itself; only not in such Order as he ought to have done, and one Passage he never mentioned at all which drawed the Delaware Indians' heart from the English and their Indian Allies [the Six Nations]."[30]

The passage which Teedyuscung failed to mention had to do with the causes of the alienation of the Delawares. He had been instructed to stress the threats of the Connecticut people to settle Wyoming as a basic reason for the Delawares' desertion of the English.[31] Instead, he charged Pennsylvania with fraud in the Walking Purchase, and the Six Nations with fraud in the Purchase of 1749.

In the following discussions of the charges of fraud in connection with the Walking Purchase, the writer is going to try hard not to pass a moral judgment. The evidence, which was presented in Chapter II, seems to show conclusively that the Purchase itself was, on the part of the whites, somewhat less than generous. But the Purchase was perpetrated in 1737; this was 1756, and a lot of water had flowed under the bridge since Logan's time. Other white men, acting in good faith on the assumption that the Purchase was fair, had bought land and settled with their families in the Forks of Delaware. And new issues had arisen on which the Walking Purchase could only throw a confusing shadow. War and peace, French and English ambitions, trading privileges and military necessities, were problems more immediately demanding solution. In the ensuing controversy neither party was wholly actuated by the best motives; neither side's motives were wholly bad. It will be enough to try to tell what actually happened when Teedyuscung charged Brother Onas with fraud.

Conrad Weiser, the ablest Indian agent in Pennsylvania's service, regarded it as a mistake when, on October 12, 1756, Governor Denny asked the "King" what had caused the war and whether it was anything that Brother Onas had done amiss. Weiser's interest in the treaty was pragmatic: his objectives were the neutralization of an enemy (the Susquehanna Delawares) and the retention of an ally (the Six

Nations). Both ends were to be achieved by a quick peace, with no questions asked about who hit whom first and why. But Colonel Denny was inexperienced in Indian diplomacy and unsure of himself. He was hamstrung by an anti-Penn Assembly, on which he had to depend for the money to effect any decisions he might make. At the innocuous-sounding request of Franklin, Pemberton, and the Quaker commissioners, he asked the "King," "Have we, the Governor or People of Pennsylvania done you any Kind of Injury?"[32]

Teedyuscung himself was unprepared for the question, and he made no answer that day. He had come down with excuses designed to ingratiate himself with Pennsylvania. He could blame the French, the Six Nations, the Connecticut people, and Charles Brodhead for the war. These allusions were not intended to *explain* anything. They had been prepared for Teedyuscung by the council at Tioga for the purpose of banishing ill feeling by deliberately side-tracking the real bones of contention between the Delawares and Pennsylvania. Now here was the Governor inviting him to make all the bitter accusations which a lifetime of privations had brought him to feel were just. "Indeed," wrote Weiser, "Teedjouskong would have openly scolded had he not been prumped with an Answer from that Party which so manifestly endeavoured to ruin the Proprietaries' Intrest and Character."[33]

That evening, after the Governor's speech, Israel Pemberton told Moses Tattamy, Teedyuscung's adviser, that "now was our [the Delawares'] time to speak bold, and to be strong and fear nothing, and to remember well what was said to us by him before."[34]

Next day, November 13, Teedyuscung burned his bridges behind him. He charged the proprietaries with forging the deed on which they based their claims to the Walking Purchase; he suggested that the walk itself had been unfairly performed; he stated that the Six Nations had no right to sell the lands included in the Purchase of 1749. He said:

This very Ground that is under me (striking it with his Foot) was my [i.e., the Delawares'] Land and Inheritance, and is taken from me by Fraud; when I say this Ground, I mean all the Land lying between *Tohiccon Creek* and *Wioming,* on the River *Sasquehannah.* I have not only been served so in this Government, but the same Thing has been done to me as to several Tracts in *New-Jersey,* over the River. When I have sold Lands fairly, I look upon them to be really sold. — A Bargain is a Bargain. — Though I have sometimes had nothing for the Lands I have sold but broken Pipes, or such Trifles, yet when I have sold them, though for such Trifles, I look upon the Bargain to be good: Yet I think I should not be ill used on this Account by those very People who have had such an Advantage in their Purchases, nor be called a Fool for it. *Indians* are not such Fools as to bear this in their Minds. — The Proprietaries, who have purchased their Lands from us cheap, have sold them too dear to poor People, and the *Indians* have suffered for it. It would have been more prudent in the Proprietaries, to have sold the Lands Cheaper, and have given it in Charge to those who bought from them to use the Indians with Kindness on that Account. . . . Now, although you have purchased our Lands from our Fore-Fathers on so reasonable Terms, yet now at length you will not allow us to cut a little Wood to make a Fire; nay, hinder us from Hunting, the only Means left us of getting our Livelihood.[35]

When the Governor asked him to specify what he meant by fraud, he said:

When one Man had formerly Liberty to purchase Lands, and he took the Deed from the *Indians* for it, and then dies; after his Death, the Children forge a Deed, like the true One, with the same *Indian* Names to it, and thereby take Lands from the Indians which they never sold—this is Fraud. Also, when one King has Land beyond the River, and another King has Land on this Side, both bounded by Rivers, Mountains, and Springs, which cannot be moved, and the Proprietaries, greedy to purchase Lands, buy of one King, what belongs to the other—this likewise is Fraud. . . . I have been served so in this Province: All the Land, extending from *Tohiccon,* over the *Great-Mountain,* to Wioming, has been taken from me by Fraud; for when I had agreed to sell the Land to the old Proprietary by the Course of the River, the young Proprietaries came and got it run by a straight Course by the Compass, and by that Means took in double the Quantity intended to be sold.[36]

Teedyuscung, however, was not too well convinced of the relevance of his own statements. He repeatedly assured the Governor that the land grievances were "not the principal cause" of the war. Weiser observed, "Many Expressions Teedjouskon made use of, were no Indian Phrases, and he could not afterwards answer to them, before he spoke with Israel, or some others."[37] When the Governor offered to give the Delawares immediate satisfaction in goods, Teedyuscung, no doubt under instruction from Pemberton, refused. His reply is interesting because it reveals that he had not come to Easton prepared to press charges of fraud; and because it notified Pennsylvania that what had been a peace treaty was now a court of equity:

I will now, in a few Words, according to my Abilities, give you an Answer. You desired me to acquaint you what the Grounds of my Uneasiness were, and I complied, tho' it was not the main Thing which I came about. But when you put me in mind, I was pleased, for before I thought it not proper to mention it in these difficult Times; it was not the Cause of the Stroke, tho' it was the Foundation of our Uneasiness. Now, Brother, in Answer to your Question, What will satisfy us? It is not usual, nor reasonable, nor can I tell you what the Damage is, and adjust, as in a Ballance the true Value at that Time and these Times; formerly it might be lighter, but being delayed, it is now the heavier; the Interest is to be added. Besides, there are many more concerned in this Matter, not now present; and tho' many who have suffered, are now in the Grave, yet their Descendants feel the Weight, and the more now for the Time they have waited.[38]

The conference ended officially on a high note of satisfaction. The peace was virtually (but still not formally) settled. Goods valued at £400, contributed largely by the Quakers, were presented to the "King" and his retinue. The Indians held a condolence ceremony for the late Captain Newcastle, who had died of smallpox in Philadelphia, and Teedyuscung delivered a speech. Captain Newcastle, he said, was a good man and had promoted the good work of peace. "His Death would put him in Mind of his Duty, as it should all of us."[39] And on the seventeenth Teedyuscung parted from Israel Pemberton.

Taking leave of Pemberton was an ordeal for Teedyuscung. He and most of his people went down to the ferry, where the Quakers were making ready to depart, to dine with their new-found supporters. Just before the final farewell Teedyuscung took Pemberton and Isaac Zane aside and told them that their pious exhortations had gone to his heart and had brought tears to his eyes. At that very moment, suiting his actions to his words, he burst into a flood of tears. He withdrew for a moment to weep in privacy. When he returned he told them that, "in the course of this business, he had endeavoured to turn in his mind, and look up to God for direction; that when he was alone in the woods and destitute of every other counselor, he found by doing so, he had the best direction; that he hoped God would bless their [i.e., the Quakers'] endeavours, and wanted Friends to remember him." He followed the Quakers to the boat, and at the last was so affected that all he could do was cry.

The Friends were duly edified. It "was a humbling scene," they reported, "and excited reverent and thankful sentiments, in the minds of those immediately observing it."[40]

Teedyuscung was now a great man. That night the Moravian stable boys in Bethlehem gave hay to the horses of the lesser Indians; but there were two quarts of oats for the "King's" horse.[41] The only sour note, in fact, was sounded by Teedyuscung's wife, Elisabeth. She refused to accompany him back into the Indian country "because for his debauched way of living." It took all of Weiser's short supply of tact to convince her that, as the wife of a king, policy came before preferences.[42]

XI

Quaker Politics and Proprietary Honor

1756

Teedyuscung had Conrad Weiser for companion on the road from Bethlehem to Fort Allen. Along the way he badgered the interpreter for rum to treat the Munsees, who had stayed five miles beyond the fort all during the treaty. He was anxious to satisfy his vassals, and began dividing the presents on November 20. The apportionment of the loot was completed the next day. That night there was a frolic at the Indian camp outside the stockade; Conrad Weiser contributed five gallons of rum to the festivities. At midnight the "King" returned to the fort and was let in to spend the night with Elisabeth and the children. "He behaved well," said Weiser, as if the fact were worth recording.[1]

Weiser's sentiments about Teedyuscung were mixed. He simply did not know what to make of him. The Jersey Indians whom he represented already had a bad name. He observed, too, that the Munsees who had stayed in the woods during the treaty "seemed to be very friendly, but notwithstanding they appeared to be guilty of a great deal of mischief: some of them could not look into my face."[2] Teedyuscung himself was a bundle of contradictions. When Weiser left him, he was sober, and his eyes were filled with tears. "Though he is a Drunkard and a very irregular Man, yet he is a man that can think well, and I believe him to be sincere

137

in what he said," was Weiser's estimate of his character.[3]

But Weiser had no sooner left the "King" than ominous news came from the Wyoming trail. A Mahican Indian, on his way to Bethlehem to live with the white people, had met the "King" and his party just eight miles beyond Fort Allen. The Delawares, this Indian said, were already organizing into scalping parties. These Indians paid no attention to their "King." When the powder and lead given by the province was distributed, they said cynically, "Now we have something to kill our Brethren with." Tattamy, who was not overfond of Teedyuscung, told the Mahican that Teedyuscung had little or no authority among his own people and was not employed by any other nation.[4]

* * *

Sir William Johnson, when he heard of Teedyuscung's charges, did not believe that the Delaware "King" was putting off the peace in order to rake up old grievances. He thought that the treaties of July had ended the war between the Susquehanna Delawares and the English, and that the charges of fraud were raised by the Ohio Delawares, whom also Teedyuscung once had claimed to represent. Therefore he wrote to his deputy, George Croghan, in Pennsylvania, inviting the Ohio Indians to come to New York; Croghan was to tell them that Johnson had authority from the King of England and would "endeavour to have Justice done them."[5]

When Johnson learned that Teedyuscung had still not come to terms and that his charges of fraud were backed by the Quakers, he was furious. Sir William Johnson bore a royal commission as superintendent of Indian affairs for the northern colonies. He executed imperial policy, and the imperial policy was to cultivate the friendship of the Six Nations. Pious Quakers meddling with Indian affairs obstructed this policy and infringed on his prerogatives as Indian superintendent. His antipathy to the Friends was soon to be as animated as that of the proprietary party.

Johnson's concern over the dangers of Quaker meddling was an honest one. The Six Nations, who held the balance of power between the French and the English, were only lukewarm in the English interest. Historically they were for the English and against the French; but the languishing of trade, the success of French arms in the Ohio, the raids into Pennsylvania and New Jersey, the fall of Oswego—all these had cooled their ardor. The Geneseo Senecas in the west, about Fort Machault (Venango), were already in the French pay; the Mohawks in the east were carrying arms under Johnson, but grumbling; the Onondagas, Cayugas, Oneidas, and Tuscaroras wavered this way and that. Johnson's chief concern was to hold the Six Nations to their alliance with the English.

Now Teedyuscung's Delawares were among the inferior allies of the Six Nations, at least as far as the Onondaga Council was concerned. The Council was angry with them, first because they had gone to war at all, and second because they had defied their "uncles" in refusing to lay down the hatchet. The defection of the Delawares from the Six Nations was a threat to Iroquois prestige, and a military threat as well, because the Susquehanna Delawares lay on the flanks of the Iroquois country. If, at this ticklish point, the Delawares, prompted by the Quakers, were allowed to blame the war on land frauds concerted between the Six Nations and Brother Onas, and were allowed to assert their independence of the Six Nations, the wavering loyalty of the Six Nations to the English might collapse altogether.[6]

Johnson, therefore, when he had thought the matter through, came to the conclusion that the Quakers must be stopped, by fair means or foul. His deputy, George Croghan, was of the same mind. Croghan had lost a fortune in his vast trading empire in the Ohio, a fortune which the Quaker Assembly had refused to defend in 1753 and '54, and for

which the Assembly now refused to make any reimburse-
ment. Johnson and Croghan repeatedly forbade the Friends
to deal with the Indians, and circulated rumors designed to
discredit them. The Quakers, they said, through their storekeeper at Shamokin were carrying on a profitable Indian
trade with Teedyuscung. Quaker financiers were whispered
to have invested heavily in the Susquehanna Company of
Connecticut. And Johnson transmitted to Lord Loudoun a
"speech" purported to have been sent by the Society of
Friends to the Six Nations, inviting them to a treaty at
Lancaster. The Quakers, in this document, offered the Six
Nations "everything fitt to Kill Men with in plenty" and
asked only that the warriors, when they invaded Pennsylvania, should not kill any of the Quakers, who supplied them
with their arms and ammunition.[7]

None of these canards was true. Israel Pemberton indeed
had supplied the post at Shamokin (now Fort Augusta) with
£200 worth of goods in the fall of 1757, but only at the request of the Assembly, which then had no funds available.[8]
(Of course, had the Assembly been able, no doubt they would
have had to buy the goods from a Quaker firm.) The "speech"
offering the tools of murder for sale of course was a fiction.
Leaving aside its distortion of the traditionally humanitarian
character of the Friends, it is impossible to believe that such
a proposal should ever be sent by any sane individual, liable
as it would be to capture or betrayal; furthermore, internal
evidence, in the form of explanatory footnotes, points to an
enemy of the Quakers as the author.

It is unfortunate that the Friendly Association chose the
middle of an Indian war for the time to champion the rights
of the Indians. Calm discussion was impossible as long as
Delaware tomahawks flashed in the bushes. For anyone desiring to see justice done, a worse occasion could not have been
selected.

*   *   *

There is no doubt that many of the honest men who were members of the Friendly Association did desire to right an old wrong when they prompted Teedyuscung to charge the proprietaries with fraud. But justice was not the only goal which they hoped to achieve. Quaker merchants and business men dominated the financing of Pennsylvania's Indian trade. Quaker commercial interests thus demanded peace, for the sake of the trade in skins and furs; they also demanded friendship with the Indians. Quaker political interests demanded freedom from proprietary apron strings. With the diligence of men who realize that God has made His aims dependent on their prosperity, the Quakers worked to make peace and to lay the blame for the war on their political opponents.

The Quaker-dominated Assembly had delayed appropriating funds for the military defense of the province, both before and after the outbreak of hostilities in 1755. It had also failed to supply Pennsylvania's Indian allies with arms and ammunition. A direct consequence of the Assembly's dilatoriness was the alienation of the Susquehanna Delawares.

The reason for this neglect was not wholly stiff-necked pacifism. When the scalping parties struck in the fall of 1755, the Quaker party chose that moment to try again to wrest political advantages from John, Thomas, and Richard Penn, the proprietors. They would not, they insisted, vote appropriations for defense unless proprietary estates were taxed as well as citizens. This attitude was "radical." The old charter granted by Charles the Second to William Penn had been almost a feudal document, with both executive authority and the land itself assigned to the proprietors; and subsequent constitutional reforms had preserved the vast proprietary estates exempt from taxation. The Governor, appointed by the Penns in England as their lieutenant, was under personal oath and bond to them not to sign any bill taxing the proprietary estates. The implications of the squabble over taxing proprietary holdings were far-reaching. "The power to

tax is the power to destroy." The threat of taxation could, if
such a bill were approved, be used to extort any desired con-
cession from the proprietors. The ultimate ambition of certain members of the Quaker party (including Benjamin
Franklin, who was not a Quaker) was the expulsion of the
Penns and the introduction of a crown administration: an
ambition, however, which Pemberton himself did not share.

A compromise bill was finally passed on November 27,
1755, which appropriated money *without* taxing the proprietary estates, while Thomas Penn made a free gift of
£5,000 to aid in the defense of his province. But much blood
had flowed on the frontiers by then. Each side searched for
a scapegoat.

The proprietary party laid the blame for Pennsylvania's
military unpreparedness, and the consequent massacres, on
the shoulders of the Quaker party. Quaker pacifism had caused
the shedding of innocent blood! cried the Reverend William
Smith, proprietary pamphleteer. The Quakers were placed
on the defensive.

The Quaker party countered in 1756 by putting the blame
for the war itself on the proprietors. According to the charter,
all land purchases from the Indians were to be handled by
the Penns or their personal representatives. The Indians
would never have attacked Pennsylvania, argued the Quakers,
if they had not been swindled out of their lands. This argument had the advantage of being consistent with the generally pacifistic and humanitarian inclinations of the Quakers
themselves, but no doubt much of the moral fervor with
which Pemberton and his comrades castigated the proprietaries, and defended Teedyuscung, arose from their consciousness that doing justice coincided very nicely with their
political schemes.[9] Teedyuscung himself they puffed up to
a position of nobility most uncongenial to the democratic
usages of the Delawares and Iroquois. "He is," they declared,
"really more of a politician than any of his opponents,
whether in or out of our Proprietary Council, and if he could

be kept sober, might probably soon become Emperor of all the neighboring nations."[10]

This exaggerated Quaker esteem for the "King" recoiled upon the Friends at times. Teedyuscung, mild enough in the face of prominent men like Pemberton and Norris, traded on his reputation as "one who makes the earth tremble" when he was among lesser folk. On one of his visits to Isaac Norris' estate at Fairhill, near Philadelphia, he and his cohorts entered the house when its master was away, and playfully terrorized the servants. The hired girl declared that she fully expected to be killed.[11] Conrad Weiser said that Teedyuscung would "do nothing but in the most popular and publick Manner."[12] And Teedyuscung, in English and in public, continually referred to himself as "the King"[13] and "the Head of all Nations."[14]

In vain the Quakers tried to cure him of his drunkenness. A boisterous Friend named John Hughes rallied Teedyuscung about his penchant for alcohol. Teedyuscung had told Hughes that he needed to have a little writing done. "If," said he, "they would not allow him a Clerk there was a Cousin of his an Indian who had been bred at College who could write."

Hughes answered jovially,

If you Indians would learn Your Children to write You would be clever Fellows, But Teedyuscung You are a damn'd Fool, You shou'd go over to Your Brother, King George and shake hands with him and tell your own Story and Then You would have justice done You; for many an one has made themselves clever Fellows, who could not tell so strait a story as you can. But you would get so damned Drunk you would fall over Board and be drowned.[15]

Teedyuscung resented being told that he drank too much. "The Indians think it no harm to get drunk whenever they can," he said on another occasion. "But you white men say it is a sin, and get drunk notwithstanding."[16]

The first tentative move to blame the Penns was made as

early as November 1755. Then the Assembly had inquired why the Delawares and Shawnees, traditionally the friends of Pennsylvania, had struck the frontiers.[17] William Smith in 1756 excoriated this inquiry in his pamphlet *A Brief View* as talking while the house was on fire. But the idea lay fallow until the fall of 1756, when Teedyuscung, at the behest of the Quakers, charged the Penns with fraud.

Teedyuscung's charges in 1756 came at a time when the constitutional war between the Quakers and the proprietaries was nearing its crisis. The new governor, Denny, was proving to be as obdurate as the unhorsed Morris, about the business of taxing the proprietary estates; and the bill which the bucking Assembly passed in September 1756 (before the second Easton treaty), raising £30,000 on the proprietary terms, was put through under protest and accompanied by the resolve to send a remonstrance to England. The Quaker politicians were already preparing a dramatic checkmate in London, in which Teedyuscung was to be an enthusiastic pawn, with the role of blackening the name of Penn in Indian affairs. When in January 1757 the Assembly did resolve to send Benjamin Franklin to England to represent the interests of the Quaker party before the crown and parliament, Franklin was able to take over with him Teedyuscung's damaging charge that the Penns had alienated the Delaware Indians by fraud in the Walking Purchase.

*　　*　　*

The proprietary faction was indignant. They knew very well that land grievances were not the principal cause of the war; but the charges involved the integrity of the whole Penn administration and, unless disproved, could be represented in England as a reason for removing the Penns from political control of the province. Conrad Weiser was called before the Governor's Council the day after Teedyuscung's speech and questioned concerning the truth of the accusations. Weiser said that few or none of the Delawares present at the treaty had ever lived in the disputed territory and that those who had lived there were either dead or had migrated to the Ohio country.[18] The Council then reviewed the history of the lands claimed by Teedyuscung and came to the conclusion that they legally belonged to Pennsylvania.

Most attention was paid to that part of Teedyuscung's charges which alleged fraud in the Walking Purchase. These charges centered about two points. First, declared the Quakers (through Teedyuscung), the copy of the deed of 1686 (the original had been lost) which the Penns had brought forth in 1735 was a forgery. Second, the manner of the walk itself was fraudulent. The Indians had intended the walk to parallel the Delaware River; the Penns had made it proceed almost directly north by compass course. The Indians had understood by "walk" an easy strolling gait with time out for hunting, smoking a pipe, and so forth; Edward Marshall, the only one of the three walkers who finished the eighteen hours, had traveled hard. The northern boundary was understood by the Indians to be Tohiccon Creek; the Penns had run a line back to the Delaware River along the line of the Kittatinny Mountains, some sixty miles parallel to the river it was supposed to meet.[19]

The proprietary party defended the justice of the Walking Purchase by citing old letters referring to the deed of 1686 and the price paid to the Indians, and by laborious arguments to show that the walk as performed had not violated any literal prescription in the deed itself.[20] The terms of the copy used in 1737 were indeed so vague that the walk might have included even more land than it did.

In addition to the desire to defend the honor of the Penns, the proprietary party was motivated by the same considerations which moved Johnson. The Susquehanna Delawares were not as important in a military sense as the Six Nations, and the proprietary officials were sincere enough in the fear that encouraging Teedyuscung's pretentious claims to independence and his wholesale accusations against both Brother Onas and the Iroquois might quickly lead to a break with the Six Nations. The Indian affairs of the province had always been largely in the hands of the executive branch, which was responsible to the Penns and was much more aware of the ins and outs of forest diplomacy than were the Quakers.

*   *   *

The position of Teedyuscung himself in the controversy is strangely obscure. At first glance it would seem that he was a simple patriot; that as soon as he knew that a wrong had been done to his nation, he rushed to right it. But there are too many incongruities to make this interpretation possible; in fact, patriotism very likely was the least of his motives in raising the Walking Purchase charges.

In the first place, the Delaware "nation" was, in 1756, a scattered people with no central governing body of any kind. Many Delawares were out in the Ohio country; some were settled here and there along the Susquehanna; a few were along the Allegheny; and stragglers still remained in their territory, which had been overrun by the whites, as for example at Bethlehem. The Delawares had never, even in the late seventeenth and early eighteenth century, developed a national conception of land. Land rights were enjoyed by local communities composed of a few related maternal lineages, who exploited lineage hunting territories. Teedyuscung himself, being a Jersey Delaware, had no personal responsibility for any of the land included in the Walking Purchase, and his own followers had no claim, except perhaps a very few.

Among this very few was the old chief Nutimus, whom Teedyuscung had more or less supplanted along the Susquehanna in 1755 and 1756. Nutimus, although he was allowing Teedyuscung to steal the limelight, was still a power. It was

Nutimus who ordered Teedyuscung to raise the Walking Purchase question in 1756[21]; it had been Nutimus in 1737 and 1742 who, as the chief Delaware landowner in the Walking Purchase area, had most vigorously opposed the Walk.[22] In 1762 Teedyuscung admitted to Johnson that it was Nutimus and the Quakers who had made him bring up the fraud charges.[23] Nutimus was influential among the Susquehanna Delawares, and he was the one man whom Teedyuscung never dared to order about.[24] Teedyuscung himself declared, "Neutimus . . . gave me his place of Chief man of the Delawares."[25] Nutimus during the war was living at a little village on the Cowanesque, a few miles below Pasigachkunk, where Teedyuscung's cabin and cornfields stood.[26] There is no doubt that Nutimus' sentiments carried a good deal of weight with the "King."

The importance of the Quaker interests in the motivation of Teedyuscung cannot be overemphasized. It may seem strange that Teedyuscung, who had come down to Pennsylvania with the firm intention of making peace, should at the behest of the pacifistic Friends launch a barrage of accusations at Brother Onas. It was of no use to him to make the charges at the moment when he was endeavoring to win back the favor of the proprietary officials: no advantage, that is, if he thought the proprietary party was the important one. But Pemberton in 1756 made sure that Teedyuscung realized that it was the Quakers who ruled Pennsylvania. He dazzled the "King" with lavish gifts and made the portion contributed by the government look pitifully small. He flattered him by affirming the Quakers' belief in his importance. And he offered him a way out of the humiliation of admitting that the war was a mistake. He gave to Teedyuscung, the despised "heathen savage," the chance to embarrass one group of white men while he was enjoying the admiration of another. Thus at one stroke Teedyuscung could satisfy both his love and his hate for the white people.

Weighed against these opportunities, the dangers of antagonizing the Six Nations, Sir William Johnson, and the government of Pennsylvania seemed trivial indeed.

He was to learn his error.

◄ XII ►

The Land Affair Which Is Dirt
1757

Teedyuscung's great problem now was to keep his Susquehanna Delawares behind him. He was at best only a "pine
tree chief"; what claims he had to the loyalty of his followers
must be based on demonstrated and continued ability as a
diplomat to win them advantages from the whites. His new
policy of antagonizing the Penns by playing Quaker politics
meant more presents for the time being, but in the long run
less security.

Most of the Tioga Delawares had been glad enough to
listen to Nutimus when he proposed an early peace. They
were tired of fighting French battles and tired of living on
short French rations. When, late in the fall of 1756, one hundred Ohio Delawares called at Tioga on their way against the
English, some of Teedyuscung's followers told their visitors
that they had made peace with the English and were determined to keep it.[1] As far as they were concerned, the definitive
peace between the Susquehanna Delawares and the English
had been made at Onondaga in July 1756 by Nutimus and
Sir William Johnson. Thus Teedyuscung's separate treaties
at Easton were technically irrelevant.

Actually, however, Teedyuscung's treaties were very important indeed to whoever—like Denny and Pemberton—
saw in them some lever of political usefulness, and to those
Indians who had not heartily subscribed to Nutimus' treaty.
Teedyuscung's treaties had two functions: to air the Walking

149

Purchase; and to provide a few as yet unreconciled Susquehanna Delawares with an opportunity to join the peace *for
pay*.

Not all of the Susquehanna Indians were anxious to make
peace. The "heathen Munsees" along the upper reaches of
the river were not so much like the whites in their way of
living as was Teedyuscung's band. They had no emotional
bonds such as tied Teedyuscung to the English. They were
willing enough to hear what Brother Onas had to say; and,
of course, they were willing to announce politely that they
were anxious to lay down the hatchet. But it would seem that
actually the Munsees did not want an end of the war.

When Teedyuscung came back that winter he did not
spread broadcast the details of his new contract with the
Friendly Association. To a few chosen ones he unburdened
himself. "King" Nutimus, the old politician behind the
scenes, the one man whom Teedyuscung never ordered
about, was pleased with the news that Teedyuscung had
charged the proprietaries with fraud. And Nutimus was not
the only Delaware of Teedyuscung's acquaintance who nour-
ished a grudge on account of the Purchase. His own half-
brother, Captain John, had disputed the right of the Moravian Brethren to occupy his plantation at Nazareth, and he
and Tattamy, another of Teedyuscung's counselors, had sent
the petition to the Governor in 1742, asking permission as
Christians to remain on their lands. These three men and
no doubt others encouraged Teedyuscung to continue his
claims. But these erstwhile "Forks Indians" were few; the
rank and file had never had any interest in the Forks of Delaware. To the majority of the Susquehanna Delawares, peace
was the main object—a peace which would bring a renewal of
trade—peace at once and without delay.

News that the Tioga Delawares were dickering over peace
terms with the English reached the ears of the French. In
January two French officers and seven French Indians visited
Tioga, where they did everything in their power with bribes

and persuasions to turn the Delawares there against the English.[2] Teedyuscung, however, remained firm and in February sent word to Easton that in March he would come down "with a great number of Indians."[3] March and April were the hungry months in the Indian villages, when the winter's supply of corn was almost exhausted, and the woods were too wet for hunting.

The Six Nations, however, now began to take an active interest in Teedyuscung. Since his charges involved their honor and their authority over the Delawares, they too decided that they had better be represented at the next treaty. They were encouraged by Sir William Johnson to go down to Pennsylvania. Toward the end of March Teedyuscung's advance guard, consisting of members of his family and some other Indians, reached Fort Allen. On April 1 the Six Nations delegation arrived at Harris'. Croghan, as Johnson's deputy, welcomed them and urged them to use their influence on Teedyuscung to bring about peace. Scaroyady, speaker for the Six Nations, removed the council fire to Lancaster, where they would await the coming of Teedyuscung and the Delawares.

Throughout the month of April vague messages arrived from Teedyuscung, somewhere up the river, explaining that he was delayed. The explanations varied. First it was because "the Mohock Indians were not quite ready to march."[4] (The Mohawks were already waiting for him in Lancaster.) On the thirteenth one of his counselors, Tapescawen, came to Bethlehem with the news that Teedyuscung had been far back among the Six Nations, gathering delegates to the treaty.[5] Later on his tardiness was said to be due to the scarcity of provisions.[6] On May 9 messengers reached Lancaster who said that a week or so earlier they had met Teedyuscung at Tioga. He had told them then that he had not come down because the invitations sent by the whites had not been formal enough. The runners had been too young; the belts did not contain enough wampum; and be-

sides, some Delawares were still being kept prisoner at Bethlehem and in New Jersey.[7] These objections were stuff and
nonsense. Invitations to a treaty, of course, were quite properly carried by young warriors, and the confirmatory strings
of wampum were not supposed to be belts, especially when
the treaty had been agreed on long before, as had this one.

But by this time hope had died that Teedyuscung would
ever come down to Lancaster. The Delawares who had been
waiting for him at Fort Allen had gone back to their homes
along the Susquehanna to plant corn. The Six Nations had
finally got down to talking with Croghan and Weiser at Lancaster about the Delaware peace. The Six Nations blamed the
alienation of the Delawares in general (including both Ohio
and Susquehanna groups) chiefly on the invasion of their
hunting lands at Wyoming and Juniata by the whites. Aggra-
vated by this, they had been an easy prey to French diplomacy. Little Abraham, the Mohawk speaker, advised Brother
Onas to "treat them kindly, and rather give them some Part
of their Fields back again than differ with them. It is in your
Power to settle all the Differences with them if you please."[8]

The Six Nations were moderate indeed in their assessment
of the Delawares' guilt. Their logic was pragmatic. The
Delawares had declared their virtual independence of the
Onondaga Council; they had revolted against being called
"women" and had expressed willingness to look up to the
Senecas as their only "uncles." Rather than enter into an
unpleasant tussle of wills in open council, the Six Nations
were ready to make concessions in order to close up the
ranks of the League.

Why then did Teedyuscung balk at stating his claims
before the Six Nations? The answer lies partly in his ignorance of the actual polity of the League itself. Born and
raised near the white settlements in New Jersey, he knew
little more of its operations than did the whites. He saw only
its peripheral operations—its Canasetegos, its apparent arbi-
trary enforcement of mysteriously evolved plans—and failed

utterly to grasp the fact that the unity of the League was not maintained solely, or even primarily, by military power. In fact, the authority of the League was dependent entirely upon an occasional fortunate concurrence of sentiments among its members. The statesmen at Onondaga knew this, and were more anxious to obtain this uncertain unity than to maintain any particular formal balance of powers. If Teedyuscung had known this, he would have seen that he was in a strong bargaining position. He did not know it.

Another reason for Teedyuscung's inability to understand the Six Nations was the fact that his personal relations with Iroquois public men had been embarrassing to him. He had quarreled with Newcastle. John Shickellamy would not speak to him. His belts, sent north from Wyoming in 1755 asking for aid against the English, had not even been answered. Scaroyady had tried to discourage his warriors from attacking Pennsylvania. When he spoke with Canyase, the Mohawk councilor, before the first Easton treaty of 1756, he had been humiliated by being reminded of his lowness and subordination.[9] He bitterly resented the fact that the Iroquois nickname for the Delawares was "women."

Furthermore, he was temperamentally incapable of sympathy with the Six Nations. In his ways of thinking and acting, Teedyuscung was often more nearly like the pushing, aggressive, contentious European citizen than the restrained, superficially impassive, rigidly equable type of Iroquois and Delaware forest diplomat. Therefore he not only irked the many Indians who still adhered to the traditional pattern; he read into that old design of life the competitiveness he recognized and expected from himself.

When Teedyuscung learned that the Six Nations were to be present in force at Lancaster, he lost his courage. He forgot about the peace he was intent upon; he forgot about the Walking Purchase. In a flurry of fear he turned to the French

M. Pouchot, the French commandant at Niagara, and the at Niagara again.

Marquis de Vaudreuil, his superior at Montreal, by now had despaired of the "Loups of Tioga" (as the French called the Tioga Delawares). After Teedyuscung's visit in the spring of 1756, parties of Susquehanna Indians had visited Niagara, bringing prisoners, scalps, and intelligence about English activities at Shamokin. But the visits were becoming less and less frequent. The Marquis had heard of Pennsylvania's treaties with Teedyuscung's band. He had also heard of Israel Pemberton, to judge from his remark, "These Loups had been led away by an English interpreter, who had given them many presents."[10] His own efforts to win them back had been unavailing. Secretly he sent belts to Tioga. With tongue in cheek the Delawares replied that they would send their families to Presque Isle to plant corn and that all the warriors would assemble at Tioga to oppose the advance of the English. Nothing happened. Some time later the Marquis heard that everything was quiet among the Delawares and that they were planting their crops (but *not* at Presque Isle). "I have neglected nothing," the Marquis reported mournfully, "to induce the Loups of Tioga to come near me. They are established near Fort Skamoken [Shamokin]. I did not think I could succeed because the Loups have never had the slightest friendship for the French, and because they have always been with the English."[11]

What, then, was the Marquis' surprise when in the middle of April Teedyuscung himself showed up at Niagara! The Marquis wrote in a tone of fervent self-congratulation to his superior in France:

My negotiations, however, have succeeded up to the point that I actually have with me the great chief of that tribe (who is called the king), with a band of his warriors. I have received him very well, and sent him back in such a way that he assured me that he and all his tribe would be closely allied with the French and would make war against the English. I demanded that he give me a proof of the sincerity of his promise. He immediately assigned some of his warriors *to go and join the army I am sending against Fort George. The sight of this army, which consisted of*

*about 9000 men, will give these Loups nothing but an exalted
idea of the French power and strengthen the confidence they are
beginning to have in us.*

The alliance I made with these Loups will be advantageous to
us in all respects. They can send out their parties as far as New
Gersey, New Yorck and many other places which our savages are
not near enough to strike.[12]

Teedyuscung returned to Tioga with the comfortless
knowledge that if he now found himself in trouble with the
Six Nations he could turn to the French for aid. From Tioga
he went on to Pasigachkunk, where he had his plantation,
seventy-five miles to the west, and nervously awaited develop-
ments. His excuses for not coming to Lancaster had been
flimsy. Perhaps the English would wash their hands of
him. . . .

When Jo Peepy and Tapescawen arrived at the beginning
of June, with invitations to bring his "uncles" the Senecas to
a treaty at Easton, his worries dissolved. "It was as if all the
clouds were broke," he said. He had been too much troubled
in spirit even to plant his corn; now, with the help of the messengers, he sowed the seed. In a glow of relief that the English
still loved him, he stopped three French scalping parties from
going through his village. He told the messengers, who were
returning at once to the settlements, that he would start off
on June 19. Four or five horse-loads of dried meat would be
needed, he said, as supplies for his followers; could they be
sent to Wyoming, and with Indians as riders?[13] (If the horse-
men were whites, they would insist on riding back, which
would deprive Indians of transportation.)

When he got to Wyoming, he sent down for more provisions and six quarts of rum.[14]

*   *   *

There were too many Indians in Easton, that July, and the
weather was too hot. Teedyuscung himself brought down

159 men, women, and children; and there were 118 Senecas besides. The Indians had to be guarded from the savage townspeople. Teedyuscung was distinguished from the other Indians by being lodged at Vernon's tavern. Pemberton and his Quakers were present, sanctimoniously lobbying for justice. In these confused circumstances the proprietary party could not prevent the Quakers from carrying on what amounted to a separate treaty with the Delawares. Everyone's temper was on edge. A young Indian, Bill Tattamy, a Christian convert of David Brainerd's, and a son of old Moses Tattamy, was shot by an irresponsible white youth. The wound, which was in the lad's right thigh, festered for five weeks until the victim died. One of Teedyuscung's sons almost shot James Hamilton, a member of the Governor's Council; fortunately someone seized his gun before he fired. It was found to be loaded with powder and a chewed (expanding) bullet.[15]

The conference itself opened inauspiciously. Teedyuscung, pleased with the opportunity to play the major role in this frontier drama, delivered a vacuous speech decorated with noble sentiments and lofty exhortations. "Perhaps," he said, "the evil Spirit was busy in former times, but he is busier now than he was then; Let us therefore be exceeding carefull in whatever we do. Let us try to exceed our Grandfathers in Care in our Proceedings. Let us look up to the Supream Being that we may now by our faithfull Endeavours, have our End answered to the Good of both."[16] Then, following Pemberton's instructions, he requested a private clerk to take down the minutes for the Indians. "I aim," he said, "by having a Clerk of my own, to exceed my Ancestors, by having every Thing for the best."[17]

In his reply next day, Denny refused the request. It was contrary to precedent, he said. Teedyuscung, who did not understand Pemberton's strategy, mildly agreed. One clerk— the secretary of the Governor's Council, Richard Peters— would be enough.

But that evening Israel Pemberton told Teedyuscung that the Governor was making a fool of him. Teedyuscung was very sensitive to being called a fool—especially by a white man. The incident is revealing. Teedyuscung had been chatting upstairs in a room at the tavern with two militia officers, the Indian interpreter John Pumpshire, and Moses Tattamy, when Pemberton unexpectedly came in. Pemberton persuaded him to come outside for a talk. When they were alone, the Quaker told him that he was being led by the nose. The metaphor impressed the "King." When he came back to the company in the tavern, he was "pretty warm." He told Conrad Weiser that the Governor was trying to lead him by the nose, but that he was determined to have his own clerk; and as he spoke, he seized his own nose and shook it vigorously. "He had as much right to a Clerk as the Governor had!" he exclaimed.[18]

Next day Teedyuscung's demand for a clerk was an ultimatum: no clerk, no treaty. He got his clerk—twenty-seven-year-old Charles Thomson of Philadelphia, master of the public Quaker school, a notable Latin scholar, and later secretary to the First Continental Congress. The sober luster of Thomson's mind can be measured by the fact that he had read the Bible through at the age of six.[19]

The conference proceeded laboriously. Teedyuscung, under the tutelage of Pemberton and Thomson, renewed the charges of fraud against Pennsylvania and again accused the Six Nations of being "instrumental to this Misunderstanding." "Though it was not the principal Cause, that made us strike our Brethren the English, yet it has caused the Stroke to come harder than it otherwise would have come."[20] He refused to make peace before an inquiry had been held. He refused to accept Sir William Johnson (a friend of the Mohawks) as arbitrator: let King George be the judge. (By taking the case to England the Quakers hoped to attract the crown's attention to what they considered to be the Penns' abuses of power.)

Teedyuscung by now had merged his interests with those of the Quakers and had completely forgotten the purpose of the whole conference, which was to make peace. His extreme suggestibility to Pemberton and Thomson is indeed remarkable. The over-use of liquor may have contributed to it. He was equally suggestible to any white man of high status. When he was alone with Conrad Weiser, he declared that he was not interested in the land dispute, and in 1762 he said the same thing to Johnson. With his powerful longing to be like the English, he identified himself easily with any white man who treated him kindly. But the Quakers, who had more money and gentler manners than the harassed proprietary officials, like Weiser and Peters, were in a favored position in the contests of ingratiation.

But when the Governor, after delivering to Teedyuscung the deeds which he had wanted to inspect, announced that the ministry in England had ordered the dispute to be laid before Sir William Johnson, Teedyuscung overplayed the Quakers' hand. He bluntly informed the Governor that his speech was "as a Rumbling over the Earth, or Confusion about Lands," and told him to get to the point.[21]

It was Teedyuscung who had forgotten the point—peace— and it was swiftly recalled to his attention by his own Delawares. His own followers revolted. They wanted peace; the land squabble could wait. Some of them, "very grave & sober Counsellors," had throughout the treaty been "much Concern'd at his behaviour with regard to Drinkg."[22] In the council itself, under the eyes of the Governor, the agitated counselors began to talk together in angry tones. Then Lapachpitton, the sachem who in 1748 had almost been chosen as the successor to Sassoonan, and a man of great reputation among the Indians, got to his feet. In an angry tone of voice he interrupted the "King." "Why did you bring us down?" he cried. "We thought we came down to make Peace with our Brethren the English, but you continue to quarrel about the Land affair which is Dirt, a Dispute we did not hear of till now. I desire you to enter upon the Business we came down for, which is Peace.[23] We have been here these Twenty Days, and have heard nothing but scolding and disputing about Lands. Settle the Peace, and let all these Disputes stand till after."[24] The other Delawares shouted approbation of Lapachpitton's speech.

Teedyuscung suddenly realized that he was jeopardizing everything by following the Quaker line and ignoring the wishes of his own followers. If his own Indians did not support him, neither would the Friendly Association. He swallowed his own words. Without a sign of discomfiture, he at once rose to his feet, extended the two belts tied together—the symbol of peace—to the Governor, and took him by the hand. The Governor was for a moment at a loss. After a hurried consultation with Conrad Weiser and George Croghan, he too rose up and handed to Teedyuscung a very large white belt, in confirmation of the peace that was to endure as long as the sun and moon gave light. The belt showed the figures of three men, representing King George joining hands with the King of the Five Nations and with Teedyuscung, the King of the Delawares. To make the contract more precise, the letters G. R., 5 N., and D. K. were marked in, for George Rex, Five Nations, and Delaware King.[25]

The peace had been concluded, in spite of Teedyuscung and the Quakers, and to the surprise of everyone.

The immediate consequences were gratifying to Teedyuscung. Next day there was a great banquet at Vernon's tavern, and after dinner the peace treaty was publicly announced. That night there was a huge bonfire lit at the Indian camp, and a variety of Indian dances performed for the white people's entertainment.

For the rest of the treaty, Teedyuscung avoided the perilous advice of Israel Pemberton. Beyond renewing his claims to lands in New Jersey, where he himself had lived, he was careful not to raise any new controversies. He promised to bring the other tribes into the peace, and vowed to take up the hatchet against the French, asking for a scalp bounty, and suggesting joint Delaware-Pennsylvania war parties under Indian captains. The quarrel about the lands had been referred to King George. Indeed, the "King" reminded Governor Denny when they parted that if the Governor could not make good the Indians' claims, he (Teedyuscung) would "go to England to King George"—a trip which regrettably he did not make. Teedyuscung realized that now, for the time being, the Walking Purchase had better be dropped as a topic for discussion in treaty. Israel Pemberton had given him "a rod to scourge the white people," but it had been laid on his own back by Lapachpitton.

◆§ XIII §◆

Peace in the West
1757-1758

During the winter of 1757-58 Teedyuscung, as the recognized spokesman of the Susquehanna Delawares, attempted to gather up the threads of many problems facing himself and his people and to weave them into a coherent fabric. In the back of his mind was his old, familiar stereotype of the perennially hungry Indian, ill clothed, ill housed, unlettered, and abused. In 1755, in the plea for sympathy extended to Captain Newcastle at Tioga, he had said, "Brother Onas, We desire you will look upon us with Eyes of Mercy, we are a very poor People, our Wives and Children are almost naked, we are void of Understanding and testitute of the Necessaries of Life. Pity us."[1] Now, after two years of war, poverty was still the most pressing problem among the Susquehanna Delawares; and Teedyuscung himself was still almost morbidly eager to be a white man. But three new necessities had to be met now, too: the breaking of French power, the settlement of land grievances, and the extension of the peace to the Shawnees and Delawares in the Ohio.

Hunger was the leitmotif twisting through the somewhat discordant symphony of interracial relations. Since 1755, war had interrupted the normal pursuit of hunting and the normal planting of corn, squash, and beans about the villages. Enforced migrations had carried the Delaware populations of Shamokin, Nescopeck, Wyoming, and Tunkhannock far up the Susquehanna to Tioga, Assinisink, and Pasigachkunk; many

161

of the more active young men and women had continued on out to the Ohio country. Those who remained were not familiar with the hunting grounds where they now lived, and which were very likely overcrowded anyway. Much of the seed corn had probably been lost or spoiled. And the necessity of going out on long scalping raids meant time lost from the hunting and trapping. Consequently many of the adherents of Teedyuscung in his redundant peace-making were largely prompted by the hope of gaining access to the vast food supplies of agricultural Pennsylvania; indeed, as appeared at the treaty of 1757, some of them were more eager than Teedyuscung himself, who was more interested in his reputation than in his stomach.

With the covenant of peace, Pennsylvania had promised to reopen the trade at Fort Augusta. Teedyuscung left Easton about August 6, reluctantly enough, to publish the news of the treaty in the Indian country. (At the close of the treaty he had irresponsibly suggested to Governor Denny that he would like to come to Philadelphia, but Denny had persuaded him to go away with the other Indians.)[2] Teedyuscung left Fort Allen on the seventeenth, "very glad and joyful,"[3] and returned a week later, having performed his duty—at least in its minimum requirements.[4]

The news that the trade was to be reopened at Fort Augusta (Shamokin) spread through the Susquehanna populations like wildfire. On September 8 thirty Delawares arrived at the fort with skins, expecting to trade; and when they were told that the goods had not yet arrived, they went away sullenly, complaining of a breach of faith.[5] The trade at Fort Augusta did not officially begin until December 8, when John Carson, the storemaster, opened the store for business.[6] But Teedyuscung's belligerent son John Jacob, presuming, no doubt, on his father's status, bought some £15 worth of goods from Major James Burd, the commander at Fort Augusta, as early as October 15. John's purchases are revealing in the data they give on the style of dress affected by

Teedyuscung's familial followers. John bought a regimental coat, a gold-laced hat with cockade, a pair of shoes, a checkered shirt, a ruffled shirt, a plain shirt for his wife, a cotton handkerchief, two pairs of breeches, a pair of buckles, a yard of scarlet shalloon for a flag, a yard and a half of half-thicks for leggings, an English pipe tomahawk, and a rifled gun (the Indians preferred rifles to smooth-bores, to the dismay of the ill-armed militia).[7]

Burd's tact in accommodating the sartorial ambitions of the young John Jacob bore unexpected fruits. A week later John, along with some of his friends, came to Burd to say that he was going to Fort Duquesne to strike the French. "John Tidyouskung," said his comrades, "was the greatest Warrior of all the Delaware Nation. . . . He was their Capt. & they would do what he ordered them." They would not attack any of the Ohio Indians on this raid; but if at the end of twelve months those Indians had not made peace with the English and taken up the hatchet against the French, then they would strike them too.

Burd, of course, replied that he would be only too glad to see them bring back French prisoners and French scalps.

John thanked Major Burd and went on to tell him (in Burd's words):

the French had not used them as I [Burd] have done, that they kept Continually sending them to Ware agt. their good Brothers the English, by which means they had become poor, and naked, and their wifes and Children almost starved to Death, as the French made no Provision for them but used them like Doggs; that hunting was the Indians's living & they could not hunt while they went to Warr & therefore they depended that I would Continue to Cloath And provide for them & their Familys as I had done, and for their part they would go to War . . . when & where I pleased to order them, and that they would leave their familys under my care.

Next day John took up his hatchet, struck the war post, and danced the war dance; the rest of his party followed him.

On October 24 the warriors set off in high spirits, promising to leave seven captured French spears, handed over to them by Burd, in the breasts of their enemies, and to return in twenty days.[8]

The opening of the store in December brought the Susquehanna Delawares swarming around the fort. By the seventeenth the factor had received a small parcel of skins and had disposed of a quantity of goods.[9] By the end of January 1758 some forty-three Delawares, including old Nutimus and all his family, had brought skins to trade at the store and were camping about the fort, consuming the provisions they had bought, under the safety of the English guns.[10]

When Johnson heard about all this, he immediately interpreted it as a nefarious Quaker plot. "The Quakers are now carrying on a considerable Trade at Shamokin or Wiyoming, and detirmined to carry on a very great one next Spring," he wrote; and he added suspiciously that thus Fort Augusta was becoming a potential supply source for the French and their Indians.[11] But Johnson's doubts were unjust. The purpose of reopening the trade at Fort Augusta was to keep the Susquehanna Indians firm in the interest of Pennsylvania. To do this, on October 28, 1757, the loan office had advanced to Joseph Fox, one of the assembly-appointed commissioners for Indian affairs, the sum of £1,000 for goods to begin the trade at Fort Augusta.[12] The plan was to sell the goods at cost; but since strouds, blankets, and matchcoats had been commonly sold "at a very Low Rate" before the war, the prices of some other less necessary things were raised.[13] This occasional up-rating, nevertheless, did not make up the difference. By 1762 the accounts of the commissioners for the Indian trade noted: "Loss on the Trade at Augusta £197/2/2½."[14] The reason probably was that the Susquehanna populations never did succeed fully in rebuilding their shattered economy. A profitable trade in furs and skins could only be carried on with a stable Indian population. But even in the summer of 1762, canoe loads of Indians were still coming down the river from Wyoming to ask for corn, or, in the absence of that, for flour.[15]

Teedyuscung himself, of course, was almost competely dependent on the whites for support. Although he did have a cornfield and the opportunity of hunting at Pasigachkunk, and later at Wyoming, his frequent trips into the white settlements left him dependent on the whites for food and clothing during most of the year. In September 1757 he persuaded the Moravians to build him a lodge near the Crown Inn where he lived the rest of the winter, dining, of course, at the Crown Inn with his family.[16] Elisabeth apparently had become reconciled to her husband, for she moved in with Teedyuscung from the little house which the Moravians had built her "to live by herself."[17] On November 1, 1757, the Moravians at Bethlehem were credited by the provincial commissioners (who supervised the expenditure of the military defense funds appropriated by the Assembly) with having spent £75/11/5½ since 1756 for provisions supplied to Teedyuscung and some other Indians.[18]

* * *

Teedyuscung's son John Jacob and his companions, who had left Fort Augusta in October, did not return to the Susquehanna until the middle of December. They came back with an impressive tale to tell. They had gone as far as Custaloga's town, where they had told the old chief about the treaty at Easton. Custaloga had in consequence instructed his warriors not to join the French in a proposed attack on Fort Augusta next spring. John and his comrades had also learned that Teedyuscung's peace belt, which the "King" had sent to the westward, had arrived at Allegheny Town, some twenty miles above Venango.[19]

While this made pleasant hearing, it did not mean a great deal in itself. The acceptance of the peace belt by a village or two was no assurance of universal good will by the Ohio

Indians. Even the Susquehanna Indians were as yet by no means completely in the English interest. These two groups of pro-French Delawares—on the Ohio and on the upper Susquehanna—were a standing threat to Teedyuscung's prestige. Should French counsels prevail, Teedyuscung would become a broken reed.

Throughout 1757 there had been a party among the Tioga Delawares who refused to join the peace that Teedyuscung was making with the English. These Indians, largely Munsees, resorted to Niagara, where Messieurs Pouchot and Chabert encouraged them to bring their prisoners and scalps, and where they fanned the spite that the Delawares as "women" felt for their Iroquois chaperons, even suggesting that they return the *machicote* (petticoat) to the Six Nations.[20] The French had hopes of introducing a Jesuit priest into the Tioga community; but this last scheme met unexpected resistance. The anecdote is worth telling for the sake of the insight it gives us into the hodge-podge of the Delaware mind, half Indian and half European, in 1757.

In August the Marquis de Vaudreuil, the French commander-in-chief at Montreal, sent to Niagara some of the St. Francis Abenakis to make an alliance between them and their Algonkian "grandfathers," the Delawares. The Abenakis took with them their Jesuit missionary. During the council proceedings the Abenakis gave to the Delawares a fine belt to encourage them to hear the priest and receive him into their confidence. The Delawares politely replied that they were delighted to know their "grandchildren" the Abenakis, and would be pleased to hear what the Jesuit father had to say. The father then spoke, giving the pagan Delawares a short homily on the excellence of religion.

The condescension was too marked, and a baptized Christian Delaware arose to defend the spiritual sophistication of his people. "He was not ignorant," he said, "that to enjoy a happy life a person should know, that there once came into the world a little child, who having [sic] sinned in his life, at the age of thirty years was killed, and that they pierced his hands and feet. It was him who had charge of the life of the other world, and that nothing could be had without him." Then, going on to speak of the Trinity, the Delaware designated the first person as a great chief, whom he compared to a king; the second, to a war captain; and the third was like the church, or prayer. These three persons had made men, as they were found on earth, in three colors: red, black, and white; and the Trinity had destined the one for praying, one for hunting, and the third for war. But beyond that, the will of men was free.[21]

The Delaware who delivered this counterblast against papistry may very probably have been a Moravian convert. He professed to baptism; and his comments on free will do not suggest Presbyterian influence. The emphasis, even though distorted, on the life of Jesus is also diagnostic of the Moravian doctrine, which laid great stress on the saving grace of Christ.

Even while Teedyuscung tarried at Bethlehem in September, enjoying the company of the Brethren, there were new raids on the frontiers. Teedyuscung was eager to assure the Governor that his Delawares were not responsible; indeed, he asked Denny to send him a war belt for his warriors, and promised that if a scalp bounty were offered, his men would quickly disperse the skulking invaders.[22] On Conrad Weiser's advice, however, and in consideration of humanitarian ideals, the suggestion was refused. Weiser felt that the bounty would pay for Pennsylvania scalps, and would put the Susquehanna Indians in a position to say that Pennsylvania made peace with the Delawares solely to trick them into fighting Pennsylvania's battles.[23] The Indians chiefly responsible for the new murders were Munsees, who had caught the contagion of land grievances and were muttering about the expropriation of their lands in New Jersey and New York, between the Hudson and the Delaware rivers.[24] Along with the Munsees went parties of disaffected Cayuga and Seneca young men.²⁵ There is no reason to think that Teedyuscung condoned participation of his people in war parties against the English. But the persistence of these raids carried a threat to his position as the trusted agent and friend of Brother Onas. As he well knew, white people were notoriously unable to tell one Indian from another, and rumors were rife that Teedyuscung and his followers had been concerned in the murders.²⁶

But with the New Year of 1758 came a change in the complexion of things on the Ohio. Saur's newspaper carried a story about ten white men who, in the middle of January, went north over the mountains to visit their deserted plantations and to hunt deer. They unexpectedly came upon three Indians carrying peltries. The white men fired hastily, but the Indians stood still and called, "Stop! We are friends!" The whites cried, "If you are friends, drop your guns and come to us." The Indians did so, saying, *"Wir sind Freunde und sind eure Brüder. It is no more Waar! Es ist kein Krieg mehr!"*²⁷ At the end of the month it was reported that none of the Susquehanna populations, exclusive of the Munsees, were any longer the enemies of Pennsylvania.²⁸

On March 6, 1758, however, real auguries of a peace between Brother Onas and the Ohio Delawares appeared. On that date a party of five Delawares from the western regions arrived at Bethlehem with a message for Teedyuscung, who since the last treaty had been making his home at the Crown Inn with his wife and children. The news was important: the Ohio Indians were turning to the English. Three days later another party, of ten men, reached Teedyuscung with a similar message intended for the Governor of Pennsylvania.²⁹

This was Teedyuscung's great chance to show the Governor (and the whole world of white men) how important he was and how much he could help Brother Onas. He had sent his peace belt, without mentioning that he had made the peace under pressure, to the Ohio—and see, here were the results! On March 9 he and the messengers set off for Philadelphia, but not before Teedyuscung had announced that they bore the "good News" that the war in this part of the world was over.[30] The messengers from the Ohio, shepherded by Teedyuscung, reached Germantown on the eleventh. Their progress attracted considerable attention in the newspapers and private correspondence of the time. The Indian deputies, it was said, had traveled for forty-seven days on snowshoes in order to reach Fort Allen. They had been snowbound at Tioga for days by a heavy snow. Three of them had collapsed when they reached Bethlehem and were unable to continue to Philadelphia. These deputies carried various strings of official wampum and a huge tobacco pipe artistically contrived. They were described to the public as being quiet, good-natured men who refused to touch strong drink because "they believed it destroyed the understanding." In an age when notions of a "state of nature" could tickle the fancy of the sophisticated, the simple woodnotes of the Ohio Indians almost eclipsed the mock-European bombast of Teedyuscung. Christopher Saur, the editor of Pennsylvania's German-language newspaper, wrote critically: "People say they were called and invited by a message from Teedyuscung to live in peace and friendship with the English; but is more likely that the French at this juncture don't have overmuch to give to the Indians, and so poverty may have helped them to make the long journey by snowshoe."[31]

The success of his diplomacy inflated Teedyuscung's opinion of himself to an extraordinary degree. On the thirteenth, while the Indians were wiping the snow from Richard Peters' and one another's eyes with strings of wampum, and arrangements were being made for the official presentation of the message from the Ohio, Teedyuscung repeated his customary and always irritating demand for a private clerk. In fact, he bluntly announced that he would bring his own clerk into the Governor's Council, whether they liked it or not. The usual contest of wills began again, with Teedyuscung as ever holding the advantage because his compulsion to win was more insistent. The Council refused to admit a second clerk. The denial was brought to Teedyuscung. He sent back a sharp answer. He was at dinner, he said, and tired of waiting. If he could not bring his clerk, he would not speak at all to the Governor. The Council, which had originally set the meeting for noon, adjourned, notifying Teedyuscung that since this had not been planned as a public treaty, no Indian clerk would be tolerated; but if he insisted on a clerk, a public treaty could be arranged.[32]

This, of course, suited him very well: the more conspicuous his appearances were, the better. Accordingly, then, the treaty convened on the fifteenth, the meeting place was the council chamber of the State House, now known as Independence Hall. Indians present included Teedyuscung, the Ohio deputies, Tapescawen (Teedyuscung's chief counselor), his half-brother Young Captain Harris, and Moses Tattamy the interpreter. White men on hand were Governor Denny, the Council, Conrad Weiser, the speaker of the Assembly and a number of members, and various citizens of Philadelphia.[33]

The treaty, which continued from March 15 to 25, 1758, marked the pinnacle of Teedyuscung's career of self-advertisement. It was more than usually difficult to separate fact from rhetoric; and the difficulty was enhanced by the inadequacy of the interpreters, including Moses Tattamy, all of whom were Jersey Indians, brought up among white settlements from their infancy, and entirely unacquainted with the usages of the foreign deputies.[34] At most the messages the Ohio visitors had brought were simple protestations of friendship from certain well-disposed individuals who hoped intensely to encourage Pennsylvania to continue her efforts to make peace.[35] This, of course, while by no means signifying the conclusion of an alliance between Brother Onas and all of the Ohio Delawares, was a convenient basis upon which to found a later rapprochement. But Teedyuscung expanded these mild and qualified overtures into a full-fledged peace treaty. His ignorance of Indian protocol probably helped him to jump to conclusions; his desire to appear prominent certainly did.

Teedyuscung reported to the assemblage that he had given the "Big Peace Halloo" to the western nations. In response, all the nations from the sunrise to those beyond the Great Lakes, where the sun sets, had sent messages to him constituting him their plenipotentiary to make peace. All power was in his hands. Eight more nations had taken hold of the covenant chain: the Ottawas, the Twightwees (Miamis), Chippewas, Tawas (south of Lake Erie), Caughnawagas, Mahoowas (who lived "on an Island in One of the Lakes"), Pottawotamies, and Nalashawanas (north of New England). On behalf of these eight nations, and the ten whom he already represented, he handed round the peace pipe and presented an ornate peace belt.

Brother Onas did not quite know how to take this grandiose pronouncement. Abortive efforts were made to sound the Indians themselves on their reactions to Teedyuscung's speechifying. Finally it was decided to accept the claims at face value. A great peace belt was given to the deputies from the Ohio; and, when they departed, they were presented, as a special mark of favor, with William Penn's own calumet, which he had used in his first treaty.[36] It was hoped that, although no real agreement upon any of the points at issue between Brother Onas and the Ohio Delawares had been reached, the testimonials of mutual good will and respect would facilitate a later understanding.

While Teedyuscung was in treaty at Philadelphia, one of his sons was leading a party of warriors to the Ohio to take French prisoners, for the Delawares still steadfastly refused to attack one another.[37] On March 27, when Teedyuscung had just returned to Bethlehem, his son came back with about twenty foreign Indians, strangers to the Moravians, who said they had been brought along by Teedyuscung's son to make peace. A rumor quickly spread about the countryside that these Indians were actually carrying a message from the notorious Shingas the Terrible, mild-mannered speaker and war captain of the Ohio Delawares, to Teedyuscung. Shingas, it was said, wanted to come to Pennsylvania to treat with Brother Onas about the terms of peace. It was reported in Saur's newspaper that Teedyuscung leaped high into the air for joy at this unexpected news.[38]

There is no question that there was a strong peace movement among the Ohio Indians. Even the French were aware of it. Montcalm was remarking that more and more the enemy were making strenuous efforts to detach the Delawares and Shawnees from the French—and that they were succeeding.[39] Many of these attempts were being made by Teedyuscung himself, whose belts and messengers were spreading the word that peace was offered by the English, and peace not only with honor, but with profit, in the form of renewed trade in food, clothing, and ammunition.

*   *   *

As long as the military situation remained static, Teedyuscung could negotiate for peace without prejudice to his position among either the English or the Delawares, excepting a few die-hard fanatics. On the whole he was being successful in bringing Indian and Englishman together, since he was working with the inevitable stream of events. Peace would be a military advantage to the English, an economic advantage to the Delawares. But with the spring came complications. The long arm of William Pitt was reaching out into the Ohio country: General Forbes was preparing to mount an offensive to capture Fort Duquesne.

How Teedyuscung became aware of the coming campaign is not clear; but when he found out, he realized at once how it jeopardized his whole position. His appeals to the Susquehanna and Ohio Delawares had all been based on the belief

that the Indians would be left undisturbed in the possession
of their present lands. There would be no more Walking
Purchases. There would be no reprisals. There would be no
British troops on their trails. By implication, it would be
Indian hatchets which would finally knock the French on
the head, thus at once putting the English in their debt, and
securing to themselves the land upon which they were living.
But an English invasion of the Ohio country would make
his peace proposals sound like English threats. Teedyuscung
would appear to his Delaware compatriots as a man who
softened the way for the English by speaking fair words
while the white man sharpened his hatchet.

In April 1758 Teedyuscung made a special trip to Philadelphia with the rather naïve design of dissuading the British
Empire from prosecuting the war on France. Don't attack
the French in the Ohio, he told the Governor. "I will give
them one Blow, and if any escape that I will drive them to
the Sea for you." The Ohio Delawares were already cheering
him on in his peace-making endeavors; but, he intimated,
a premature military campaign might wreck all that had been
accomplished.

The reply was disappointing to this self-appointed har-
binger of peace. The English, said Robert Stretell, president
of the Council, must fight in the Ohio to drive away the
French. But, ever open to a hint from white men, Teedyuscung was not one to suffer from an excess of consistency.
Without hesitation he announced that in that case he would
fight alongside the English. "Where your Bones lie there my
Bones shall lie also," he said. Stretell then asked him to send
word to the eighteen nations who had supposedly joined
Pennsylvania, to assist Forbes in his advance. Before the end
of the conference Teedyuscung had promised, unwisely, to
recruit a party of Delawares under Delaware captains to re-
capture some white people who had recently been seized on
the frontiers.[40]

The embarrassments aroused by the Forbes campaign, and

his own unwisdom in promising to raise a ranging party from among his own followers, quickly appeared on his return to Bethlehem. On April 18, 1758, he appointed his son John Jacob to be a captain, and gave him and another son, Amos, together with some other youthful relatives, a string and three belts to carry to the Allegheny Indians to tell them to stop striking the English. (It had apparently been Indians from the Allegheny who had committed the late murders.) One of the Indians was wearing a very ragged shirt, and Teedyuscung, in a gesture of magnificent *noblesse oblige,* stripped his own new one off his back and gave it to the indigent. He also handed each of his sons a dollar. They went away in high spirits.[41]

The young men went to Fort Allen, where they celebrated their mission in liquor, and stayed drunk until the twenty-second. They were not so drunk, however, as to omit seeing the two Indians from the upper Susquehanna who came to the fort of the twenty-first. What passed between the two parties has not come to light; but Teedyuscung's sons, who left Fort Allen next day in the morning, returned the same night. They had had a dream, they said. They had dreamed that two Indians had poisoned them. The meaning of the dream was that they would die if they went to Allegheny.[42]

Meanwhile the "King" was having trouble with others of his retainers. In accordance with his promise to recruit a ranging party which would help to police the frontiers and stop infiltration by hostile Indians, he had sent five warriors to Fort Allen to assist Captain Orndt in his scouting. These five were not anxious to fight. They dragged along with them several full casks of rum from Easton, and spent their whole time at the fort drinking and carousing.[43]

These floutings of Teedyuscung's authority were straws in the wind which the colonial bureaucrats were not slow in picking up. At the end of April Richard Peters was writing that Teedyuscung would soon be "deposed" by the Susquehanna Delawares.[44] The French in the Ohio were informed by some Munsees, probably from Tioga, that the English were planning to attack Fort Duquesne.[45] These same Delawares presented a belt to the Ohio Delawares which, contradicting Teedyuscung's messages, urged them to war against the English.[46] And a Delaware family from Tioga, who were settled on the Susquehanna between Wyoming and Fort Augusta since the reopening of trade there, told Conrad Weiser that they would not be commanded by Teedyuscung. Teedyuscung, they said, among the Delawares was reported "as one that *wants to make Englishmen out of the Indians* ... his way of acting was disagreeable to the Indians about Tioga."[47] Although the Tioga Delawares were firm in the English interest, they were not prepared to become Englishmen along with Teedyuscung.

The Dream
1757-1758

During the course of the great treaty at Easton in July 1757, Teedyuscung had demanded the establishment of a tribal reservation for himself and his followers. Although he had specifically declared that land grievances were not the principal cause of the alienation of the Delawares, he had admitted that they "had caused the Stroke to come harder than it otherwise would have come."[1] His demand for land (prompted, no doubt, but not motivated by the Quakers) was made on July 28, 1757, and lay like an unexploded bomb among the council minutes for years thereafter. "We intend," said Teedyuscung,

to settle at *Wyoming,* and we want to have certain Boundaries fixed between you and us; and a certain Tract of Land fixed, which it shall not be lawful for us or our Children ever to sell, nor for you, or any of your Children, ever to buy. We would have the Boundaries fixed all round, agreeable to the Draught we give you, that we may not be pressed on any Side, but have a certain Country fixed for our own Use, and the Use of our Children forever.

And as we intend to make a Settlement at *Wyoming,* and to build different Houses from what we have done heretofore, such as may last not only for a little Time, but for our Children after us; we desire you will assist us in making our Settlements, and send us Persons to instruct us in building Houses, and in making such Necessaries as shall be needful; and that Persons be sent to instruct us in the Christian Religion, which may be for our future Welfare, and to instruct our Children in Reading and

Writing; and that a fair Trade be established between us, and such Persons appointed to conduct and manage these Affairs as shall be agreeable to us.[2]

At the time he made the speech, Teedyuscung drew a crude map in chalk on the table, showing the lands he wanted. This rough draft was later projected onto Lewis Evans' map of the English colonies and delivered to the Governor. The designated tract embraced some two million acres[3]—over three thousand square miles—centering in the Wyoming Valley and including much of what eventually became the great anthracite coal region of Pennsylvania. Beginning a little below Shamokin (leaving out the fort and a small quantity of land as an English enclave, for the trading post), the line was to run eastward along the northern boundary of the Purchase of 1749 to Lackawaxen Creek where it entered the Delaware; thence northward along the Delaware to Cushietunk (Station Point); thence on a straight course to Burnet's Hill where it crossed the Susquehanna (about ten miles south of Tioga); thence along Burnet's Hill to Big Island in the West Branch of Susquehanna; and thence down the West Branch to Shamokin.[4]

Although this claim struck the proprietary officials as wildly extravagant, as simply unthinkable, Teedyuscung and the Quakers were able for several years to use it as a lever to pry concessions from Brother Onas. Teedyuscung had thoroughly impressed the whites with the bitter resentment which he and his followers felt about the loss of their lands; and rather than give them the lands he asked for, Pennsylvania would grant many other smaller favors. The land problem was puffed up by Teedyuscung into a threatening monster. When Governor Denny delivered the Grand Peace Belt to Teedyuscung on August 3, 1757, he told him that as peace was now concluded, all white captives must be punctually restored. Teedyuscung, turning short on the Governor, replied, "They should certainly be restored, but he [the

Governor] must remember, They [the Indians] must first be Satisfied for their Lands."[5]

In discussing the formulation of this demand of Teedyuscung's for land, security, and Europeanization, it is impossible to disentangle what he himself originally conceived from what was suggested to him by Pemberton, Thomson, and other Quaker advisers. Certainly the Friends helped him with legal advice and encouragement, hoping through him to entangle the Penns in a coil of litigation which would eventually draw down royal frowns upon proprietors who could not remain on good terms with their Indian populations. But just as certainly the demand for land grew immediately out of Teedyuscung's own experience. The insistence upon secure title was an outgrowth of his own observations of what had happened to Indian territory again and again in New Jersey and Pennsylvania, especially in the case of the Walking Purchase; and the plea for instruction in the European way of life was of the very essence of his personality.

After his return from the Indian country in August 1757, Teedyuscung spent a few days at Bethlehem. While he was there, Bishop Spangenberg invited "the Apostate, who had raised himself to a King," together with his family, to have a cup of coffee with himself, Peter Boehler, and Martin Mack. Teedyuscung appeared to advantage in this interview. "The King," wrote the Bethlehem diarist, "was animated and strictly attentive. He is naturally quick of apprehension and ready in reply." With great tact and some sincerity, Teedyuscung during the course of conversation frequently alluded to his baptism and his former communion with the mission. He observed "with apparent regret" (as the diarist cautiously wrote), that he had lost the peace of mind he had once enjoyed, but that he hoped it would return. And he told the Brethren that it was his sincere desire to remain in connection with them, in preference to any other people among the whites. It is noteworthy that during this chat, in which he impressed the Brethren with his good qualities, he also was

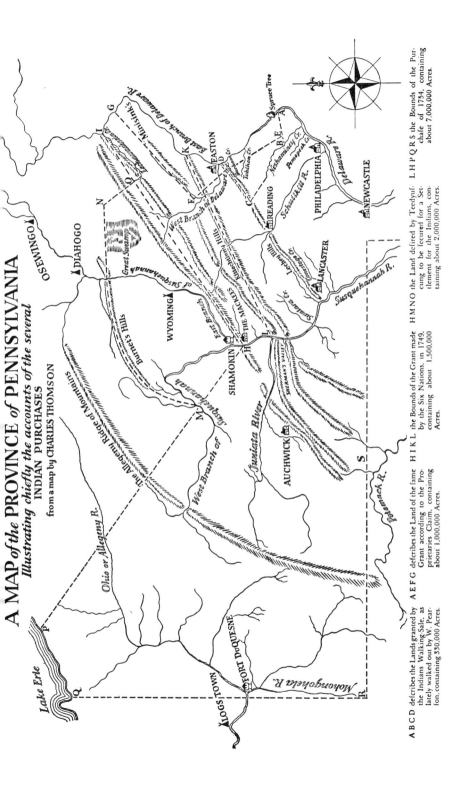

A MAP of the PROVINCE of PENNSYLVANIA

Illustrating chiefly the accounts of the several

INDIAN PURCHASES

from a map by CHARLES THOMSON

A B C D defcribes the Land of the fame Grant according to the Proprietaries Claim. containing about 1,000,000 Acres.

the Indians Walking-Sale, as lately walked out by W. Pearfon, containing 330,000 Acres.

H I K L the Bounds of the Grant made by the Six Nations, in 1749. containing about 1,500,000 Acres.

A E F G defcribes the Lands granted by the Indians Walking-Sale, as lately walked out by W. Pearfon, containing 330,000 Acres.

H M N O the Land defired by Teedyufcung to be fecured for a Settlement for the Indians, containing about 2,000,000 Acres.

L H P Q R S the Bounds of the Purchafe of 1754, containing about 7,000,000 Acres.

able politely but firmly to disagree with them on several important points.

There were several bones of contention between Teedyuscung and the Brethren. For one thing, Bishop Spangenberg still wanted to build Gnadenstadt (the City of Grace) on the site of the old Shawnee town in the Wyoming Valley. As we have seen, this dream of the Moravians for a Christian metropolis in the heart of the Indian country, first conceived by Zinzendorf in 1742, had touched off the train of events which eventually led Teedyuscung and some of the Gnadenhütten congregation to settle at Wyoming in 1754. Now Spangenberg suggested to Teedyuscung that the Moravians would like to buy the tract. Teedyuscung refused.

Teedyuscung had a request to make too. The Brethren had recently purchased a piece of land about a mile east of Bethlehem, on which they proposed to establish the Indian congregation who were living in crowded quarters in Bethlehem. Teedyuscung observed that if an Indian settled in the white man's country, he was subject to the white man's law. Then he asked, "Why cannot the Indians who love the Saviour remove to the Indian country and plant along the Susquehanna? The Brethren surely can visit them, preach to the men and women, and instruct the children."

Spangenberg rejoined by stipulating that in such a case the Christian Indians should have a town of their own, with a school and a church, and no pagans or wicked persons should be allowed within its precincts.

Teedyuscung agreed to the reasonableness of these conditions, and then expressed the wish that all the Indians who loved the Saviour might live together.[6]

Teedyuscung has often been accused of being perversely opposed to Christianity in general, with being an apostate, a renegade, a traitor. The opinions brought forward by him at this interview indicate that another evaluation might be more just. It seems, to this writer at least, that Teedyuscung had intuitively grasped some of the essential factors of the whole problem of interracial accommodation. His experience with the formal mission life at Gnadenhütten had been unsatisfactory, for the professions—and deeds—of the Christian missionaries did not accord well with the behavior of the Christian settlers. The Brethren themselves, honest and sincere, and fair to the natives, spoke of the brotherhood of man in Christ. One of them, Christian Frederick Post, had married Teedyuscung's son's sister-in-law. At Gnadenhütten there had been relatively little racial antipathy, relatively little economic injustice. But among the whites in general there was a rapidly growing sentiment of spite toward the Indians, which had been greatly magnified by the war. "Intermarriage," wrote the famous botanist John Bartram in 1756, "would be reconed A horrid crime with us."[7] Rough frontiersmen, exasperated by the war, called friendly Indians dogs and rogues, and damned them to their faces. At the second Easton treaty in November 1756, for instance, a bloodthirsty peddler had to be jailed for conspiring to murder the Indian ambassadors. He had offered to furnish some of the militia with knives to cut the throats of the Indians, and he himself had promised to kill Teedyuscung.[8] The unctuous openness and friendliness displayed by the proprietary officials and the Quakers at the treaties did not blind any Indian to the prevailing sentiments of the majority of whites.

Hence segregation was the only thinkable immediate policy. Without lands of their own, lands which were inalienable and able to support the Indians at a standard of living comparable to that of the white people, the natives would be thrown on to the chilly hospitality of the Europeans.

But mere segregation would create more problems than it would solve. For one thing, the marginal Indian, as represented by Teedyuscung, did not want tó be native; he wanted to be a white man. This admiration for white culture undoubtedly prompted many a Delaware to accept the Christian religion. But taking over the white man's religion was merely taking over the white man's shadow: the substantial differences remained, and these were technological and economic, social and psychological. Teedyuscung wanted not just the right to call himself the white man's brother in Christ; he wanted to be able to read, and write, and do blacksmith work, and live in a permanent log house; he wanted to fence his corn, and plow his own land instead of letting his women till it with hoes. In other words, mere theological democracy was no substitute for economic equality. Inferiority feelings were not relieved by the experience of baptism, because white prejudice and economic hostility did not end with conversion.

The Indian and the white man did have a common measure of interests, however, in the Indian trade, whereby manufactured articles were exchanged for fur and peltries.

It seems that Teedyuscung, whether or not he was able to express it philosophically to himself, had come to the conclusion that the solution of the Indian's urgent need for emotional and economic satisfaction could not be met by allowing alternate exploitation and evangelization to proceed uninhibited. The Indian needed a secure territory where he could gradually adjust himself to the growing white society, and where he could control the processes of culture change by choosing those elements of European life (including religion and technology) which would enable him to fit into, or articulate with, white society as a member of a self-sufficient Indian society.

*   *   *

After his chat with Spangenberg, Teedyuscung went on to Philadelphia to report that certain Ohio Delawares had announced their intention of abiding by the peace made at Easton. At Tunkhannock he had met the messengers, who had given him a belt for Brother Onas testifying to their pacific inclinations. He had sent his son Amos back with them to Venango to spread the good word of peace. Teedyuscung added that the Shawnee Paxinosa, old Mahican Abraham, and one of the Unami Delawares on the Susquehanna had told him, "Teedyuscung, You must go soon to Wioming you must go and live there and wee three Nations will soon come to you—Be sure let the Governor know this and desire him to build a little Fort at Wioming for the safety of Our Wives and Children."[9]

Governor Denny replied, "I have communicated all you have said to me to my Assembly, who were fortunately sitting, and . . . they have promised to enable me to send and employ proper Persons forthwith to build a Fort for your Protection and some Houses to live in."[10]

Although his misison was successful in this respect, Teedyuscung fell afoul of the Governor over trivial misunderstandings. His actions in Philadelphia were in significant contrast to his pleasant behavior at Bethlehem a few days before. He had initially embarrassed Denny at a state banquet by asking after the health of Mrs. Denny, an error which did not improve their relations, for the Governor's wife was having an affair with a Mr. Way and had already or would in a few months elope with her lover.[11] Denny, nettled by Teedyuscung's importunate and haughty manner, expressed to Johnson his suspicions that Teedyuscung had come back to Philadelphia because his arrogant ways had offended other Indians, or perhaps because the villainous Quakers had summoned him.[12] Teedyuscung, for his part, on September 5 presented himself before the Governor to demand "in a very sower manner" to know why the treaty of 1757 (as yet only a month old) had not been printed. Governor Denny said that George Croghan, the deputy superintendent of Indian affairs, had desired the printing be delayed until the minutes were submitted to Sir William Johnson—a legitimate request. But on hearing this, Teedyuscung fell into a "Violent Passion," called Croghan a great rogue, and said he would henceforth have nothing to do with him, or with Johnson either.[13]

Denny's peevish behavior threw Teedyuscung right into the waiting arms of the Quakers. Next month he came again to Philadelphia to tell Denny that he had decided not to accept the war belt from Brother Onas. "It would be better to postpone it till the Spring," he said, "when it would be seen by how many the Peace was approved."[14] Tactlessly, the Governor omitted to give him any presents, and Teedyuscung was forced to beg him for gold to pay his reckoning at the inn. He got two pieces of eight.[15] The Quakers, on the other hand, presented him with a plain coat and jacket, which he carried back to Bethlehem and had refurbished with forty-two buttons, silk, mohair, brown linen, and buckram.[16]

It was also the Quaker element of the Assembly who supervised and carried out the Governor's promises for the construction of houses at Wyoming. On October 21, 1757, £500 was drawn out of the Loan Office "towards erecting Indian Houses at Wyoming."[17] The four commissioners appointed to the task recruited some 150 laborers and carpenters and proceeded northward toward Hunter's Fort on the Susquehanna, a little above Harris'.

When Denny's letter of notification reached Teedyuscung at Bethlehem, the "King" was upset. By this time most of his followers were away, including his own counselors and interpreters, doing their winter's hunting. He waited four days for his interpreter, who never came, and finally set off for Wyoming by way of Fort Allen with nine or ten companions. When he arrived at Wyoming, the town was deserted except for three or four persons; all the rest were out hunting. Meanwhile the 150 carpenters and laborers were struggling up the Susquehanna on "battoes," escorted by a company of militia. The whole party included over two hundred white men.

When Teedyuscung learned of the little army that was poling its way up the river toward the deserted town, he sent a messenger down to intercept them. The messenger met the party at Namesesepong or Fishing Creek, some twenty miles above Fort Augusta. His news was disheartening. "Teedyuscung says he is very sorry that the Season is so far advanced before his Friends came to Wyoming to build the Houses & that he was not prepared for them with any Provisions." The messenger intimated that it might be wiser to wait until next spring.[18] The white men, nevertheless, decided to push on.

Teedyuscung met them a few miles south of the valley and guided them to the chosen spot, on the east bank near the middle of the plains. He carefully asked them to build no fort, only houses, fearing no doubt to arouse the suspicions of the Indians that the English were occupying the valley. But by the time eight house frames had been erected and two covered in, Teedyuscung realized that the business could not be completed that winter. "I looked at their Horses," he said, "and saw there was no Hay; I looked to the Clouds and Sky; I felt it then cold, and expected it would snow, and become much colder." So he suggested to the commissioners that perhaps it might be wiser to give up and return home. He himself was planning to spend the winter in Bethlehem. In the spring they could all come back and complete the task.[19] By December 1 he was once again in Philadelphia.

During the winter, as we saw in the last chapter, Teedyuscung occupied himself with extending the peace contracted at Easton to the Delawares on the Ohio. This, of course, was entirely in harmony with his other plans. Security for the Susquehanna Delawares was contingent upon peace among all nations and tribes. As long as scalps were being taken, no man could be secure in his home, whether he was a white settler or an Indian hunter.

In the spring, true to his promise, Teedyuscung made ready for the actual building of the town at Wyoming. On April 28 he arrived in Philadelphia and on May 2 he was advising the government to make haste. Indians were waiting to move in as soon as the houses were built; corn-planting time was fast approaching, and it would take three weeks for the same

number of men as were at Wyoming last fall to do the job.[20]
He had also announced that he wanted two schoolmasters,
some Christian ministers, and political advisers.

The government would have preferred to have Teedyuscung forget the whole thing. General Forbes was in the
city, preparing for the campaign which within the year would
shove the French out of the Ohio country; troops were scarce
and so were supplies. But Forbes, no doubt realizing the diplomatic importance of the gesture, endorsed Teedyuscung's
request, stipulating only that no troops be detached to guard
the workmen. Let the Indians take care of that themselves.[21]
Forbes apparently hoped that if the Indians were satisfied
they could be persuaded to guard the back settlements during
the summer so as to free the militia for the campaign in the
west.[22] Accordingly Teedyuscung was notified that the commissioners would set out immediately to build "Teedyuscung's Town."

Teedyuscung, his wife, and family left Bethlehem for
Wyoming on the sixteenth, to the infinite relief of the Brethren, who had been entertaining the sportive monarch and
his hungry minions since the preceding fall. As William C.
Reichel, the Moravian historian, acidly put it, "on the going
out of these spirits 'The Crown' was swept and garnished,
and Ephraim Colver, the publican, had rest."[23] They traveled
with Hughes and the other commissioners to Wyoming,
where they arrived on May 22 "after a very Fatigueing Journey." On the twenty-third the fifty-odd carpenters, masons,
and laborers were put to work.

Difficulties beset the builders from the start. The "battoes"
with supplies from Fort Augusta had not arrived as planned,
and the bread was exhausted within a few days. The workmen became uneasy, understandably enough, in the lonely
valley in the heart of the Indian country. On the twenty-
seventh the supplies from Fort Augusta still had not arrived,
and to cap the climax, one of the workmen was killed and
scalped by skulking Indians who fired on a wood-cutting

party. The young man, Joseph Croker, a mason, was found in the woods with a club beside him neatly lettered "R. J.," and a scalping knife.

Later it was learned that the murderers had been a band of six French Shawnees. But at the time Teedyuscung mistakenly suspected the Six Nations of having killed Croker as an indirect blow against the "King," out of jealousy of his new Europeanized town. The white laborers laid down their tools, refused to work any more, and made ready to go home. Teedyuscung burst into tears "for his sad Disaster in the Death of J. Croker." This accident threatened to shatter his dreams of a new life at Wyoming. The stroke was intended for him, he said, not for the English; indeed, Teedyuscung's tears were none of them for Croker, but all for himself. He told the commissioners "that he believed the man was kild in order to make him run away that they the Six Nations might laugh at him and say ah see Titeusquand is still without a home see what is becom of the thing he so mutch talked of." And he sent a message to the Six Nations, remonstrating against this harsh treatment. "Uncles," he complained, "you told me to cum & setle in this place & I have Done as you directed and sat Down & gathered a few sticks together & made a Fire & got my Friends about me and Now I am strock in a Cruel manner."

John Hughes and Isaac Zane, a Quaker representative of the Friendly Association, who had arrived on the twenty-eighth with additional laborers and horses, reproved Teedyuscung for his lack of spirit. If the Indians stayed, said Hughes, the whites would too, and finish the houses to boot. And on the same day the "battoes" at last arrived from Fort Augusta. All this put everyone in a less dolorous frame of mind, and in the morning work was begun again, with the building of houses, the splitting of rails, and the making of plows and rakes.

On the evening of the thirtieth, however, another ominous incident occurred. A canoe came drifting down the river at twilight, in the rain, carrying three Indians painted black—the color of war. Teedyuscung from the shore hailed them and invited to shelter in the town. The travelers, when they landed, turned out to be Bill Sock, a Conestoga Indian of ill repute; an old Seneca warrior; and a Conestoga youth. Teedyuscung learned from them that the Six Nations resented the building of European houses at Wyoming. In the dead of night Bill Sock crept up to one of the watchmen and asked him how long the white men intended to stay there. The three Indians set off again at ten o'clock next morning.

A little while after the three black-painted Indians had set off downstream, an empty canoe came floating down the river. Pulled ashore, it was found to contain nothing but twenty-eight paddles! A crowd gathered around the canoe with its strange cargo, chattering about the mystery. The general opinion was that hostile warriors were descending upon Wyoming.

At this critical moment Teedyuscung suddenly stepped forth "in an heroick manner." He himself thought enemy warriors were coming. Almost naked, with only a mantle about him, and a belt in his hand, he cried, "Hear, Brothers! I'll take this and I will go and talk with them . . . and may be they will hear me, but if they will kill me and not hear me, I will Dye." Then he called for his horse, mounted, and rode off with two Indians running afoot behind him.

He returned a little after dark. "I have been," he announced, "seven miles up the river where I have found more canos & paddles which was brought here by french Indians who have been and stoal horses; for the tracks on the shore of those yt. came with the canos are old and a most worn out but the horse tracks are fresh to be seen." Three friendly Indians, he said, had collected the paddles and floated them downstream as a warning.

The whites were panic-stricken at this report. They wanted to go home. The commissioners decided that the whole party would leave as soon as ten houses had been completed; and they did. They departed on June 2, after finishing ten houses of ten by fourteen feet, and one for Teedyuscung of sixteen by twenty-four feet, built out of squared logs dovetailed together, and after plowing and fencing some ground for a garden at the end of the valley. The Indians were as glad to see them go as the white men themselves were glad to leave. The season was late, they said, and the grass was so high that the ground would not be fit for planting, except "in a few Places such as Old Towns and the Like." They suggested that the commissioners come back some day when the times were more propitious.

Just before the exodus, Bill Sock and his companions returned, carrying a French flag. Bill Sock had just murdered a pro-English Indian, Jagrea, and a white man in Lancaster County, but the news had not yet reached Wyoming. Teedyuscung was aware that something was amiss, however, and confiscated the French flag, giving them an English one in return. Commissioner Hughes took the *fleur de lys* along to show to Governor Denny.[24]

*   *   *

The building of the new town at Wyoming really had stirred up a hornet's nest of suspicions along the Susquehanna. A rumor was circulating among the Susquehanna Indians, and in the Seneca country too, that the English had built a fort at Wyoming and garrisoned it with eight hundred men.[25] This of course aroused the jealousy of the Six Nations, who regarded the Wyoming lands as their own. Paxinosa and his family, at Tioga, were making preparations to go to the Ohio, where he had been born, because they thought that the whites were going to take the Susquehanna lands away from the Indians. It was said also that the Nanticokes and Mahicans at Otseningo were making ready to leave. All along the Susquehanna, Indians were packing up and moving toward the Ohio country. And to add the final fillip to this stampede, word was going around that the English had summoned the Cherokees and Catawbas from the south to annihilate the Susquehanna Indians.[26] What Forbes had actually done, of course, was to invite a party of Cherokees to join his army in the Ohio as scouts and raiders; but with the misunderstanding about the fort at Wyoming fixed firmly in their minds, the coming of the Cherokees and Catawbas seemed to the Susquehanna Indians like the last blow.

Poor Teedyuscung was at his wits' end. In the very moment of his greatest success, when his long-dreamed-of English houses were built and he and his followers living in them; when most of the remaining Delawares and Mahicans along the Susquehanna were planning to gather at Wyoming —this rumor about the "English fort" was bidding fair to ruin his prestige and perhaps cost him his life. The Geneseo Senecas sent down an enormous war party of some two hundred warriors to attack Pennsylvania. Teedyuscung met them at Wyoming and desperately persuaded them to turn aside and attack the settlements in northern New Jersey.[27] But a company of seventy-eight of them continued on south from Wyoming to cut the road from Fort Allen to Wyoming. Teedyuscung was in a panic lest depredations committed by these pro-French warriors should arouse the English to retaliate against Wyoming.

Meanwhile Brother Onas was viewing with concern the deterioration of the carefully built-up pro-English sentiment of the Susquehanna Indians. In the second week in June, Christian Frederick Post and Teedyuscung's "clerk," Charles Thomson, were sent up to talk with Teedyuscung. They carried two messages: one, from Governor Denny to Teedyuscung and the Wyoming Indians, assuring them that the Cherokees who were with Forbes were taking up the hatchet against the French, not against the Delawares, and asking Teedyuscung to explain that the English had no ulterior motives in the building of the houses at Wyoming; and the other, from Forbes and Denny to all of the Susquehanna Indians, asking them to send a white belt to the Ohio Delawares, warning them to stay out of the way of Forbes's army.

Post and Thomson got no farther than Nescopeck, where they were stopped on the eleventh by some Indians from Otseningo. Next day Teedyuscung and four councilors came down to speak with them. Teedyuscung told Post and Thomson, "I am very uneasy, even at Night I cannot enjoy rest."[28] He explained that the road was blocked by the Seneca war party, and positively forbade Post to go any farther. But he had some cheerful news. The French at Niagara were said to be starving, and in the Ohio his own son had caused a party of French Delawares to mutiny against Father Onontio. John Jacob had killed two Frenchmen. The commandant at Fort Duquesne had blamed the *Ohio* Delawares for the murder, whereupon some of them, who had been innocent bystanders, in disgust had turned away from the French.

Teedyuscung also asked that some corn and ammunition be sent up from Fort Augusta. There was no need to ask for rum: he was getting contraband liquor from Bowman's, five miles south of Fort Allen[29]—liquor in such quantities, in fact, that when Post finally managed to get through to Wyoming on the twenty-seventh, he found the Indians in a perpetual carouse. Two of Teedyuscung's followers beat their wives almost to death while Post was there.

But Post's second visit was more gratifying both to Brother Onas and to Teedyuscung. Post could say that Fort Augusta would supply Wyoming's needs and that Pennsylvania would guarantee Teedyuscung's tenure of the valley. And Teedyuscung could introduce Post to Pisquitomen, the brother of Beaver and of Shingas the Terrible, and the man who had led the Indians at the Penn's Creek massacre. The Ohio Indians, said Pisquitomen, were ready for peace; the French were "a broken Reed" and the Indians were starving.[30]

A Bird on a Bough

1758

During the winter after the Easton treaty of 1757, Teedyuscung had resolved the warring halves of his spirit and developed a policy. His policy, on behalf of the Susquehanna Delawares, demanded universal peace, guaranteed by interlocking alliances; territorial security for the Delawares in their new home, the Wyoming valley; and the gradual initiation of the Delawares into English ways. But now, in the execution of this policy, his greatest obstacles were the antagonisms which he himself had created by his charges of fraud; the suspicions of his followers that he was a better friend of the English than of the Indians; and the extreme suggestibility to white men which made him an easy prey to Quaker flattery and thus the avowed enemy of the proprietary party.

The Six Nations in August 1758 notified Brother Onas that they had something to say. This something concerned Teedyuscung. For a year and a half the Iroquois had heard the "King" ranting against them, and they had seen Brother Onas encouraging the rant. "[We] had little to say then," they observed, "because our Cousin Teedyuscung was busy, and we had not time to say any thing. We only came to hear him. Now when we come we will speak for ourselves fully."[1] There was more in the resentment of the Six Nations against Teedyuscung than either he or the Quakers realized. The Six Nations were not merely reaffirming their ancient claim to the Delawares' allegiance: they were demanding that the English support that claim. It was almost an ultimatum. As allies of the English king, they expected to be given tangible assistance in maintaining the integrity of their League. There were real apprehensions in official circles of an approaching war with the Six Nations, which would have been, in the opinion of Goldsbrow Banyar—a confidant of Sir William Johnson—"more to be dreaded . . . than the War we sustain already against five times their Number."[2] The treaty, therefore, was critical for the English in North America. Forbes was slowly invading the Ohio country; military and naval contests were nearing the decisive phase. At this crucial point, the Six Nations *had* to be kept from joining the French.

The immediate purpose of the treaty, however, was the settling of the land-fraud charges. The Board of Trade, informed of Teedyuscung's charges, had sent Sir William Johnson the Penns' recommendation that he settle the matter. Johnson had referred the task to George Croghan, who, in conjunction with the Pennsylvania authorities, went ahead and arranged the meeting. It was hoped that the differences among the Iroquois, the Delawares, and Brother Onas could be ironed out and all interests accommodated in a united front against the French. Teedyuscung's own policy envisaged just such an arrangement, and this is probably the reason why he was willing to appear before the Six Nations in 1758 instead of bolting to the French at the last minute as he had done in the spring of 1757. Security for the Delawares at Wyoming was dependent on the good will of the Six Nations, who owned the land; Anglicization was dependent on the good will of Pennsylvania; and general peace could be obtained only by general agreement.

This ambitious program could have been accomplished by Teedyuscung alone, simply and with dignity, if he had withdrawn the fraud charges and asked the Six Nations to grant the Delawares the right to live at Wyoming forever. Eventually Teedyuscung did these things, but only after two weeks of wrangling and hysteria.

*   *   *

Teedyuscung came to Easton in fear and trembling. He was not so much afraid of physical punishment (although one Six Nations Indian thrashed him for his pompousness) as of being made to look foolish. His prestige among the Susquehanna Delawares was uncertain and he knew it; among the Munsees and Mahicans it was almost nil. The Six Nations despised him. George Croghan, before the "King" arrived, remarked, "I have a bad opinion of this Treaty ye Indians are Much Divided and Jelious of Each other. ye Muncys & Mohickenders Dispise Teadyuscung as Well as ye Six Nations and ye Quaker party hear I faer will Indevour to supert him if So ye Six Nations will be much Displesd with us."[3]

As soon as Teedyuscung reached Easton he began to drink heavily. A proclamation had been issued forbidding the sale of rum to the Indians, but the Commissioners of the Assembly (who were of the Quaker party) were dispensing it at provincial expense. When the Governor had sentries posted to guard the rum barrels, the Quaker party shrieked that the liberties of the people were being infringed. Teedyuscung, dependent upon the Quakers for rum, clothing, and food, forgot his laboriously developed policy and identified himself again with Quaker intrigue. At that very moment he was probably wearing his new vested suit, given to him by the Quakers, made of snuff-colored broadcloth and shalloon, trimmed with linen, buckram, and silk, and adorned with twenty-six buttons. He was doubtless riding around the town on the bay horse the Friends had presented him with a few months before.[4] But there is no reason to suppose that the Quakers, as Croghan charged, deliberately kept Teedyuscung drunk "on purpus to serve some end."[5] Teedyuscung's psychopathic need for liquor was enough to keep him drunk without encouragement from anybody. (Croghan had a flair for canards: he even charged that Quakers were investing in Connecticut's Susquehanna Company, which proposed to take Wyoming from the Indians, while they raised the ghost of the Walking Purchase to bedevil the proprietors!)

One of the things that Teedyuscung brooded about was being called a "woman" by the Six Nations. The word rankled, and the shame he felt on its account led him to the misconception (which his clerk, Charles Thomson, has embalmed in his famous *Alienation of the Delawares*) that the Six Nations' sole interest in the Delawares was to grind them into the dirt.

The history of this "Delawares-as-women" business is obscure but intriguing. Some time in the seventeenth century, probably at the close of the Five Nations' war with the Susquehannocks, the Delawares, in order to avoid continuous warfare with hostile Iroquois tribes, seem to have petitioned to become sustaining but not active members of the League. By calling them "women," the Six Nations in the eighteenth century were popularly supposed to have meant that the lowly, effeminate Delawares were henceforth not allowed to own their own land or to make war. What precise political status the "women" metaphor actually symbolized is not altogether clear; but certainly it did not originally refer to a blanket prohibition of all military activity and land ownership on the part of the Delawares. The Six Nations had other things to do besides exercising a gratuitous and unprofitable tyranny over neighboring Algonkian tribes. Technically, being "women" meant only that they were expected to entertain official emissaries from the Great Council with food and lodging,[6] a "feminine" obligation in a society where women were responsible for the cultivation of maize, the preparation of food, and the maintenance of the household economy. The Delawares were also not given the privilege of speaking in the Great Council except on specific invitation; they were enjoined (as were all other subordinate adherents of the League) not to engage in irresponsible warfare. Not only the Delawares were called "women": the Mahicans were "women" too, and the Nanticokes, and the Siouan Tuteloes, and even the Iroquoian Tuscaroras—the "Sixth Nation" of the confederacy.[7] Thus it would seem that the "women" metaphor meant at first, for the Delawares as well as for the other "props of the confederacy," simply a non-voting membership in the League.

But with the growth of bad feeling between the Delawares and the Iroquois after 1737, the "women" epithet began to come into use as a term of opprobrium, as an insulting nickname with which Six Nations speakers would taunt the down-and-out Delawares.[8]

To Teedyuscung, goaded by the Quakers, who raised before him every grievance he had or could imagine having, the "women" epithet now became a matter of life and death. During the treaty he metaphorically threw his petticoat at the Seneca chief Tagashata and told him to wear it himself. "I am a man!" he crowed. "He calld himself King of the Quakers & was very rude to the other Indians."[9]

Punishment for these affronts was quick in coming. Next day a Tuscarora Indian beat him up "for affecting the Great Man."[10] It may be significant that it was a Tuscarora who avenged the Iroquois' wounded dignity. The Tuscaroras— the "Sixth Nation"—were "women" who could not vote in open council. In other words, the five original nations did not revenge themselves; they accomplished it indirectly, through a deputy.

But, not satisfied with insulting the Six Nations, Teedyuscung also turned on Brother Onas. On one occasion, laying a belt of wampum on the council table, he demanded that Pennsylvania submit to him as her king, and he offered the province a petticoat to wear as the symbol of submission. The English were less reluctant than the Six Nations to enter a personal quarrel openly. A certain officer, probably Conrad

Weiser, who told the story, seized the belt from the table and informed Teedyuscung that if he insisted upon an answer to that belt, "The point of the Sword should decide it, upon the first mention thereof."[11]

With admirable restraint the Six Nations ignored Teedyuscung's vagaries, publicly at least, and proceeded to the preliminary business of the treaty—the private Indian councils. Indian protocol insisted that the issues be clarified before public debate by having the policy to be taken by the group discussed and agreed on beforehand. First of all, the Six Nations wanted to get to the bottom of the confused and contradictory charges which Teedyuscung had raised concerning the causes of the war. Coming directly to the point affecting themselves, the Six Nations, through the mouth of Tagashata, asked the Delawares, "If your Uncles had wronged you out of any land, pray don't mince the matter. Say so boldly."[12] It was an opportunity for Teedyuscung to gain the support of the Six Nations in pressing for satisfaction of his claims against Pennsylvania. The Six Nations were willing to make concessions in return for Delaware acceptance of their hegemony.

But Teedyuscung was afraid and fumbled his chance. He mumbled evasively that he would leave everything up to the Six Nations; let them decide about their own honesty. It was a sulky answer. The Six Nations patiently tried again. Nickas, a Mohawk chief, asked him privately why the Susquehanna Delawares had gone to war. Teedyuscung at first refused to make any answer at all: he was afraid of the Six Nations and afraid of the Quakers too. Finally he said that some years earlier a New Jersey Delaware had been unjustly hanged by the whites for a murder he did not commit.[13]

Teedyuscung was referring to the celebrated case of Weequehela, which agitated the consciences of both Indians and whites in Pennsylvania and New Jersey in 1728. Weequehela was a Delaware sachem who, like Teedyuscung, had owned land and lived in New Jersey; and, again like Teedyuscung, he admired the white men. Weequehela was "an Indian of great note and account both among Christians and Indians." On his plantation along the Delaware he pursued the life of an English country gentleman, "with a taste much above the common rank of Indians, having an extensive farm, cattle, horses and negroes, and raised large crops of wheat, and was so far English in his furniture as to have a house well provided with feather beds, calico curtains, &c. He frequently dined with Governors and great men, and behaved well." Among the domains of Weequehela's lineage was a cedar swamp. His neighbor, an Englishman named Captain John Leonard, not knowing of Weequehela's rights in the swamp, purchased it from some other Indians. When Weequehela remonstrated against this buying from one what belonged (in part at least) to another, Leonard denied that Weequehela had any right to the land. Weequehela thereupon declared that he would kill Leonard; and in the spring of 1728 he did so, shooting him as he walked in his garden. Weequehela, who had made the threat in the presence of witnesses, made no attempt to escape, was tried, and hanged at Perth Amboy.[14]

From the white man's viewpoint, of course, the case was plainly murder. But not so by Delaware customary law. As is the case with many other primitive societies, among the Delawares trespassing on another's land was an offense which the owner could punish by killing the trespasser. The threat of the exercise of this right functioned importantly to reduce poaching among a people who depended on the chase for part of their larder, but the rule was not blindly enforced against travelers who were hungry, or against occasional or accidental violators. It was the only recourse for a persistently wronged owner in a society which supported no organized, state-administered judiciary and police system. Thus from the Delaware standpoint, Weequehela was legally justified in killing Captain Leonard, who had first of all, perhaps in ignorance, trespassed on Weequehela's land, and, when informed of his error, had refused to make restitution. And therefore, from the Delaware standpoint, the execution of Weequehela himself was murder.

The murder of a Delaware Indian sometimes began a blood-feud or vendetta, for the members of the victim's lineage felt themselves to be obligated to avenge his death, if satisfactory compensation were not forthcoming. Not to make the attempt, at least, would be disgraceful. (Here again the absence of state-controlled police and judiciary organs meant that punishment had to rest with the injured party himself or those who identified themselves with him. Nevertheless, except where the white man's liquor had been introduced, the incidence of crime in Indian communities was very low.) Accordingly, with the predictability of clockwork (but to the amazement of the provincial officials, who knew practically nothing about Indians), Weequehela's relatives took up the hatchet to avenge his death.

Weequehela's most prominent kinsman was Menakihikon, a Munsee (Delaware) sachem of considerable eminence, whose influence radiated from his home (in 1730) in the Minisink region in northern New Jersey, throughout that state, southward in Pennsylvania to Tohiccon Creek, and westward to the Susquehanna. (In 1737, when he signed the Walking Purchase deed, Menakihikon had moved to Wyoming.) Menakihikon correctly understood that the murder of Weequehela had been accomplished by the white people as a whole, acting through their government. Accordingly the white people as a whole had to be punished. Menakihikon therefore in 1728 made a strong effort to stir up a war between the Indians and the provinces of Pennsylvania and New Jersey. Immediately after the hanging, he traveled north to talk with the Six Nations, and especially the Cayugas, among whom he had friends and acquaintances. (At the present time the Delawares, as allies of the Confederacy, are "under the Cayugas' armpit," i.e., under their especial care and guidance.) He asked their assistance in obtaining revenge.

The Six Nations, who were bound to the English by ties of trade and a hatred of the French, were sympathetic but did not wish to engage in a war with their English neighbors. So they sent "a very large Belt" of black wampum to the Twightwees (Miamis) in the Ohio, desiring them to launch a raiding party against the offending provinces. Menakihikon dispatched four belts to the Munsees hunting on the upper Allegheny River, warning them to return to their homes, because they would be in danger, if they remained in those parts, "from some Strangers that are to march that way."[15]

Menakihikon's plot failed; the Miamis' war party never set forth. Vengeance was delayed until 1755 and 1756, when the Munsee descendants of Menakihikon and Weequehela satisfied their honor with English scalps and prisoners in abundance.

Teedyuscung, in ascribing the war to the Weequehela imbroglio, was no doubt correct, in so far as the descendants of the principals in the case were concerned. For them, the war was an opportunity to pay off old scores. But blood-feuds, by their very nature, are not national affairs; the engagement of the thousands of Delawares scattered from the Susquehanna westward almost to the Mississippi could not be laid to the Weequehela case. Thus this answer to the Six Nations' question, What was the cause of the war? was patently inadequate. And it could hardly have been pleasing to the Six Nations, reminding the world as it did of the part they had played in Menakihikon's plot to make war on the English.

Since no satisfactory answer could be had from the sulky Teedyuscung, the Six Nations decided that the public treaty should begin on the morning of October 11. They, the "uncles" of the Delawares, would do the explaining, and Tagashata, a Seneca, was chosen to speak first. On the appointed morning Tagashata's belts and strings, to be used to endorse and remind him of the points of his speech, were duly laid on the table. But before he could say a word, Teedyuscung jumped to his feet and asked that he be heard first.

To smooth over the *faux pas,* Governor Bernard of New Jersey, a more or less neutral party who was present simply to settle the Munsee and Delaware claims to certain lands in New Jersey, made a short and innocuous speech of welcome.

Teedyuscung, however, would not be put off. When Bernard had taken his seat, the "King" got up and delivered himself. It was not a long speech he gave, but it was a significant one, for by it he meant to forestall any discussion whatever of his land charges in the presence of the Six Nations. "I have made known to the Governor the reason why I struck him," he said evasively. "Now I and the Governor have made up these differences between him and me, and I think we have done it, as far as we can, for our future peace."

Tagashata, with the wind taken out of his sails, could only adjourn the council until the next day. "Publick business requires great consideration," he said.

Teedyuscung's convulsive effort to have the conference avoid all the issues embarrassing to him was calmly disregarded next day by the Six Nations. Tagashata was doing his best to come to an understanding with the Delawares and the English; he was probing for some common ground of agreement. His speech held out hope for a firm tripartite alliance on terms agreeable to the Delawares. He confirmed the peace between Teedyuscung's band and Brother Onas. He announced that the Munsees (whom Teedyuscung had not been able to control) "have at last listened to us, and taken our advice, and laid down the hatchet." He apologized for the misguided young men among the Iroquois (chiefly his own Senecas) who had shed English blood, and testified to the desire of the Six Nations that the Ohio Indians make peace. It was a pleasant speech but Teedyuscung unfortunately ruined its effect.

Teedyuscung had come to the meeting drunk. "Teddy," observed Secretary Peters, "had a bottle of rum with a straw cork which he put under the table and which Charles Read overset that the rum might run out."[16] He was just drunk

enough to have lost whatever sense of discretion he had.
While Tagashata talked, Teedyuscung kept up a running fire
of comments which were highly inappropriate to the occasion. Swearing "prodigiously" in English, he mouthed sentiments which sounded strangely like those of a small boy
frightened out of his wits and defying his elders. Benjamin
Chew, who was present, wrote down a graphic account of the
scene:

Teedyuscung came in very drunk soon after we met, was very
troublesome the whole time and interrupted the conference very
much, swearing that he was King of all nations and of all the
world, and [that] the Six Nations were fools and said in Indian,
as Messers Croghan, Weiser, and Montour afterwards informed
us, and as he had often been heard to say before, that they did
not know how to behave to the English, that the way to be well
used by them was to make war on them and cut their throats,
that he had struck them and would continue to do so as long as
he lived. The Indians and even his own counsellors seemed angry
and much disgusted with his behavior, but took little notice of
it at that time.

The "disgust" of the other Indians at Teedyuscung's provocative behavior was not simply the normal disapproval by
sober businessmen of an indiscreet colleague. It went deeper
than that. The traditional Iroquois and the Delaware personality structure was in a very real and fundamental way ori-
ented toward the suppression of hostility-arousing behavior,
physical or verbal, in face-to-face relationships. In war the
pendulum might swing to the other extreme; but in civil
life, and especially in councils and treaties, a grave decorum
and agreeable manner, occasionally leavened by bantering
humor, were absolutely *de rigeur*. To the Indian mind,
Teedyuscung's antagonizing behavior was a terrible breech
of morality. It is noteworthy that, as Chew observed, the
councilors "took little notice of it at the time": to do so
would have been to commit the same fault as Teedyuscung
had committed. But what happened in the following days
affords a fascinating study of the equable Iroquois and Dela-

wares trying to cope with the rogue male in their midst without themselves openly displaying their anger.

Next day (Friday the thirteenth) the heavens fell on Teedyuscung. After Pisquitomen had spoken on behalf of the Ohio Indians, advocating peace, Nickas got to his feet and, pointing at Teedyuscung, spoke angrily in Mohawk. Nickas in doing this was violating the code of equanimity which Teedyuscung himself had broken, and the Indian interpreters refused to translate his speech into English. It was too inflammatory to be put on record. The burden of Nickas' remarks was inescapable, however: Who, he asked, had made the upstart Teedyuscung a great man? Had he any right to represent the Delawares at all?

Teedyuscung's back was against the wall. If the Six Nations publicly refused to deal with him as the representative of the Susquehanna Delawares, the government of Pennsylvania would have to desert him too. If that happened, his own followers would no longer support him. Some of them would be only too glad to see him go; others accepted him only because he was able to negotiate with the whites. If his own followers left him, even the Quakers would be powerless to help.

He had two alternatives: either to submit to the Six Nations on whatever terms he could get; or, with the Quakers behind him, fight it out as "King" of the Delawares.

Rather than undergo, after boasting that he was the king of eighteen nations, the humiliation of begging the forgiveness of the Six Nations, Teedyuscung chose to fight it out. He lost the first round on Sunday. (On Saturday the Indians were too drunk to do business.) The chiefs of the Six Nations met, in the absence of the object of their spite, with the two Governors and their councils in a private room at Scull's tavern. With Teedyuscung not there, they could say what they thought of him. One after another, the chiefs rose and denied the authority of Teedyuscung. Nickas, the Mohawk chief, spoke first. "Brothers, We thought proper to meet you here, to have some private Discourse about our Nephew Teedyuscung," he began. "You all know that he gives out, he is the great Man, and Chief of Ten Nations; this is his constant Discourse. Now I, on Behalf of the Mohawks, say, we do not know he is such a great Man. If he is such a great Man, we desire to know who has made him so. Perhaps you have, and if this be the Case, tell us so. It may be the French have made him so. We want to enquire and know whence his Greatness arose." The other chiefs, representing each of the other nations, in turn addressed the Governors, demanding, Who made Teedyuscung a great man?

On Monday, Governor Denny and Governor Bernard replied that as far as they were concerned, Teedyuscung was only as great a man as the Delawares and Six Nations were willing to make him. They disclaimed responsibility for making Teedyuscung a great man.

On Tuesday the Six Nations themselves took Teedyuscung to task in person at a private Indian council. "Old Ted," observed James Pemberton, Israel's brother, that day, "looks very serious & [I] believe is very thoughtfull how he shall acquit himself of some matters."[17] The Quakers, however, rallied to his call for help. Let the Six Nations say what they would, Teedyuscung should be a great man, they declared. Their concern was natural: if Teedyuscung's pretensions to represent the Susquehanna Delawares collapsed, their attempt to blame the war on the Penns would collapse too.

Teedyuscung spent Wednesday morning closeted with Pemberton. He put himself abjectly into the Quaker's hands. Pemberton, in order to gain favor for Teedyuscung in the Indians' minds, distributed presents wholesale. And that afternoon Teedyuscung made his last bid against the Six Nations. Addressing the Governor of Pennsylvania, he pressed his charges of fraud:

Brethren, I did let you know formerly what my Grievance was. I told you, that from Tohiccon as far as the *Delawares* owned [to the northward], the Proprietaries had wronged me. Then you and I agreed that it should be laid before the King of *England;* and likewise you told me you would let me know, as soon as ever he saw it. You would lay the Matter before the King, for you said he was our Father, that he might see what were our Differences; for as you and I could not decide it, let him do it. Now let us not alter what you and I have agreed. Now let me know if King George has decided the Matter between you and me. I don't pretend to mention any of my Uncles Lands, I only mention what we the *Delawares* own, as far as the Heads of *Delaware.* All the Lands lying on the Waters that fall into the Sasquehannah, belong to our Uncles.

"As far as the Heads of Delaware!" That was Six Nations country. One by one, the Six Nations chiefs got up and left the meeting. When Teedyuscung turned with another belt to speak to the Six Nations, there was no one to hear.

The renewed charges made by Teedyuscung accomplished nothing. The Quakers, of course, hoped by bringing the matter to King George's attention to discredit the Penns. But the Six Nations flatly contradicted Teedyuscung's statement that the Delawares owned the lands above the hills as far north as the headwaters of the Delaware. The Delawares, they said, had never owned lands (in Pennsylvania) above the northern boundary of the Walking Purchase. They reaffirmed their own right to sell the lands included in the purchase of 1749 (which would have been fraudulent if Teedyuscung's claims were admitted). They stood by their affirmation in 1742 that the Walking Purchase lands had been fairly bought by the Penns. And, to cement the friendship between the Six Nations and Pennsylvania, a release was drawn up by Benjamin Chew, the attorney general, of all the Penns' claims to the Ohio lands which had been bought of the Iroquois, but not paid for, in 1754.

Against this solid front Teedyuscung was helpless. And so, as he had done at Easton the year before, he abruptly changed his strategy. On Thursday he went to the Governor and told him that the Delawares "did not claim Lands high up on

Delaware River; those belonged to their Uncles; and he thought proper to let the Governor know this, that there might be no Misunderstanding of what he had said in the publick Conference."

And on Friday he said what he should have said two weeks before. He acknowledged to the Six Nations that neither he nor his people had any right to any lands above Lackawaxen. Having thus patched up the quarrel with his "uncles," he made a short and eloquent plea for a deed from the Six Nations to the lands at Wyoming:

Uncles, [he said, addressing the Iroquois] You may remember that you have placed us at *Wyomink,* and *Shamokin,* Places where *Indians* have lived before. Now I hear since, that you have sold that Land to our Brethren the *English* [i.e., the Susquehanna Company, in 1754]; let the Matter now be cleared up, in the Presence of our Brethren the English.

I sit there as a Bird on a Bow; I look about, and do not know where to go; let me therefore come down upon the Ground, and make that my own by a good Deed, and I shall then have a Home for ever; for if you, my Uncles, or I die, our Brethren the English will say, they have bought it from you, and so wrong my Posterity out of it.

Teedyuscung's Bird-on-a-Bough speech has the ring of sincerity as well as art. But John Pemberton, who knew the "King," in later years observed that Teedyuscung's oratory was comparable to that of William Pitt, the Earl of Chatham, whom also he had heard speak.[18] It would be difficult to say with certainty whether Teedyuscung's change of policy proceeded from conviction or from the Quakers, who may have decided that after all the important thing was to maintain Teedyuscung's position for the sake of future agitation, even if it meant temporarily making concessions to the Iroquois. It seems likely to the writer, however, that Teedyuscung probably did realize that in defying the Six Nations and Brother Onas at once over an issue as remote as the Walking Purchase, he was endangering his own dream of land, peace, security, and acculturation, which depended on the favor of the Iroquois and the proprietaries both.

* * *

The Six Nations responded agreeably enough if not very generously. Teedyuscung had come under the wing of the League again, and no more questions were asked about who had made him a great man. They promised to recommend Teedyuscung's plea for tenure of the Wyoming Valley to the Onondaga Council, which was ultimately responsible for the disposition of the land. They used their influence to raise the New Jersey settlement of the Munsee and Wappinger land claims in northern New Jersey from eight hundred to one thousand Spanish dollars.

The Easton settlement signalized the beginning of the end for the French in the Ohio.[19] When, on November 20, 1758, Christian Frederick Post, escorted by Teedyuscung's son Captain Bull,[20] brought the news of the Easton agreements to Kuskusky in the Ohio, the Delawares there raised the British flag. Five days later General Forbes occupied Fort Duquesne.

For Teedyuscung, however, the treaty's end signified only the reascendancy of the Six Nations over him and his minions. He himself might make one of his characteristic gestures of grandiloquent generosity, by demanding that the government of Pennsylvania give an ancient and infirm Wappinger chief a horse to carry him home. The white people granted this request. But Tom King, the Oneida, reminded Teedyuscung pointedly that he was small fry indeed in the eyes of the Iroquois. He scolded the "King" for not having brought in some white prisoners whom he had pledged to return. And he said icily, "To tell lies does not become a Great-Man; a Great-Man always keeps his word and performs his promises."[21]

The Forbidden Trail

1759-1760

Forbes's taking of Fort Duquesne virtually ended the war in the Ohio; henceforth the French, still resisting in the more remote northern and western outposts, were chiefly a nuisance. Teedyuscung's role in preparing this event had not been inconsiderable: his peacemaking had had a sort of snowball effect, rolling on, with the help of many hands, from a minor armistice on behalf of some Susquehanna Delawares to a general, although informal, cessation of Indian warmaking.

The peace which now descended over the snow-covered fields and forests was not a peace of relaxation, however. In the Ohio, the presence of British troops at Fort Duquesne (now renamed Fort Pitt) stirred the Ohio Indians, including the Mingoes (Six Nations Indians living in the Ohio), Delawares, and Shawnees to mutter against the English. Time and time again the English were told to get out, to evacuate the Ohio country, and to open the Indian trade again. English relations with the Ohio Indians were discolored by mutual distrust on both sides, the English suspecting with justice that at Kuskusky and elsewhere lived concealed Frenchmen and irreconcilable pro-French Delawares,[1] and the Indians suspecting, again with justice, that now that they were in possession of the fort, the English would try to seize more and more of the surrounding lands. A treaty was sorely needed, to ratify the peace and to settle the doubts and suspicions concerning the occupancy of lands and the reopening of the Indian trade. But in the meantime the English were going ahead on the bland assumption that peace with the Indians had been automatically reëstablished with the expulsion of the French. By April 1759 white settlers in large numbers were flocking back to their farms along the charred and blackened frontiers of Pennsylvania.[2] White troops and auxiliary civilian services poured westward to Fort Pitt.

Teedyuscung was delighted with the success of English arms, which he credited himself with having promoted, and looked forward to leading his people into a closer and more intimate connection with Brother Onas. When certain Pennsylvania officials proposed that a road be built from the inhabited parts of Pennsylvania up to Shamokin, in order to transport goods to that place for the Indian trade, Teedyuscung was all in favor. But when Benjamin Lightfoot, the professional surveyor, set out from Fort Henry to lay out the projected route, Teedyuscung was suddenly alarmed. He was at Fort Augusta when he learned of Lightfoot's activities. Rather than meet Lightfoot and be implicated in the survey, he left the fort "with some precipitation and discomposure of Mind." His alarm had been aroused by the disapproval expressed by some of the Six Nations and Nanticokes to a road being built through the Indian country around Shamokin. The Six Nations, said Lightfoot, were afraid that if the white people got a wagon road through to Shamokin, they would come in droves to settle the land. "We will not part with the Shamokin Lands as they are the Burying Place of many Kings and great Men," said the Indians.[3]

Teedyuscung, as a matter of fact, was now in an embarrassing position among the Indians. Even though the Geneseo Senecas had at last turned from the French to the English, thus practically forcing the Ohio tribes (who seem generally to have followed their lead) to act a friendly part to the English troops west of the Alleghenies, the sentiment in the Indian towns was distinctly cool toward the English. Just as the diplomatic success of the French had been owing to their military control of the avenues of trade, so now the ascendancy of the English was owing to their military victories and to the implication thereby that Indian livelihood depended on the English trade. Teedyuscung's notoriously pro-English leanings, which went so far as the virtual Anglicization of the Indians under his influence, did not recommend him to those communities who still insisted on the integrity of an Indian culture. By June rumors were flitting from town to town that the Ohio Indians had concocted a plan to capture an English fort east of Fort Pitt by stratagem and to seize the powder there; with these supplies they would then invest and reduce the other English establishments west of the mountains.[4]

Governor Denny in Philadelphia was sensitive to these currents of dissatisfaction. In April he sent a message to Teedyuscung at Wyoming, asking him "to hear and see" for Brother Onas, and to use his influence with the Ohio Indians to promote a general treaty of peace in Philadelphia.[5] Teedyuscung was certainly in a position to furnish confidential information: his son Captain Bull was even then serving as a spy for Colonel Mercer, the commander at Fort Pitt, and his half-brother Captain Peter (Young Captain Harris) was the chief of the pro-French die-hards at Venango.[6]

Teedyuscung, in compliance with the Governor's request, spent the summer of 1759 in making a journey through the Ohio country. His perambulations fortunately coincided with Johnson's victory at Fort Niagara on July 25, which ended the threat of a French counterattack on Fort Pitt, and left the Ohio Indians without the support of their Father Onontio.[7] It was this repulse to the French, rather than Teedyuscung's suasions, which probably brought his anti-English brother from Venango to Fort Pitt in August.[8] Teedyuscung of himself does not seem to have accomplished a great deal on his tour. "I met with one that told me," he reported to the Governor in December, "that Eleven Nations had heard of my Sitting Face to Face with the Governor of Pennsylvania at Easton." These eleven nations seemingly approved of the peace which had been concluded there. But this was all he had to say. He did not mention that at Pittsburgh he had come to blows with his old enemy George Croghan, now the deputy superintendent of Indian affairs under Johnson, and crown representative in the Ohio valley. (On August 20, 1759, Charles Kenny, the Quaker factor in charge of the trading post, noted in his journal, "Croghan has a black eye this morning & I have been informed, that he was drunk & fought with ye Indians, & that Teedyuscung gave him ye black eye."[9])

Teedyuscung was back in Philadelphia on October 4, 1759, to report, somewhat gratuitously, that the wounds of war were all healed. He promised to bring in some white prisoners later in the fall. There were only about five among the Susquehanna Delawares, he said (a notable understatment); it was the Munsees and the Mohawks who had most of them. Governor Denny, who did not have much use for Teedyuscung, replied with a broadside of complaints. If the prisoners were not brought in, every last one of them, he declared, "we are afraid it will Occasion a Breach between us." He told Teedyuscung that British arms were victorious at Niagara, Crown Point, Ticonderoga; that Quebec was besieged; that the British flag floated over Lake Champlain, Lake George, and Lake Ontario. And he demanded the return of six horses which had been stolen by some Susquehanna Delawares near Fort Allen.[10] For Teedyuscung, the only pleasant part of the meeting was the gift made to him by the Friendly Association: six strouds, six matchcoats, and three thousand pieces of wampum.

From Philadelphia Teedyuscung repaired to Assinisink, where a general meeting was being held to which he had been invited by the upper Susquehanna Indians. His anxiety about his equivocal status, partially rejected by both white man and Indian, was making itself obvious now in continual drinking[11] and in the commission of diplomatic gaucheries. At Assinisink Teedyuscung—only a guest at the conference at the Munsee town—bluntly demanded that Ekoan, the Munsee chief, deliver up to him the thirteen prisoners which Ekoan admitted having. Ekoan refused even to answer this presumptuous request, and Teedyuscung was obliged to collect as best he could two elderly white women and two boys, "quite naked and destitute," to carry down to Brother Onas. He also managed to find the six horses, and to detach them from their new owners. This task also was doubtless a thankless one. The thieves, who had been questioned earlier by Captain Orndt at Fort Allen, had been impudent enough, saying, "When the People were murdered and their creatures taken away two years since, there was not so much said about it, but now there was a great Noise about a few Horses."[12] Teedyuscung was getting the unenviable reputation among Indians of being a better friend to the white people than he was to his own Delawares.

At the end of November Teedyuscung returned to Philadelphia with the four prisoners and the six horses to prove his loyalty to the English cause. He was drunk on December 4, when the formal conference was scheduled to begin at the State House, but he insisted on speaking none the less. He reported on the meeting which he had just left at Assinisink, where two messengers from the Ohio (whom he brought with him) had testified that fully eleven western nations were anxious to join the peace. Next summer there was to be a great treaty in the Ohio country. He ought to be there, he said, as the representative of Pennsylvania.[13]

William Hamilton, the newly appointed governor of Pennsylvania, was very much in favor of this suggestion, and so was the House of Assembly. Teedyuscung was "encouraged to go."[14] In accordance with his suggestion, Christian Frederick Post and Isaac Stille were to be appointed to accompany him. After the treaty, Teedyuscung returned to Fort Allen to spend the winter.[15]

*   *   *

Making ready for the trip exercised the minds of the intending travelers during the winter and spring. Teedyuscung, at Fort Allen, sent word to the Governor that he was sick, and had neither sufficient clothes nor wampum for the journey. In March he made a special trip to Philadelphia to be outfitted. There he was given, among other things, a good suit of clothes and a hat "that he may make an Appearance answerable to the Occasion."[16] The Friendly Association voted £50 to outfit the party, and proposed to board the daughter of Moses Tattamy while he was gone (Moses had been appointed to accompany the other three men). Israel Pemberton, on Post's request, lent them a portable tent, which Post regarded as a marvelous modern invention.

Post was in poor health when he set forth. On a recent trip to New York he had met with a serious accident, which left him weak and dizzy after any exertion. Throughout his journal of their daily adventures occur complaints of fainting spells, dizziness, pain, and a constant struggle against malaise. Only courage and devotion to his duty as he conceived it carried the preacher-diplomat on during a journey on horseback over difficult and mountainous terrain, in the face of hostility from the communities they visited and the disloyalty of Teedyuscung.

The purpose of the trip was to attend the great treaty at Fort Pitt, scheduled to be held between the English and the Ohio Indians in July 1760. Their function before and during the treaty was to use their influence to bring the Ohio Delawares into agreement with the English. To this end Post carried a message from General Jeffrey Amherst, the British commander-in-chief in North America, advising the Indians that the English did not intend to preëmpt their lands. The prosecution of the war, however, said Amherst, required that the English man certain forts in the Ohio country as long as the threat of French counterattacks (still theoretically possible from lonely outposts in the northern and western regions) remained. Post had been selected for the mission because he had a high name for integrity among both whites and Indians. An omen of Amherst's bluff, aggressive policy toward the Indian nations was contained in a threat of reprisals if the Indians were disorderly and interfered with the conduct of the war.

Post left Philadelphia in company with Teedyuscung's son, Captain Bull, on May 3, 1760. Teedyuscung himself was waiting for them at Wyoming. Post was very weak and had to ride in Israel Pemberton's chaise. The first day they got no farther than Germantown. Next morning Post took time off to pay several old accounts of Teedyuscung's at taverns along the road. On the ninth, Post reached Fort Allen.

At Fort Allen the prognosis for the mission looked discouraging. The goods previously cached there for the use of the party had already been squandered, and no other provisions were procurable. Post felt very ill. Moses Tattamy, "in one of his drunken Fits," had left essential articles behind at the house of John Hays (a white man whom Post was taking along for a companion), and Post had to gather them up. Captain Bull was not sanguine about the prospects of the Ohio Indians giving up their prisoners. "He thought it would be difficult for them to resolve to deliver them all up." Behind this probable refusal, as Post well knew, stood the force of the aboriginal morality: prisoners captured in war were, contrary to the popular conception among the whites, usually neither tortured nor killed nor enslaved; they were adopted into families to replace persons who had died, and thenceforth were accorded almost equal social status with the original members of the community. Not infrequently white prisoners found the easygoing Indian way of life more to their liking than the class- and money-conscious society from which they had been removed, and flatly refused to be restored to their homes.

When Post got to Wyoming on the eleventh he found that Teedyuscung had left a few hours before. A messenger was sent after him, and he returned next day. Post then pro-

ceeded to inform him, as co-agent in the embassy, of everything that had been concerted in Philadelphia, including
Amherst's pronunciamento. Teedyuscung boggled at the
word "retaliation" in the General's message, and the two
men sat up together till midnight, drinking coffee and indulging in "agreeable Conversation" about their mission.
Teedyuscung's opinions about the proper policy to be pursued in regard to the Ohio Delawares are important enough
to quote, because the opposite policy, enforced by Amherst,
helped mightily to produce the various uprisings collectively
entitled "Pontiac's Conspiracy." "We shou'd first see to establish a firm Peace with them," said Teedyuscung. "There are
many Nations that will come in & when they hear of threat-
ning it will startle them & incline them to draw back instead
of coming Nigh. I think we sho'd be Mild & loving until we
have gain'd them into our Interest. Then if they will not
behave well we may take a Rod or Whip to chastise them
with & bring them to Reason." It is noteworthy also in this
passage how completely Teedyuscung identified himself with
English interests.

During the next four days everyone stayed at Wyoming.
Teedyuscung had Post write a letter to Nathaniel Holland,
the factor at Fort Augusta, requesting him to supply Teedyuscung's wife Elisabeth from time to time with provisions and
other necessaries from the fort. Teedyuscung strung the
beads for the belts and strings to be used in the conferences.
Post and Hays "help'd to set up Teedyuscung's fence" and
assisted him in planting his field of corn. The need for provisions for themselves was still pressing. Not much was to be
had from the Indians at Wyoming, for they were in straitened
circumstances themselves. "Hardly anything of all ye Goods,
Horses, &c. that was distributed among the Indians was now
to be seen amongst them." Molasses, butter, milk, and rum—
items in the normal dietary of the Wyoming Indians—were
prohibitively expensive. The party consequently decided that
they would have to support themselves by hunting en route.

This decision was the occasion of Teedyuscung's delivering a little sermon to the ten or eleven Indians who were to accompany the ambassadors at least as far as the Allegheny. Everyone, he said, must help everyone else in making fire, fetching wood, and in the mornings hunting up the horses (which would be set loose at dark to graze in the woods). The Indians must share their food with the two white men, "for," said he, "they are not used like us, we fall foul of every Thing like wolves, but they are regular & have their stated Times for eating & drinking, & so would come short, if not carefully provided for." The pleasure which Teedyuscung felt in assuming responsibility for the two white men, as well as his willingness to cater to their habits rather than expecting them to conform to the ways of the majority, was painfully obvious.

The Wyoming Indians, however, were not much impressed by Teedyuscung's patronizing, pseudo-European air of authority. When, at dinner on the second day out from Wyoming, he delivered another little homily to his followers, he was embarrassed by their indifference. After telling all of them that they had neglected God and wandered from the path of righteousness, he pointed to Post as one who was able to tell them what was good and what was bad. "We sho'd not," said Teedyuscung, "live like the Beasts in the Woods." The Indians paid no attention, and Post noted carefully that Teedyuscung, "observing his People did not mind much what he said, it gave him some concern." Apparently Teedyuscung's admonitions to his followers concerning their table manners were also disregarded. Later on, Post expressed his thankfulness that his companions were good hunters, for "when the Victuals is dress'd they fall to like so many Wolves."

When at last they arrived at Assinisink, the Munsee capital, after the long and arduous ascent of the Susquehanna trail, it became apparent that Teedyuscung's authority was practically nil. The Munsees of Assinisink were busily en-

gaged in celebrating a religious celebration, with feasting
and dancing going on day and night. Teedyuscung even left
his card-games to join the pagan services. The ceremonies
continued for a full two weeks. Many of the townspeople
and perhaps some of the ceremonial participants used this
season of general celebration to indulge in drinking bouts—
a practice bitterly condemned by the religious group, including Teedyuscung, but difficult to discourage. The twenty-
sixth proved to be a hard day for both Post and Teedyuscung.
Two casks of rum had been brought to town. Teedyuscung,
realizing what would happen, called his people together and
asked them to remember the importance of the mission on
which they were traveling. They had not come here to drink
but to do business. Teedyuscung's son, Captain Bull, who
knew very well how dearly Teedyuscung himself loved rum,
paid no attention to this exhortation, and quickly became
intoxicated. In his state of inebriated good humor he then
rolled up a whole half-cask of rum and set it at his father's
feet. Teedyuscung, on his dignity before Post, the man of
God, and the jealous Munsees, as well, said flatly that he
would not taste a drop of it, and ordered it to be taken
directly away.

The behavior of the Indians soon became ugly. Drunken
Munsees threatened to kill Post and Hays; others promised
to roast them alive. The sachem of the lodge in which they
were staying did his best to defend his troublesome charges,
driving the rowdies three times out of his house. At last Post
and Hays were obliged to retreat into the woods, "where by
God's Assistance & Protection [they] ended this Dolorous
Day in Safety."

Further humiliations followed quickly on the heels of the
riot. On the very next day a messenger named Shamokin
Daniel arrived from the Six Nations country with bad news.
The Mingoes, he said, saluted Teedyuscung and Post, and
were glad that they had arrived safely at Assinisink. "Nevertheless they were surprised that Teedyuscung had brot.

[them] so far up in the Country without letting them first know of it, that therefore they wish'd [them] a safe journey back again." Post was furious; he refused to go back without delivering his message to all the Indian nations. Teedyuscung, his nose out of joint, scolded Post for Pennsylvania's entering into "secret agreements" with the Mohawks. As for himself, he would persevere and go to Allegheny; Post could go back alone to Philadelphia. Teedyuscung's ignorance of Indian diplomatic procedure evidently was so profound that he had not known that travelers through Six Nations territory—especially white travelers—must first receive permission before entering the country. (Or was he ignorant of that requirement?)

The next week was an unhappy one for Teedyuscung. On June 1 the Munsees of Assinisink sent a message to Pasigachkunk, where Teedyuscung had lived a few years before, inviting the Indians there to come to meet Teedyuscung and Post. Post sent a message of his own along with the Munsees', insisting on his right to go on to the Ohio with his important belts. The replies were negative. The Pasigachkunk Delawares refused to come to Assinisink, and the Six Nations Indians who lived nearby refused Post passage, saying, "It is agreed on by the 5 Nations that White Men shall not travel this Way." Teedyuscung took these refusals badly. "Teedyuscung was so vex'd & grieved at it that he hardly knew what to do," observed Post.

But every cloud has a silver living. As on two earlier occasions—Lapachpitton's challenge in 1757 about "ye Land Affair which is Dirt," and the Bird-on-the-Bough speech in 1758—Teedyuscung was able to do an abrupt about-face. At the moment he was beginning to think that perhaps this *contretemps* at Pasigachkunk might lead to a solution which might be more satisfying to his ego than the older plan. If he went on without Post, alone, all the honor would be his. He told Post not to be distressed. He, Teedyuscung, would carry on in the great work of peace. "I will cry very loud & strong when the Nations come," he declared, "& particularly I will speak in strong terms abt the Prisoners. I don't speak because I want to be great," he added apologetically; "when I am alone I am very little in my self."

Next morning Teedyuscung, Post, Hays, and Moses Tattamy held a council to discuss their problem. Teedyuscung (tongue in cheek now, we may suspect) declared to Post, "I am concern'd & my Heart is ready to break, to think that our Undertaking sho'd be thus frustrated, & as it wer knock'd on the Head, I can't see how we can do without you." Moses told the group that he had been talking with the Munsees in the town. The Munsees were not enthusiastic about Teedyuscung, who talked too much about the return of prisoners; they refused to listen to him. They were not going to give them up. The prisoners, they said, were needed to replace those members of the community recently lost through disease and war.

On the fourth a messenger brought two belts from the Great Council at Onondaga. The Six Nations expressed gladness that Teedyuscung was determined to go to the conference in the west, and they joined him in endorsing a peace between the English and the western Indians. Post, however, was still forbidden passage through the Seneca country. Teedyuscung was not agreeable to this implicit participation of the Six Nations in his peacemaking endeavors, and declined to carry any message from Onondaga to the western Indians, because, as Post understood him to say, "they wo'd then boast, that they had concluded the Peace." Post by now had sized up Teedyuscung's attitude, and his conclusion was emphatic. "I find that he is always jealous that his Honour & Character will [be] lessen'd by my bringing the Message to the Indians, & that he wo'd much rather do the Business alone, than with any body else."

But in spite of the prohibition against going any farther, Teedyuscung decided to take Post on to Pasigachkunk. There was no question now of his going on to the Ohio, although Post himself seems to have hoped that he might persuade the Six Nations to let him proceed. During their two weeks' stay at Pasigachkunk the Delawares there were brought to take hold of the chain of friendship with Brother Onas; but the Six Nations remained adamant against letting Post go through. Post finally gave up and handed over all the belts and strings to Teedyuscung. Sick and tired, he suspected Teedyuscung of having engineered the whole fiasco. The established road for ambassadors was "the great King's Road" across the Alleghenies almost due east from Harris' Ferry by way of Aughwick or Frankstown; it was entirely at Teedyuscung's request that he had come this way to the council. Post's suspicions may have been unfair. The route Teedyuscung chose was one with which he was familiar, the one along which he had friends, and a trail which was often traveled, although not by white men. But Post had his little moment of revenge. "At Parting," he wrote in his diary, "I wished Teedyuscung all the necessary Strength & Wisdom he stood in need of."[17]

* * *

Teedyuscung pushed on alone. At Salt Lick Town, up Beaver Creek, far out in the Ohio country, he gave the great halloo and called the tribes together. Beaver, the spokesman of the Ohio Delawares, left Fort Pitt for a few days to hear what Teedyuscung had to say; but he told Croghan that "they would do nothing untill they met" at Fort Pitt.[18] When the nations had assembled at Salt Lick Town, Teedyuscung treated them to a narrative of his four years' transactions with Brother Onas, and his son Amos spoke to the warriors in praise of peace.[19] The great conference convened by Teedyuscung amounted to nothing. On August 5, 1760, five days after he had left, Beaver returned to Fort Pitt, along with Teedyuscung and some other councilors of the Delawares.

Teedyuscung tried to make a spectacular entrance at Fort Pitt. When he and his party got to the river bank, they saluted the garrison with the firing of their rifles. The garrison dwarfed their compliment with the discharge of three cannon.

At the great conference itself, held at Fort Pitt from August 12 to 20, 1760, Teedyuscung never spoke. Beaver and Delaware George did the talking for the Delawares, and General Amherst's message was read by General Monckton. Over a thousand Indians were present. Among this crowd the "Jersey Basketmaker" cut no great figure; indeed, he was treated with marked contempt.[20] Rumors circulated in Philadelphia about "the very bad behaviour" of Teedyuscung at Pittsburgh and other places in the west.[21]

The issues were really too large for Teedyuscung to grasp. What was happening was a wholesale realignment of forces. English demands for additional lands for the building of new forts (gloved in earnest denials of any ultimate designs on Indian territory) brought the Ohio Delawares, who had recently been given the status of "men" by the Six Nations, to announce publicly that the whole Ohio country belonged to their "uncles." This rapprochement of the Delawares and the Six Nations was potentially a military alliance against the English. It embodied the threat that if the English did not stop meddling about lands, and instead reopen the desperately needed Indian trade, the Six Nations, the Delawares, and the Shawnees would make common cause against them.

In such an alignment of powers there was no place for Teedyuscung and his Anglicized Wyoming band. Teedyuscung had just a few days before given voice to spiteful sentiments concerning the Six Nations. To Post he had said, "You have spoil'd the Mingoes by giving them great Presents, that makes them proud & Lofty. If you English are afraid of them, we Delawares are not."[22] With his history of anti-Iroquois attitudes, he could hardly gain their sympathy or the sympathy of their allies, the Ohio Delawares. But his very value to Brother Onas lay in his acceptability to the Indians. If he was despised by them, Brother Onas would despise him too. Furthermore, his pro-English policy itself was rising to destroy his influence among Ohio and Susquehanna Delawares alike. At Pasigachkunk, Post had been told by Quetekund, the chief man of the Unami Delawares there, that it was Teedyuscung's own fault that more prisoners were not returned to the English. "He hath taken upon himself the whole Rule & Management, excluding all others, therefore they have left him alone to see how far he can bring it."[23] Teedyuscung's bumptious self-assertiveness and autocratic manner were not congenial to Delaware morality; among the equalitarian, laissez-faire Indians, a man like him was abnormal, a misfit, a flaw in the pattern of their smooth, unhurried social life. And along the Susquehanna, especially at Assinisink and Wyalusing, there was developing a strong Indian renaissant movement, characterized by adherence to old religious forms, the exclusion of rum, and the requickening of the old social organization. In the eyes of these nativist Delawares, too, Teedyuscung had small prestige.

Thus Teedyuscung now was almost a man without a country. No matter how hard he strove, he could never become a white man; yet something ("when I am alone I am very little in my self") drove him to identify himself with the whites. He was coming to be known among his own people as one who "wants to make Englishmen out of the Indians," and as such his status in the Indian community was dissolving. It is significant that at this very time his drunkenness increased and his unreliability became more marked in his dealings with the whites.

When Teedyuscung and Christian Frederick Post stood in the narrow, steep-walled valley at Pasigachkunk and looked up the forbidden trail, they had thought that one of them was free to go where he liked. But there was a forbidden trail for Teedyuscung too—the road to Philadelphia—and henceforth he was to travel it at his peril.

Powder Famine
1760-1762

Teedyuscung's need to drink had, by the time of his return
to Pennsylvania in the fall of 1760, become almost a disease.
Richard Peters observed in the following spring that in "ye
habit of drunkenness that he has got into" he neglected even
the most pressing business.[1] This sharpened appetite for
liquor seems to be significantly associated with a metamorphosis in his policy toward the white people.

His doings on behalf of the English government of Pennsylvania had hitherto earned him the reputation, among the
Susquehanna Indians, of being one who wanted to make Englishmen out of Indians, and of being personally a pretentious,
officious busybody. As soon as he was no longer valuable to
the Delawares for his interest with the whites, he was rejected
outright by his followers and tribal brethren. Apparently he
was brooding over this rejection. Drinking was an effort to
alleviate the pain, affording, as it did, release from the gnawing need for affection, and permitting him freedom to express
his hostilities in mayhem and abuse against both whites and
Indians. But drinking was not a permanent solution of the
difficulty. He sought a solution in events rather than in with-
drawal and fantasy.

It was the renewal of the encroachments of the Connecticut
people which gave him his chance to show off a new, aggres-
sively pro-Delaware policy. On September 17, 1760, while he
was still in Philadelphia reporting to the Governor on his

trip with Post, he was told that there were Connecticut men snooping about again, as they had in 1754, on the west bank of the Delaware River. Teedyuscung, with his memory full of the humiliations he had just undergone in the Ohio for his pro-English sentiments, and remembering the efforts of the Yankees in 1754 to settle Wyoming, seized on the occasion to reorient his position toward the whites. With a considerable show of warmth he requested Governor Hamilton to send "a Smart Letter" to the officials of the place where "those intruding People came from." If the Governor couldn't warn them off, he said, then "the Indians will put a Stop to it"; and that would "certainly bring on another Indian war."[2]

The Governor promptly sent some of Northampton County's justices of the peace up along the Delaware to investigate. The report they turned in, in October, revealed an extensive settlement by Connecticut pioneers. At Cushietunk, in the region called the Minisinks, there was already living a community of forty men, with some women and children. They had built three log houses, a sawmill, a gristmill, and thirty workers' cabins. A hundred more families were expected to join them in the spring. These settlers claimed the right to plant there by virtue of a purchase from some straggling Jersey Delawares; their claim stretched north and south along the river about thirty miles, and westward to a mountain halfway to the Susquehanna. Governor Hamilton, when he was informed of these activities, wrote a letter to Governor Fitch of Connecticut protesting the settlement and mentioning Teedyuscung's formal complaint, together with the threat of force which it embodied. He also issued a proclamation forbidding Pennsylvania settlers to join those from Connecticut and asking that the Connecticut people be brought before the justices of the peace of Northampton County as disturbers of the peace.[3] In this proclamation Teedyuscung's threats were published aloud to the world; they must have come to the attention of the Connecticut men themselves, sooner or later. "The *Delaware* Chief, *Teedyuscung*," announced Hamilton in the document, "hath made a very earnest and formal Complaint and Remonstrance to me, against the said Practices, insisting that the Intruders should be immediately removed by the Government to which they belonged, or by me; and declared, if this was not done, the Indians would come and remove them by Force, and do themselves Justice; with which he desired they might be acquainted beforehand, that they might not pretend Ignorance."[4]

But many of Pennsylvania's frontiersmen had no love for the Penns, who insisted on trying to collect the nominal but annoying quitrent of one halfpenny sterling per acre, and preferred the more democratic forms of local government which the New Englanders imported. Consequently, various Pennsylvania planters were buying shares in the Susquehanna Company's enterprise and were identifying their interests with those of the Connecticut people. This meant that there was no real opposition to the Connecticut settlement on the part of the Pennsylvania settlers or their justices of the peace.

Apprehensive that trouble would ensue from this disputed settlement, the Six Nations now began to take a hand in the controversy. In March 1761 two Six Nations ambassadors, Tom King (an Oneida) and Robert White (a Nanticoke), arrived in Wyoming with news for Teedyuscung. They had been at Cushietunk, they said, to warn the planters off. But the Connecticut people not only refused to leave Cushietunk; they announced that next spring, when the grass was high, they were going to settle the lands at Wyoming. "And if," the New Englanders had threatened, "the Indians who lived there should hinder their Settlement they would fight it out with them, and the strongest should hold the Land." Robert White added darkly that in the spring the Connecticut people would be four thousand strong, and that they were all going to descend on Wyoming.[5] Confirming what the North-

ampton County justices had told Hamilton, he described
Cushietunk as an armed camp. Those people were not hoping to make a peaceable settlement; they carried arms with
them everywhere, and at night set a guard, as if they were the
garrison of a fort.

In April Teedyuscung's confidence suffered another blow.
The Munsee Indians and stragglers of other bands who lived
near Cushietunk had been won over by the threats and the
trade goods of the Connecticut settlers. They now sent two
belts, one white and the other black, to Teedyuscung at
Wyoming, demanding to know what he was going to do when
the Connecticut people began to settle in his valley. If he
replied that he intended to oppose the Connecticut men,
"then they, the said Indians, who sent the said Belts, were
resolved to join with the Connecticut People, and settle them
there by force and in spite of such opposition by Teedyuscung & his Indians." The Cushietunk settlers were reported
to be building a fort, and to believe that the Wyoming Indians were ready to fight for the valley.[6]

These threats, this show of force, and the reputed invinci-
bility of the Connecticut horde so alarmed Teedyuscung that
in April 1761 he made a quick trip to Philadelphia to lay
his fears before the Governor. The ominous talk of war had
already prompted several Wyoming Indian families to desert
their homes. He himself, he said, would soon be obliged to
flee to the westward unless the Connecticut people were
stopped.[7]

Governor Hamilton, realizing that Teedyuscung was Pennsylvania's first line of defense against Connecticut's threatened anticipation of what he regarded as the Penns' prior
option on the valley, was very much upset at this deterioration of the situation.[8] On April 11 he hinted to Teedyuscung
that he would support him with troops, arms, and ammunition if the controversy came to blows. But a week later he
took these commitments back, suggesting that it might be
wiser for Teedyuscung to "collect the ancient and discreet

men" of his nation, and with them go to Cushietunk "in a peaceable Manner" to persuade the Yankees to desist. Violence should be avoided if at all possible. Hamilton was beginning to see, in these mutterings of fear and hate, the danger of a general Indian war involving both the Six Nations and the Delawares.[9]

In July and August 1761 Teedyuscung, the Six Nations, and Brother Onas entered into a three-cornered conference at Easton to discuss the issue. Some four hundred Indians gathered in the little frontier town, "orderly and sober except Teedyuscung,"[10] who was as usual being tortured by unsatisfied longings for eminence among both red men and white. On July 29, before the meeting formally opened, Teedyuscung waited on the deputation from Onondaga. Presenting the Onondaga chiefs with a large belt, he openly begged them for a deed to Wyoming for himself and his children. The Onondagas, who were not eager to save Wyoming from the English only to give it to the Delawares, replied evasively that they had already sold the land to the New England people. Teedyuscung on hearing this thought that he was betrayed, and loudly declared that he and his people would move westward to the Ohio country.[11] On August 5 he publicly announced this intention to Brother Onas, citing as his reasons the refusal of the Six Nations to grant him a deed, and the too convenient invitation they had extended to him to move into their country if the whites came over the mountains.[12]

But in the end he was persuaded not to leave Wyoming. Governor Hamilton, not anxious to see his buffer prince emigrate, urged him to stay. The Six Nations heartily seconded this request. Probably in order to put Teedyuscung under an obligation, and to give him a reward for staying, they recommended to Brother Onas that he furnish the Walking Purchase Delawares the satisfaction they had so long demanded for their lost lands. These arguments seem to have prevailed over the "King": at least, he did not leave Wyoming.[13] The Governor may even have encouraged him to believe that eventually he would be given a legal deed to the valley. Thomas Penn twice testified in writing to his willingness to see Wyoming and "a proper extent of Country about it" reserved as "a perpetual Settlement" for Teedyuscung's band—but only on condition that the Six Nations agree.[14] This concurrence of the Iroquois was never to be secured. When the Susquehanna Delawares later formally and specifically asked Brother Onas to execute in their favor a deed to the Wyoming lands, to be effective only on condition of their obtaining the written consent of the Six Nations, Pennsylvania refused. They were unwilling, they said, to meddle in the affairs of the Six Nations, who already had "positively told Teedyuscung in open Council, that they would not make him a Deed for those Lands."[15]

*   *   *

Teedyuscung's resistance to the designs of the English settlers at Cushietunk was part and parcel of a general agitation against Europeans along the Susquehanna, in the Iroquois country (among the Geneseo Senecas particularly), and in the Ohio. When Teedyuscung and C. F. Post, in the spring of 1760, had visited the Indian town of Machachlosing (near Wyalusing) on the upper Susquehanna, they found there a strong cultural renaissance in full swing.

The town was located on a fine piece of river-front land: so fine, indeed, that even as late in the spring as May the inhabitants, who must have numbered at least four hundred, still had plenty of corn stored up from the last harvest.[15a] There were some forty houses built close together. They measured eighteen by thirty feet in ground plan, and were constructed of a framework of split planks planted upright in the ground and covered with bark. Within each of these longhouses were several compartments for related conjugal families.[15b]

Even Post, who was inclined to look down his nose at the

"Stupid & Tragical" ways of the heathen, spoke of this community in admiring terms. "It is a large Town," he wrote, "& according to the Indian way fine Houses. They are religiously inclined & by no Means allow of drinking Rum. Their Religion consists in strictly adhering to the antient Customs & Manners of Their Forefathers, thinking it is pleasing to God That they strictly observe & keep the same, On which Account they are much afraid of being seduced & bro't off from their Ways by the White People, from whom they will receive no Instruction." Nevertheless these pagan Indians were "very kind & civil" to Post and his companions, and politely heard him deliver a Christian sermon—a mark of courtesy which the Brethren in Bethlehem would hardly have been willing to match. Their opposition to the whites was implemented by a requickening of their native culture, rather than by physical aggression. On Post's representation of Brother Onas' desire that all their white captives be restored, they promptly turned theirs over, apologizing for their laxity. "We thought to please God" by keeping them, they said. When the party left, they entreated Post that no liquor be introduced among them. "Pity us," they prayed.[16]

The cultural renaissance was not, however, always accompanied by charity toward the whites. At Assinisink, during Teedyuscung and Post's visit in May and June, 1760, religious rituals in the pagan tradition were being enthusiastically performed. The alarmed travelers saw, in the sun-drenched meadows, dancing men and women, naked from the waist up, who wore flowers in their hair and carried green wands and were painted with vary-colored images of snakes and birds and squirrels and other animals. In smoky lodges they dined heartily at feasts of bear-meat and venison and melted fat. They lay awake with the noise of night-long singing keeping them from sleep. They saw the sacrifice of a hog performed in the manner anciently associated with the bear; and they saw old Nutimus, the oldest man of all, draped in the skin of the first deer slain in the spring. They heard the recitation of dreams by sleepless devotees, grateful to their guardian spirits, and the prayers chanted by a "priest" who carried a mnemonic "picture-book" in which was detailed a new cosmology, half Christian and half pagan. . . .[16a] All this was a far cry from the sober Christianity which the Moravians had been trying so industriously to inculcate at Gnadenhütten. And it was at Assinisink, too, that Post and Hays, besieged by drunken Indians who threatened to roast them in the fire, had felt themselves to be at once so nearly in the hands of Satan and so close to Heaven.

The general mood of the Delawares was a dour, bitter, ill-repressed resentment of the octopus-like expansion of British power. It came to view in isolated outbursts of fury which, like flashes of lightning before a storm, confused the British observer rather than illuminated the landscape. In March 1760, for instance, an Indian who was trading at Fort Augusta suddenly went berserk and assaulted Nathaniel Holland, the storekeeper. Murder was prevented only by the interference of Colonel Burd and the hurriedly assembled guard.[17] The motives of this widespread, sulky anger were not far to seek. They were grounded in the memory of four generations of continual British and French encroachment upon and expropriation of Indian lands; in the abuses of the Indian trade; in the almost complete cutting off of this trade during the war; and in the failure of the English to reopen the trade following the expulsion of the French from the Ohio country. This last factor, the failure of the English to reopen the Indian trade promptly and fully after the war in the west, was the precipitating development.

In 1758 Pennsylvania's Quaker-led House of Assembly passed a law regulating the Indian trade in the interest of the Indians. This law provided for trading posts in the Indian country (as at Fort Augusta, for example), operated by provincial officials and supervised by a committee of the Assembly, which would sell needed trade goods to the Indians at fair prices in skins and furs. By placing the Indian trade under the control of Provincial Commissioners it was hoped to put an end to the too common practices of the conventional commercial trader, who preferred to sell watered rum rather than bulkier, heavier, less profitable, but economically necessary goods. Rum and debauchery, introduced and perpetuated by the traders, had brought about a progressive deterioration of the morale and the public health of Indian communities wherever they appeared. The plea of Papoonan's Indians against the introduction of rum was not just a piece of stuffy morality: it was a coolly considered request, and only the last of literally scores of similar Indian demands on the provincial governments. Virtually every prominent Indian who ever entered into protracted negotiations with the whites at one time or another asked that the rum trade be stopped. Pennsylvania, like the other colonies, had indeed from the earliest years carried on its statute books laws forbidding the transporting of rum to the Indian towns. But these laws were deliberately and openly violated. There was no serious effort made to enforce them; the legislators themselves depended to some extent for their livelihood on the maintenance of the rum trade, which involved a complex network of international finance, and was able to exert considerable political influence.

The sincere effort of the Quakers (who largely financed the Indian trade) in 1758 to put a stop to the traffic in rum, while continuing the trade in consumer goods and hunting equipment, was not a success. A bill was passed according to which no licenses were issued to private traders, and all trade was concentrated at Fort Augusta and Fort Pitt, where a store was opened in 1759. There the trade was supervised by commissioners appointed by the Assembly. This arrangement worked a hardship on the Indians themselves. The posts were easily accessible to near-by Indians, but hunting was poorest near the white settlements. The Indians living in the hinterlands had to make long journeys through regions unsettled by war and famine in order to reach the stores. No longer could they meet the traders in their own towns, as they had been used to do heretofore. Furthermore, the supply of goods was insufficient to meet their demands. In 1759 and 1760 the Indian populations brought great loads of skins and furs to Fort Pitt and Fort Augusta, but the factors there refused to accept a large part of them, probably because they did not have goods on hand. The Indians were greatly disappointed. At Fort Pitt, in August 1760, a Delaware spokesman said to the whites, "Brother, take pitty on our Women, Children and Warriors, we are a poor People, and Cannot Live without your Assistance; let a Fair and Open Trade be continued to be Carry'd on by your People amongst Us."[18] George Croghan, Johnson's deputy at Fort Pitt, tried to remedy the situation at Fort Pitt (and to recoup the losses he had sustained from the French seizure of his assets in 1754 and 1755) by selling contraband goods, including liquor and large quantities of powder, in defiance of his own regulations.[19] Other traders doubtless smuggled rum and ammunition, at exorbitant prices, to the hungry Indians.

In 1761 the trickle of goods was still further dammed by a directive from Sir William Johnson restricting the sale of liquor and ammunition. And in 1762 young, forty-five-year-old General Jeffrey Amherst, governor-general of British North America, acting against Johnson's advice, issued a blanket prohibition against all trade in rum, and severely limited the sale of ammunition, as a military measure to wither any Indian uprising before it could begin. Sir Jeffrey also saw to it that the time-honored policy of both French and English of making large presents in goods, at treaties and occasional conferences, out of military and other governmental stores, was abruptly stopped.[20]

Amherst's repressive measures with regard to the sale of ammunition caused immense suffering amongst the Indians. In 1763 the Geneseo Senecas complained, as the reason for their bitterness against the English, that for the last two years powder had been scarce and prohibitively dear: it cost them two deerskins to buy a quarter of a pint of powder. These Allegheny, Susquehanna, and Ohio Indian populations were not composed of story-book savages living a care-free, wandering life in the woods, indifferent to European inventions. The whole structure of eastern woodlands Indian culture in the eighteenth century rested on the Indian trade. Trap and gun, powder and lead, were not luxuries: they were absolute necessities. With the gun and the metal trap the Indian was able to hunt much more effectively than he could with bow and arrows and laboriously contrived taking-devices. With the skins and furs secured in the hunt and by trapping he was able to buy such necessaries as rifles, powder, lead, repair parts, flints, traps, knives, iron hoes, steel axes, copper kettles, files, awls, nails, wire, wampum, paint, blankets and blanket cloth, shoes (which were much drier than moccasins in damp weather), shirts, buttons, needles, thread, stockings, and breeches. The old, time-consuming arts of manufacturing the aboriginal substitutes for these articles were rapidly being forgotten. The Indian towns in the Ohio were geared to a trading economy rather than the aboriginal hunting-horticultural one, and the sudden cutting off of powder meant starvation.

Amherst was inexperienced in Indian relations; moreover, he approached the problem with a heart full of unfortunate dogmas about racial superiority. His comment on the natives in 1763, during Pontiac's conspiracy (which had been generated by his own stupid trade policy), was that the Indians were "more nearly allied to the Brute than the Human Creation." He told his junior officers, "I wish to hear of no prisoners, should any of the villains be met with in arms." He even asked, "Could it be contrived to send the Small Pox among these disaffected tribes of Indians?"—a proposal effected by the whites during the siege of Fort Pitt by handing out infected blankets at a treaty.

There were other things galling to the Indian who stood helplessly at the factor's window, denied, after a long journey with his skins and furs, product of a winter's hunting, the right to buy the necessaries of life for himself and his wife and children. All about him (at Fort Pitt, especially) there was the sound of hammering and sawing. Houses and cabins, mills, warehouses, and tan yards were rising in the forest. Pack trains with supplies destined, not for him, but for the white garrisons living on his private family hunting grounds, wound endlessly through the woods, their bells jingling merrily and mockingly. And haughty English officers constantly demanded the return of prisoners; at every conference the white people complained that the prisoners were not being restored fast enough.

The question of the return of prisoners involved a difference between the European and Indian cultures. Europeans traditionally exchanged prisoners after wars. But among these Indians, war prisoners were seldom if ever restored to their former country. Most of them were adopted into bereaved families to replace husbands and wives, sons and daughters, who had died recently. Shingas the Terrible, for instance, who had a price on his head, treated prisoners indulgently, even adopting two young white captives as his sons, and according them equal treatment with his own offspring. Teedyuscung's own brother had adopted a young white man. These adoptees were an exceedingly important population increment (in Iroquois communities, sometimes two-thirds of the population would be white or foreign-Indian adoptees), and they were generally treated as well as native members of the community. This, of course, seemed harsh to many an unhappy white man and woman, and a few prisoners were tortured and killed; but most prisoners were regarded as being potential new members of the community.

The surrender of these people meant a real sacrifice to the adopting families. No sachem had any authority to compel any Indian family to give up a son or a daughter to the whites; and these prisoners *were* now sons and daughters, husbands and wives, nephews and nieces and cousins. In some instances strong sentimental ties formed, difficult and cruel to break. Many of the young childern were orphaned in the massacres when they were captured. When orphaned children were brought back to Philadelphia, advertisement was made in the newspapers for relatives willing to adopt them. If no one offered to accept the responsibility of raising them, they were bound out as apprentices or indentured servants. The Indian foster parents called this "slavery" and objected to giving up their newfound children. All sorts of conjugal complications developed. The white wives of Indian men sometimes escaped from their "freedom" in Philadelphia to run back to their husbands in the forest. White men, rather than face the economic competition of their old communities, where they would not be at a disadvantage after years of separation, preferred to stay with their Indian families in the close-knit solidarity of native community life.

And then there were the Christian Indians at Bethlehem. Why, they argued, should the Indians return white people who wanted to live in the woods, when the whites refused to send back Indians who wanted to live in the towns?

Yet within two years (from 1759 to 1761), at Fort Pitt alone, no less than 338 white prisoners were given up. At other places, and at other times, hundreds more were released. Taking everything into consideration, it seems remarkable that so many Indian households could individually be persuaded to accept the white man's viewpoint and to give up persons whom they had legally adopted.

Even Amherst's prohibition of the rum traffic had its politically disadvantageous aspects. There is evidence for thinking that intoxication functioned as a sort of emotional safety valve in Indian communities. While from the sociological viewpoint drunken orgies were socially disruptive, from Amherst's position they should have appeared as providing a way for the Indians to work off the anger engendered by their privations. By simultaneously restricting rum and powder, he produced a multitude of Indian communities that were both sober and hostile: a dangerous combination, as he was soon to learn.[21]

By 1761 the situation had become explosive. The Indians were immediately dependent upon the forts for their daily food, for they were prevented from hunting by lack of ammunition, and agriculture had lapsed during the war. To make a little ready cash, restless young warriors were stealing pack horses (which were customarily set free by their drivers at night along the trails to graze, with bells about their necks to assist their finding in the morning). Then they would sell the bells and the horses back to the English.[22] In Detroit, Captain Campbell learned that the Geneseo Senecas, the Delawares, and the Shawnees were planning a general uprising against the English in the Ohio region. Bouquet at Fort Pitt was constrained to publish a proclamation forbidding any further white settlements in the unpurchased territory west of the Allegheny Mountains, and banning hunting by white men in this area. Martial law sanctioned the declaration.[23]

In 1762 the famous "Delaware Prophet" stirred up a general wave of revulsion against the English among the Ohio Indians, preaching a return to the ways of their forefathers as the only means of regaining the spiritual integrity needed to drive out the whites. The Prophet's words inspired Pontiac and the tribes who joined him in the summer of 1763.[24]

This restlessness was not confined to the Ohio Indians. Along the Susquehanna too the native populations were in a stew of discontent. During the summer of 1761 Charles Brodhead (the same imprudent young man who had stampeded the Wyoming Indians into war in 1755) in his happy-go-lucky way led six pack horses up the Susquehanna to Assinisink. There he was told that he was being held as a prisoner and would probably be executed. With the help of Teedyuscung's son, he was able to escape with his life, but he had to leave the six horse-loads of goods behind. The threat was probably a ruse to separate Brodhead from his merchandise, which the Indians, being unable to hunt, could not buy.[25]

In August 1761 the Indians who attended the treaty at Easton left a swath of destruction through the settlements from Fort Allen to Bethlehem, giving rise to a rumor that the Indian wars had begun anew. A drunken Indian threw a torch at his wife in a straw-filled barn; the barn burned down; the white people in the neighborhood fled their homes in a panic. At one Kleiser's plantation, in the Lehigh gap, the Indians ate up all his chickens, killed his ewe, and destroyed his orchard. North of the mountains, Indians were seen hunting sheep with a dog. At Fort Allen itself, now ungarrisoned except for a sleepy-headed Lieutenant Wacker-burg who was living with the wife of a local farmer, the Indians settled down at last to drink and to eat the rations they had been given at Easton to support them on their way back to their homes. When their food was all gone they ransacked the fort in search of provisions, surprised the Lieutenant sleeping in bed and scared him off with a shot, tore off his lady's clothes before she escaped into a cornfield, and finally took away the furniture and the chickens which she had hidden in the cellar.

The upshot of all the disorder was the popular conviction, among Indians and white people alike, that another Indian war was imminent. At Cushietunk the Connecticut settlers sent their women and children back to New England. In the Jerseys four Indians were murdered.[26] And in the fall Teedy-uscung, passing through Bethlehem on his way from Phila-delphia, predicted that war would soon break out again. The Indians, he said, blamed the Christians and their rum trade.[27]

*   *   *

It would seem that Teedyuscung, in his resistance to the threatened invasion from Connecticut, was acting in moral concert with the rest of the Delawares. It had become necessary for him, if he was to maintain status in the Indian community, to champion the rights and interests of the red men against the whites. But his stand was not taken with either the intention or the prospect of creating a rift with *all* of the whites. With Brother Onas he still kept up a friendly correspondence; and Governor Hamilton testified to his desire of keeping him as an ally in his proclamation of September 1761 against the Connecticut men, in which he stressed the perilous likelihood of an Indian war if the Wyoming valley were invaded.[28]

The Susquehanna Company, however, was not concerned with war or peace: it wanted the Wyoming lands. On January 5, 1762, the company voted ominously to "use proper Means to prepare The minds of the Indians for the admition and Carrying on Setlements on the Lands and Transact any other affairs that shall be necessary for the Setlement of Sd Lands and That the Com[mit]te[e] have Liberty To Imploy one hundred men for That purpose att the Cost of This Company."[29] On May 19 the company recommended "the speedy beginning a Settlement of our Susquehannah purchase." One hundred persons were ordered to go immediately to Wyoming to plant themselves down on the lands. This advance guard was to be given a ten-mile stretch of river front, in addition to their rights as members of the company, as compensation for the risks involved in thus taking possession. Only "wealthy and proper" persons were selected; and these were given special directions in how to conduct themselves "in this critical affair." It was reported at this time that the minutes of the meetings of the company were regularly burned at the next following session. On May 30 it was news in Philadelphia that "some people were actually cutting a Road" from Cushietunk to Wyoming.[30]

The battle lines were now drawn. Teedyuscung, at Wyoming, faced toward the east at the head of his little band of Delawares and waited for the Connecticut men to come over the mountains.

Royal Investigation
1762

The unhappy experiences of the Easton treaty of 1758 had taught Teedyuscung the perils of pulling Quaker chestnuts out of the fire. At the close of the treaty the Delaware "King" had formally given up pressing his claims against Pennsylvania and the Six Nations, and had asked only that he be assured of his right to live in peace at Wyoming. Teedyuscung and the Quakers would have been very well satisfied to let King George decide the whole land question in England. But the ministry in England went about the matter more carefully than either Teedyuscung or the Quakers desired. An issue had been raised which involved British security on the continent of North America. The fall of Fort Duquesne had not ended the war. The Indians were still worth appeasing. It was thought important to hold a thorough investigation of the Walking Purchase in order to satisfy all Indians everywhere that the English were just in their dealings and ready to right a wrong, if a wrong had been committed.

Benjamin Franklin, who represented the Quaker-led Assembly in England, laid a petition before the Privy Council in 1759, requesting action by the crown. The Privy Council referred the request to the Board of Trade, which had already endorsed the Penns' recommendation that Sir William Johnson adjudge the case. In June 1759 the Board of Trade again recommended that the investigation should be made by Sir William Johnson, who was superintendent of Indian affairs for the northern colonies. By a royal Order in Council dated August 29, 1759, Johnson was instructed to examine thoroughly into the complaints of the Delaware Indians that they had been defrauded out of some of their lands by the proprietors of Pennsylvania.[1]

There is no reason to suppose that the order was given with tongue in cheek; Johnson does not seem to have been chosen simply because he was considered to be biased against the Quakers. The issue, after all, was not whether the lands should be given back to the Indians, who themselves had not suggested that, but whether the Indians could be reconciled to the presence of the whites. That Johnson, prejudiced as he was against the authors of the charges, was chosen to carry out the investigation, was not the expression of a conspiracy against the Delawares. The task was in line with his official duties. Furthermore, Johnson up to this time had been rather the rival of the Penns in Indian affairs than their collaborator, and the fact that the Penns themselves suggested him argues that they were well convinced of the justness of their position. The report of the committee appointed by Governor Denny to look into the complaints of the Indians, presented to the Governor in January 1758, had exonerated the proprietaries, so the Penns thought. Johnson's separate inquiry would be the final proof of the sincerity of the Penns and of the English.

Accordingly, on March 1, 1760, Johnson sent a letter to Teedyuscung by one of the "King's" sons. He asked for a meeting as soon as possible, and requested Teedyuscung to be ready with his warriors to assist the English in battle.[2]

Teedyuscung was not at all anxious to meet Johnson. So far, his charges had brought him only trouble and humiliation. He was willing to let the matter slide. He and his people were living peacefully at Wyoming, and he himself was continually being employed by the province of Pennsylvania in the negotiations with the western tribes. A meeting with Johnson, to whom he had already violently objected because

Johnson was intimate with the Mohawks, could only involve him in more quarrels. Writing from Bethlehem, he regretted that he was leaving next day for the Ohio to invite the Wyandots to a treaty at Easton. He was sorry, but he could appoint neither a time nor a place for the meeting Johnson desired.[3] The Delaware "King" was taking no chances with Brother Warraghiagey.

That fall, on his return from the Ohio, he angrily complained to Governor Hamilton about Johnson's letter. He had received it just as he was setting out for Assinisink. He declared he would have nothing to do with Sir William. He wanted his good friend Governor Hamilton to conduct the investigation. Hamilton parried the proposal by saying that he would consider the matter; meanwhile Teedyuscung would have to gain the consent of all the Indians concerned to Hamilton's interference.[4]

In 1761, however, Teedyuscung came to something of an understanding with the Six Nations. They were becoming dissatisfied with the way in which Johnson was treating them. Trade languished; the Connecticut men were pressing their claim to the Wyoming Valley on the grounds of the disputed deed obtained by Lydius at Albany in 1754. "We see Death coming upon us," said the Six Nations.[5] Teedyuscung, occupying the valley, was in effect guarding the land for his "uncles," who had decided not to give the Delawares a "deed" to the land, but were very willing to have them live there. If he and his people removed, there would be no immediate obstacle to the Susquehanna Company's making a settlement.

The Governor too was forced to request that Teedyuscung stay at Wyoming. Teedyuscung then asked for settlement of the Delaware claims—and this time the Six Nations seconded his demand, saying, "Brother Onas, We would have you make some Satisfaction to our Cousins here, the *Delawares,* for their Lands, as we suppose they desire it."[6]

But all that Teedyuscung achieved by this too clever move was the reminder that he himself, a year and a half before, had refused to meet the King's representative, Sir William Johnson, to discuss just such a settlement as he wanted.

*   *   *

In the spring of 1762 Teedyuscung took matters into his own hands, writing a letter to Johnson appointing a meeting at Philadelphia by May 19.[7] Zeisberger, the Moravian missionary, delivered Johnson's reply at Wyoming on May 13, along with an invitation from Governor Hamilton to a treaty to be held that summer at Lancaster between Pennsylvania and the western tribes under Beaver and Shingas.[8] Johnson's reply suggested postponing the conference about lands until June 15, because he had already promised to attend a meeting with the Six Nations in May.[9] Teedyuscung wrote to Johnson that June 15 would suit him very well, adding mournfully, "I shall bring no other Indians along with me but such as are necessary to be present, because the other Nations will not be obedient to me, but gets drunk and do a great deal of mischief, for which I cannot be answerable, but I can answer for my own people."[10]

Teedyuscung talked over the proposed meeting with the Governor in Philadelphia. Hamilton asked him why he had so suddenly decided to lay the question before Sir William Johnson. Teedyuscung, apparently interpreting this as a reproach for changing his mind about the desirability of having Hamilton for a mediator, made a long series of excuses, and then asked the Governor to write to Johnson not to come. The Governor of course refused. Teedyuscung then complained about the long delay in settling the case. Hamilton reminded him of an occasion in 1761 when the Delaware chief had disclaimed any knowledge of the proprietors' cheating the Indians, and suggested that if Teedyuscung would publicly retract his accusations, he, the Governor, "would not be against making them a present in Composition to their Circumstances, but not on account of the Lands which had long since been bought & paid for."

Teedyuscung said he would gladly affirm in public what he had said to the Governor in private. When the Governor asked him how much the Indians had decided the lands were worth to them, he said £400.

Isaac Stille, the "King's" interpreter, interrupted angrily, "This was a Bustle, indeed, and was all this Bustle about such a Sum as £400?"

The Governor, in a huff at this, declared that if Johnson decided that the Penns had not cheated the Indians, he would not feel himself obliged to contribute a farthing.

At this, Teedyuscung hastily requested the Governor to tell Johnson not to come; and the Governor again refused![11]

This little by-play can be interpreted as a piece of skul-duggery on the Governor's part, as a successful attempt to bribe Teedyuscung. It does not really appear to be so, how-ever. In the first place, if the Governor were actually bribing Teedyuscung, it is not likely that the whole transaction would have been written down for posterity in the minutes of the Provincial Council by the Governor's own secretary. And in the second place, it was no longer in Teedyuscung's power to decide the issue. The machinery of royal justice had been set in motion, and it was not to be halted by last-minute recantations. What Hamilton very likely intended was to draw the "King" out, to see what value he himself set on his own claims, and to hold out to him the chance of gaining some money if he abided by Johnson's decision, which would certainly be to acquit the proprietors.

The news that the investigation would be held by Johnson in June was not regarded as good news by the Quaker party, who realized that his sympathies did not lie with them and the Delawares under Teedyuscung. The Pennsylvania com-missioners for Indian affairs (adherents of the Quaker fac-tion) wrote to Johnson suggesting that his inquiry be made at the time of the projected general treaty with the Ohio Indians at Lancaster a few weeks later.[12] Johnson of course refused to agree to this. He had heard too much about the near-disaster of 1758, when Teedyuscung and the Quakers came close to wrecking the whole British system of alliances with the Six Nations, to want to mix Teedyuscung's affairs with any other business.

The Quaker party also tried to break up Johnson's treaty by intrigue. On June 9 Governor Hamilton received from the hand of Mr. Fox, one of the Commissioners of the Assembly, an undated letter supposedly written by Teedyuscung at Wyoming:

Brother, You have put me to a great Stand to think that the Thing that was made by Sr William Johnson & me, that you have put a Stand to it, and calls the Treaty to wait for the Indians that come from Allegheny; them people has nothing to say to the Lands, they are coming to talk about Life Affairs, therefore, let me know as soon as you can what you think.

I was just in readiness to go down, all my people but waiting I received your Letter, it put a stop to.[13]

Hamilton had not written to Teedyuscung, but evidently some time before the ninth Teedyuscung had received a letter from someone telling him not to come to Easton on the fifteenth. From Philadelphia to Wyoming was at the very least a three days' journey on horseback. Counting back, therefore, six days from the ninth leaves June 3 as the latest date at which the message could have been sent from Philadelphia. Whoever wrote the letter to Teedyuscung could hardly have received or heard of Johnson's reply to the commissioners, which was written in New York on the second. There is no question by whom the mysterious letter to Wyoming was sent. Joseph Fox, one of the commissioners, and an adherent of the Quaker party, paid ten pounds for a horse for the messenger.[14] And the Pennsylvania Archives contain a letter by Mr. Fox to Teedyuscung, erroneously dated June 9, 1762 (probably because it was brought to the attention of the Governor on that date). The letter deserves to be quoted in full because it indicates the methods employed by the Quaker faction to *prevent* a settlement of Teedyuscung's charges:

Brother Teedyuscung: We find the Allegheny Indians are not likely to come so soon as we expected, and that the time & place you have appointed Sr Wm. Johnson to meet at Easton, will not be so suitable as to meet him when all the Indians are together. We have, therefore, informed Sir Wm. Johnson that it will be better to put off the intended meeting till that time, and to meet you all together; And as we think, Brother, you will be willing to have the Business well done, we desire you not to come from Wyoming till you hear the Western Indians are come to Shamokin, and then to come down with them to the same place they do, where we shall order provisions to be ready for you.[15]

Hamilton sent two duplicate replies to the "King," informing him that the government of Pennsylvania had not sent the earlier letter, and ordering him to be at Easton on the fifteenth as planned. The first copy was written on the tenth. A second letter was written on the eleventh, to be forwarded by Mr. Fox.[16] The Governor was taking no chances on his instructions being misunderstood or misdirected, it seems.

The hand of Israel Pemberton was probably in these desperate efforts to keep Johnson out of the case. As early as 1759, Pemberton had planned to have a grand treaty at Philadelphia, at which all the Indians who had once lived in eastern Pennsylvania and New Jersey would proclaim their independence of the Six Nations, and would elect Teedyuscung their emperor. The new nation under Teedyuscung would then publicly announce its refusal to have Sir William Johnson judge their case.[17] Although the grand treaty never materialized (fortunately for Pennsylvania), Pemberton had not given up.

*   *   *

Johnson reached Easton on the thirteenth, but could not proceed to business until the eighteenth, "the Indians being until that day drunk." Teedyuscung, it would seem, was in no hurry to be proved in the wrong.

The two parties came to grips on the nineteenth, when Teedyuscung, no doubt prompted by the Quakers, as usual demanded a clerk. But this was not 1756, and Johnson was not Governor Denny (who, as John Pemberton once remarked, "was a poor, weak-minded creature: he was a native of Ireland"[18]). Johnson said *no*. Teedyuscung meekly allowed his demand to lapse. It was symbolic of his whole attitude: eagerness to be on both sides.

Johnson now proceeded to pin Teedyuscung down to particulars. Where exactly did the disputed lands lie? Teedyuscung described the boundaries of the Walking Purchase, and told a tale of hearing James Logan at Pennsbury in 1735 warn Nutimus ("then Chief of the Delawares") that he would be wise not to complain about the legality of the deed of 1686. Was this the whole of his accusations against the Penns? asked Johnson quickly. Teedyuscung, apparently taken aback by the briskness of Johnson's manner, said that it was.

On Monday, in "the Bower" at Easton, the Penns' lengthy defense of the legality of the Walking Purchase was read. It was a complicated web of closely knit argument which, while exhaustively demonstrating that the letter of the original deed of 1686 had not been violated by the walk itself, never touched upon the main point, which was whether the Indian signers of the 1686 deed had ever intended, or had ever had the right, to sell any lands north of Tohiccon Creek. At the close of the reading, which occupied nearly four hours (and which was not translated into Delaware), Teedyuscung, without being asked, announced that he had "very well understood the purport, or meaning of what had been read." It is doubtful that he had understood it: a legal defense in a foreign language would be difficult enough to understand at best, and doubly so when it was heard without access to documents. But Teedyuscung was heartily sick of the whole affair. He had already offered to Hamilton to withdraw his charges. Although he had not yet publicly done so, he was not anxious to be dragged farther into this embarrassing dispute between the Quakers and the proprietary party.

But Pemberton had other plans. That night he must have told Teedyuscung again that the Governor was leading him by the nose, because next day the "King" was in a sour temper. When Johnson asked him to prepare his answer to the proprietary defense (a written copy of which was to be given him), and to have it put into writing (thus affording him full opportunity to consult with his Quaker advisers), his reply was provocative:

Brother, Please to hear me what I am going to say. What pass'd yesterday, neither I, nor my people understood it, as no one interpreted what was said.

Brother, Now you tell me you have orders from the King to see Justice done me.

Brother, About five years ago, when Mr. Croghan was here, He had orders to see Justice done me: now I desire you won't do as He did, for He went away, and did nothing at all.

Brother, I desire you'll let me have the Writings which were read yesterday, that I may have time to Consider of them, as We did not understand what was read.—I told you another Thing, which was, to let me have a Clerk, to write down what I have to say. This is the request of Us all.

Brother; I desire all my Brethren to attend to what I say.—I do not Speak this only from my Mouth, but from my Heart.

After the speech he handed over a letter, obviously composed by a white man, which in similar terms accused Johnson of injustice.

Johnson, who was well aware of the interests and methods of the Quakers, asked Teedyuscung who had put all that nonsense into his head. Attacked thus directly, Teedyuscung tried to be affable, protesting, "He did not entertain any suspicions that [Johnson] would do him injustice."

Johnson called attention to Teedyuscung's inconsistency in this. His last statement, said Johnson, contradicted what he had said a moment before; and what he had said a moment before contradicted what he had said yesterday. He appealed to the bystanders.

Teedyuscung was out of his depth now. Israel Pemberton, seeing that his front man was being treated lightly, decided that now was the time to throw off all disguises. No longer was it Indian against Englishman. The quarrel stood in its true colors: Quaker against proprietor, colonial against Britisher. Pemberton stood up and shouted, "Teedyuscung said no such thing!" Pemberton had a lot more to say, and he said most of it, accusing the conference secretary (a royal official) of taking false minutes, accusing Johnson of chicanery in allowing the proprietary defense to be read in English ("not one Sentence of which Teedyuscung understood to his certain Knowledge; and he had known him for many years"), threatening to carry the matter over Johnson's head to the King of England.

Johnson challenged Pemberton, "What right have you to interfere in this matter?"

Pemberton answered ("insolently," the minutes read), "I am a freeman and have as much right to speak as the governor."

As soon as Pemberton had done with his harangue, the commissioners took up the attack on Sir William. Johnson kept insisting that *he* had been appointed by the King to settle this case; the Quakers kept insisting on their rights as free men. John Hughes, the boisterous friend of Teedyuscung, announced that he was not afraid to acknowledge what he had said to any man. Pemberton even questioned Johnson's right to handle Indian affairs, and Johnson, it was rumored afterward, at one point drew his sword on Pemberton. Sir William failed to silence the Quakers, however, and finally had to dissolve the conference for the day. For the moment it seemed that the Quakers had had the better of the contest.

Two days later, Teedyuscung delivered to Johnson a paper

containing an itemized list of the frauds he charged the proprietaries with perpetrating in connection with the Walking Purchase, and renewing his complaints about the purchase of 1749, from the Six Nations, of land above the Kittatinny Mountains. Pennsylvania, he charged, had bought land from the Iroquois which properly belonged to the Delawares (i.e., the Munsees). This allegation was a surprise, because in 1758 he had publicly renounced on behalf of the Delawares all claims to lands above the mountains.

Johnson was angry. He asked Teedyuscung whether he knew what the paper contained.

Pathetically trying to remain friends with everyone, Teedyuscung replied, "My Cousin wrote it."

And then suddenly, without warning, Teedyuscung performed another of his political somersaults. He renounced every claim. His words broke up the meeting. "I did not come," he cried, "to have any Difference, but to Settle matters upon a good Footing.—I did not come to put my hand into your Purse, or to get Cloathing.—I give up the Land to you, and the white People."

On the morrow he delivered a document in which he relinquished all of his accusations and his claims to land. The charge of forgery, he said, had been "a Mistake," and

as to the Walk, the Proprietary-Commissioners insist that it was reasonably performed; but We think otherwise: which Difference in opinion may happen without either of Us being bad Men; but this is a matter that Brethren ought not to Differ about.—Wherefore, being desirous of living in peace and Friendship with our Brothers the Proprietaries, and the good People of Pennsylvania, We bury under Ground all Controversies about Land; and are ready, such of us as are here, to Sign a Release for all the Lands in Dispute: and will Endeavour to persuade the rest of our Brethren who are concerned, to Sign the same.

The treaty ended next day. Pennsylvania refused to accept a release, on the grounds that the deeds she already possessed were legal evidence of ownership. Johnson promised to recommend, in his report to the Board of Trade, that the Penns give the Delawares a large present. The Indians departed carrying £200 worth of gifts.[19]

*   *   *

The collapse of the Quaker charges produced a sensation in Philadelphia. George Croghan a few days later reported that since he had come home there was nothing talked of but the treaty. Pemberton and his henchmen were too dispirited to visit the coffee houses, and Croghan crowed triumphantly that the whole Society of Friends was seriously alarmed. Pemberton, Fox, and Hughes had carried things too far, it was said; it was even feared that they had drawn King George's resentment on the province. The proprietary party were gleeful. If the King did show his displeasure, said Croghan, "there is an End to Quaker Influence . . . the Luckest thing that could happen to pull down Quaker power."[20]

The Easton treaty of 1762 did not mark the end of Quaker influence, of course. The heart of the Quaker-proprietary struggle was not in the dispute over the legality of the Walking Purchase. That had been only a skirmish in the general campaign of the Quaker men to reduce the prerogatives of executives who lived in England and were at the same time the greatest landholders in the province.[21] In 1763 Pontiac's war provided another field of battle for the Quakers and the proprietaries. And in the same year the Friendly Association for the Gaining and Preserving Peace with the Indians by Pacific Measures declined and quietly died.

The weapons wielded in this constitutional quarrel have been remembered better than the quarrel itself. Charles Thomson, for long Teedyuscung's secretary, in 1759 published his famous *Enquiry into the Causes of the Alienation of the Delaware and Shawanese Indians from the British Interest*. This book has preserved for historians the tradition that it was land frauds, and particularly the Walking Purchase, which caused the Delawares to side with the French during the French and Indian War. Thomson was a patently biased witness, and Thomson himself was a schoolmaster, not an Indian agent. A careful later historian of the affair, Julian P. Boyd, does not consider the Walking Purchase as an important determining cause of the alienation of the Delawares. Our own investigation of the history of the charges on which Thomson based his book suggests a similar conclusion: that while individual Delaware families certainly resented the Purchase, the Walking Purchase never became a national concern of the Delawares, and would never have been mentioned by Teedyuscung had not the Quaker party, for political reasons, urged him to do it.

Death in the Valley
1762-1763

Following the settlement of the land charges at Easton in June 1762, Teedyuscung returned for a few days to the Indian country. On August 5 he was at Fort Augusta, buying provisions valued at £2/9/6, for which he paid £1/15/0 in cash, together with one otter skin and one beaver skin.[1] A week later he was back in Lancaster for the treaty between Pennsylvania and the western tribes.

The formal ratification of peace between the Ohio Delawares, represented by Beaver and Shingas, and the government of Pennsylvania, had been long delayed. Since 1758 Teedyuscung had been negotiating between the two parties, and by 1759 overt hostilities had virtually ceased. This happy event was owing rather to the occupation of the Ohio forts by Forbes's army than to Teedyuscung's silver tongue, but Teedyuscung claimed a large share of the credit.

In 1760, when he was at the Fort Pitt conference, Teedyuscung told Beaver that Pittsburgh was no place to hold a council; it was fit only for warriors. The old fire was in Pennsylvania. Beaver promised faithfully that he would come to Pennsylvania for the final treaty.[2]

Beaver at Lancaster did what was expected of him, taking the French hatchet out of the head of Brother Onas, and burying it, and wiping the tears from Onas's eyes. About fifteen white "prisoners" were handed over as a mark of good faith. These fifteen reported that they had all been well treated and had been adopted into Indian families. They appealed in Saur's newspaper to friends to ask for them. Some of the children were left unclaimed. On October 11 a last announcement was made: if their families did not come to Philadelphia for them, they would be bound out as servants. Among this latter group were "a boy and girl of whom it is supposed that they belong to the Peter Hess in *Northampton County*" whom Teedyuscung and his comrades had killed on New Year's Day six years before.[3]

Beaver denied any knowledge of claims by his followers to land along the Delaware River; and Teedyuscung publicly offered again to sign a release for all claims he had forsaken earlier in the summer at Easton—upon which the Governor was so pleased that he told him that "on that Occasion he had acted like an honest Man." The two men were well paid for their complaisance. Each of them received £100 in milled Spanish dollars and £200 in goods. Beaver was entrusted with goods valued at £400 for his people, and Teedyuscung's band got £200 worth. James Hamilton, after the treaty, remarked that Pennsylvania had spent £20,000 on the Indians "since the reëstablishment of peace" in 1756—a heavy price to pay for bringing Beaver to Lancaster.[4]

The Six Nations were present at Lancaster too, in the person of Tom King the speaker, and a crowd of warriors. Tom King took this occasion to refer to the explosive question of the Wyoming lands. Although he did not confer title to the land upon Teedyuscung and his people, he did the nearest thing to it: he specifically ordered him to live at Wyoming and to keep all white men away, because Wyoming was Six Nations country. Handing Tapescawen, Teedyuscung's councilor, a belt of wampum, he proposed the bargain by the remark, "By this Belt I make a Fire for *Teedyuscung*, at *Wyoming*." Tapescawen, by accepting the belt, sealed the contract.

Nevertheless, in spite of the protestations of mutual friendship on all sides, the treaty was not a success. The Indians complained that the whites were niggardly in supplying food and drink. And Teedyuscung shocked the whole town when he accused the white people of planning to poison the drinking water of the Indian delegates, so that they would all die of dysentery on the way home.

It has been remarked more than once that witch-fear and the dread of poisoning have a high incidence in persons who, like Teedyuscung, are living on the shabby fringes of European civilization, ridden by privation and anxiety.[5] Teedyuscung believed in poisons and witchcraft. Years ago, at another treaty, he had warned Captain Newcastle that he was going to be poisoned by a group of Delawares. Like all of his native associates, he was constantly observing the decimation of Indian communities by strange epidemic diseases; and these epidemics seemed to follow contact with white men. In the spring of 1762 there had been a vicious epidemic of dysentery at Wyoming, in which Teedyuscung's own wife Elisabeth had died, as well as her sister, who was the wife of the important Delaware Augustus. Augustus himself had died too.[6] Perhaps Teedyuscung was simply afraid that the whites wanted to kill him by the same means as they had perhaps killed his wife and friends.[7]

*   *   *

The departure of the Indians to the treaty had left Wyoming almost deserted. Only seven men, in addition to a few women and children, stayed behind to occupy the town. They, like their relatives at Lancaster, did not know that Connecticut men were at that moment cutting a road across the mountains from Cushietunk to their home. They did not know that 119 armed men were marching toward them over that road.

Sometime in the middle of September the woodcutters of the Susquehanna Company broke through the last of the forest and stalked out on to the great plains of Wyoming.

The Indian women and children fled into the woods, and the seven men, with guns and tomahawks in their hands, went out to meet the invaders. In angry voices they demanded to know what business the white men had. But the white men brushed their objections aside and coolly set about their work. By September 22 they had cut fifteen tons of hay at their encampment on the north bank of Mill Creek, a few miles above the Indian town, and had begun the building of three blockhouses. They had also set up huts to house themselves, and had sowed grain. They were being supplied with flour over the newly cut road from the Minisinks. They told certain inhabitants of Lower Smithfield Township, some of whom had bought £48 shares in the enterprise, that they intended to hold the land by a "strong hand." They were expecting to be joined by two hundred families later in the fall.[8]

Meanwhile the treaty at Lancaster was coming to an end, and the Indians were dispersing to their homes. On September 22 Tom King and the Six Nations delegation, traveling northward up the Susquehanna to their homes in New York, surprised the Connecticut trespassers at work. Tom King had just been telling everyone at Lancaster that the Six Nations would never permit the Susquehanna Company to steal the Wyoming lands. And now, lo and behold, here they were, trying to do just that! He and his warriors were angry. In the afternoon "a great Number of ill looking Fellows" ordered the Connecticut people to get out. The Yankees, who had largely completed what they had come to do, agreed to leave. Twelve of them set off the same afternoon, and the rest next morning. But before they went, they said that they were going to hold a treaty with the Six Nations at Albany in the winter, and that next spring they would come back, with a thousand armed men and two cannon![9]

Teedyuscung reached Wyoming a week later, and learned from Tom King, who had remained behind while his comrades went on up the river, the story of the attempt at settlement. Tom King advised him to "be quiet" until he received a message from the Six Nations to come to Albany. There the Six Nations would prevail on the Connecticut people to desist from their unlawful undertakings.

After Tom King had gone, the Wyoming Delawares met in council to consider measures for the defense of their valley. It was obvious enough that they could not ultimately stand off the better armed and more numerous invaders from New England. Their security, then, lay in alliances. After deliberation they concluded not to promise to come to Albany in the spring, where they would have to rest their faith in the Six Nations, who had already betrayed them by selling the valley, but to ask Brother Onas for advice and direction.

Scarcely had the council come to this decision when 150 New England men (probably many of them the same persons who had been chased away a few weeks before) poured into the valley. They brought with them all sorts of tools, "as well for building as Husbandry," and announced that they had bought the land from the Six Nations and now intended to erect houses and to plant at the north end of the valley. Teedyuscung scared them off with blustering speeches. "I threatned them hard," he told the Governor of Pennsylvania later that fall, "and declared I would carry them to the Governor at Philadelphia; and when they heard me threaten them in this manner, they said they would go away, and consult their own Governor; for if they were carried to Philadelphia, they might be detained there Seven Years." (Was this a sly dig at the flint-heartedness of the Quakers, who bound out the orphaned prisoners turned over by the Indians, as servants and apprentices, for seven years?) They mockingly offered to give up their claim to the land if the Delawares returned the purchase money (which of course the Delawares had never seen), amounting to several "Bushels of Dollars."

A week later, about the middle of October, fourteen more men from Connecticut entered the valley bearing "a Saw &

Saw Mill Tools." These men, Teedyuscung observed frostily, intended to "build a Saw Mill about a mile above where I live." He threatened them too with forcible detention if they persisted. Like the others, these men went away, after burying their tools somewhere in the woods. "These people," Teedyuscung reported in an offended tone, "desired me to assist them in surveying the Lands, and told me they would reward me handsomely for my trouble, but I refused to have any thing to do with them." The prospective lumbermen-surveyors departed, muttering that in the spring they would return with three thousand armed men.

And still the Connecticut men came on! Six days after the fourteen sawmill builders had gone away, eight more white men and a mulatto marched into the valley. These people actually stole Teedyuscung's horse, which he had just bought that summer at Easton. Teedyuscung was really exasperated at this. "Immediately I got together my Council," he said, "and as soon as we had finished our Consultations, I told these people that I would actually confine them and carry them to Philadelphia." After giving Teedyuscung another horse and five pounds in cash to boot, these men also departed, predicting that they would come again in the spring with "great Numbers."[10]

In November, when it appeared improbable that any more Connecticut settlers would visit Wyoming, Teedyuscung made a trip to Philadelphia to complain again to Brother Onas. He told the Governor the story of how he and Tom King had scared off the hopeful pioneers. To Hamilton, he seemed "full of anger and resentment." "He would I doubt not," said the Governor, "fall upon these people and cut their throats on the least encouragement given him."[11] But the Governor, who along with Thomas Penn was confident that the ministry in England would prohibit the settlement of Wyoming, was anxious to avoid open conflict. Although he urged Teedyuscung not to leave the valley, he advised him not to be hasty in the use of force. Go with the Six Nations to Albany, he suggested, and treat there with the New England people.[12]

This was cold comfort. During the winter Teedyuscung seriously discussed with his councilors the advisability of removing to Beaver Creek out in the Ohio country next spring, and settling about Kuskusky.[13]

But in March the Six Nations, encouraged by Sir William Johnson's opposition to the Connecticut scheme, resolved to take a firmer stand. They decided not to meet the representatives of the Susquehanna Company at Albany. Johnson told Colonel Eliphalet Dyer and the Reverend Timothy Woodbridge, who were visiting him and attempting to bribe him with tenders of land, that the Six Nations would never agree to the settlement, and that if they made one, an Indian war was certain. Some Mohawks who happened to be then at Johnson's declared that "such a Procedure must occasion a genl quarrell with all the Confederacy." Dyer and Woodbridge replied that after spending so much money they were not going to give up their plans. They *would* settle Wyoming, by force if they had to, "to a Considerable number, sufficient to maintain themselves in the possession thereof."[14]

As the spring continued, apparently encouraged by the support which he felt the Six Nations, Brother Onas, Sir William Johnson, and probably King George were now promising him, Teedyuscung made up his mind to stay at Wyoming and try to weather the storm.

*   *   *

On April 19, 1763, Teedyuscung was murdered. In the evening, as he lay asleep in his cabin (some say in a drunken stupor), the house was set afire from outside; he was burned to death within the flaming walls of the lodge which Brother Onas had built for him. Almost simultaneously the twenty surrounding dwellings burst into flames. Within a few hours the whole town of Wyoming lay in ashes. The surviving members of the community fled in terror, some of them to the Moravian mission at Wechquetank, not far from Fort Allen; some to Nain, near Bethlehem; and others across the mountains to Big Island in the West Branch of the Susquehanna.[15]

And about two weeks later, ten or twelve families from New England were comfortably planting themselves down at Wyoming, and a great many more were expected daily. They found the valley conveniently deserted, except for a few scattered Indians living here and there in the empty towns. Later in the month 150 more Connecticut settlers arrived, most of them persons who had been chased away the preceding fall by Tom King and Teedyuscung. They brought cattle with them this time, and seed corn, and that summer planted several hundred acres. They also set up massive blockhouses.[16]

The tradition has prevailed that it was the Six Nations, jealous of Teedyuscung's authority, who killed the "King." Charles Miner, the honest old historian of Wilkes-Barre (as the town founded by Connecticut settlers at Wyoming eventually came to be called), and himself a settler under a Connecticut grant, tells a tale of several Iroquois who for some weeks before the murder had been visiting Teedyuscung. They had been on friendly terms with their host, Miner suggests, in order to lull him into a false sense of security, and at the proper moment had set the town aflame.[17] Heckewelder, the great Moravian missionary, likewise intimated (although he avoided a definite statement) that it was the Six Nations who encompassed Teedyuscung's death. It was these Mingo visitors who had brought into the town the "fatal liquor" which was used to make the "King" drunk and was thus, to his mind, "instrumental to the execution of the design." But as to who the people were who employed the Mingo visitors, Heckewelder delicately hedged. They were Teedyuscung's enemies, "whoever they were."[18]

While of course it is impossible to prove that the Six Nations did not execute Teedyuscung, it is most improbable that they did. The presence of two Iroquois visitors in the town, with some rum, would be no remarkable circumstance: Six Nations hunters could be found scattered everywhere in the northeast; and Indian middlemen commonly carried black-market liquor to backwoods communities. The Six Nations had no reason now to kill Teedyuscung. He had been brought to admit their ownership of the Wyoming lands and their avunculate over himself and his band. In fact the Six Nations had a very good reason for wanting him alive. He was guarding their land; he had been repeatedly requested by them to remain at Wyoming; and the Six Nations were preparing to support his tenancy by force of arms. That the Six Nations would assassinate their chief tenant and disperse his people so as to make room for the entrance of their own enemies is so incredible an hypothesis that it may be dismissed from serious consideration. And anyway, the League of the Iroquois did not have police powers.

There does not seem to be much room for doubt that the Susquehanna Company was behind the murder of Teedyuscung and the remarkable simultaneous firing of the houses at Wyoming. Following his death, which occurred so conveniently for them, the charge was widely circulated that it was the Connecticut people who had murdered the Delaware "King."[19] The Six Nations accused the Connecticut men.[20] The Delawares themselves believed that the Yankees had committed the crime, enshrining Teedyuscung's memory in a verse of the Walam Olum:

But Tadeskung was chief in the east at *Mahoning* and bribed by the *Yankwis:* there he was burnt in his house, and many of our people were massacred at *Hickory* (Lancaster) by the Land robbers *Yankwis.*[21]

Six months after the murder, Teedyuscung's own son, Captain Bull, led the Delaware war party which massacred the Connecticut settlers at Wyoming.[22] The historian Miner himself said that Charles Thomson told him, in 1808, that he did not wonder that blood had been shed for such a beautiful valley; and Thomson gave Miner "a fact and an opinion," concerning the first massacre by Captain Bull's Indians, which the historian of Wilkes-Barre thought it "more prudent to omit than to tell"![23] And we have seen that ever since 1754 there had been developing the seeds of battle. High finance and international intrigue were involved; war had been predicted; the Susquehanna Company had publicly threatened to kill any Indians who stood in their way. In the end, Teedyuscung (and perhaps others unnamed) was killed, and immediately thereafter the settlement was completed.

It is difficult, therefore, to avoid the conclusion that the Susquehanna Company accomplished the murder of Teedyuscung. Probably the majority of the settlers did not realize the tactics which their leaders, whose schemes were concocted in secret caucuses, were using to gain the common end. But whether white thugs were the incendiaries, or whether the Company hired Munsee or Six Nations warriors to do the job, is a question of means, not of responsibility.

*   *   *

Although Teedyuscung had been killed, and Connecticut settlers were plowing up the land where he had walked, his ashes would not lie still. In the Ohio country the uprising of Pontiac was about to break forth; in the east, even among the faithful Mohawks, revenge was in preparation. By the end of the dark and bloody year 1763, no white men lived on the grassy plains of Wyoming.

On April 30 the Six Nations, perhaps not yet aware of the killing of their deputy at Wyoming, met in a general conference at Onondaga. They were "much alarmed" at the threatened seizure of the Delawares' plantations, and were expected by Johnson to take the matter into solemn consideration.[24] A month later a delegation from the Six Nations visited the

government of Connecticut at Hartford. There they stated
flatly that the deed which Lydius had procured at Albany
was illegal and invalid, and that they would not permit the
settlement of Wyoming on the strength of it. Governor Fitch
hypocritically replied that the Connecticut government had
already forbidden the settlement.[25]

Meanwhile Indian complaints about the Wyoming invasion were reaching Brother Onas. On June 2 Governor
Hamilton published a new proclamation forbidding the settlement and hinting that an Indian war would be the upshot
of an attempt at it. He also appointed Colonel James Burd
and the trader Thomas McKee to go up the river to turn the
trespassers off, if possible, by argument and expostulation.[26]

Burd and McKee were on the Susquehanna in a canoe,
just passing Kittatinny Falls above John Harris', when they
heard the first news of Pontiac's uprising in the west. The
long-threatened Indian war had begun. Fearing that Fort
Augusta would soon be under attack, they gave up their plan
and went no farther than Shamokin.[27]

The pious Quaker missionary, John Woolman, happened
to be at Wyoming when the first alarms about the western
uprising began to circulate. The remnant Indian community
there, of about twenty persons, including Teedyuscung's son
Captain Bull, were divided in council, some of them preparing to flee southward to the Moravian town of Nain;
others, up the river to the as yet pagan Papoonan's town near
Wyalusing; and a few, under Captain Bull, were going up
the West Branch of Susquehanna. They had heard exaggerated news of Indian successes in the western war: Detroit
they believed to have been already taken (actually, of course,
it was never reduced).[28] A day after Woolman's arrival,
the Moravian missionary David Zeisberger came hurrying
through the town on his way to Wyalusing. Zeisberger found
the Indians "in great Consternation not knowing wither they
moved"; but they were all "in Motion to leave the place."[29]
When Woolman, who also went on to Wyalusing, came back

to Wyoming on June 22, all the Indians were gone except one old man who inquired wistfully after Israel Pemberton.[30]

After their desertion of Wyoming, Captain Bull and his few followers repaired to Big Island, far up the West Branch, where Tapescawen, Teedyuscung's old councilor; Nutimus and his son Joseph; and at least thirty other Susquehanna Delaware warriors and sachems were living with their families. Toward the end of June, Burd invited them to Fort Augusta for a conference. They came, somber and quiet; they may have known that this was the last time that they would meet Brother Onas in friendship. When they were asked to tell what they knew about the conspiracy, the speaker replied sullenly, "I don't know nothing." It was a dour treaty, and at the end of it the speaker said, "My Boys want a little Powder I wish it could be come at more handily."[31]

In the summer the vicious circle of war swept down on the frontier settlements of Pennsylvania. It was the old story of 1755 and 1756 all over again: Indian raids; scalped corpses; burned plantations; prisoners and refugees; hysteria and frantic reprisals. In Carlisle, west of the Susquehanna, there was "not a Stable, Barn, or Hovel of any kind . . . that is not crowded with miserable Refugees." Fifty thousand acres of grain were left uncut in the fields of the province, to rot or to feed the Indian invaders.[32] In Cumberland County, the "unbridled and undistinguishing rage" of the people spurred Colonel Armstrong in September to undertake an expedition to Big Island, where Nutimus, Captain Bull, Tapescawen, and others of the Wyoming Delawares were now living. Hamilton was distressed to think that Nutimus, who had in general been a fast friend to the English (or so he thought), was to be sacrificed to the frenzy of the mob; if he had been able, he "would have protected the Old Man and his family from being butchered."[33] It seems that Nutimus and the rest of the Big Island community fortunately escaped. But Tapescawen, Captain Bull, Nutimus, and the rest of the pro-English Delawares came back to find their houses destroyed and their corn, on which they depended to live through the winter, burned by their friends the English.[34]

For Captain Bull, this was too much. Early in October he led a war party of Delawares into Northampton County, where they killed at least fifty-four persons.[35] (Bull later boasted that he had killed twenty-six white men with his own hands.) Then he led his warriors back to Wyoming, where his father had been murdered. They reached the Susquehanna Company's town on Saturday, the fifteenth.

The little village had been largely evacuated. Most of the settlers had gone back to safer country in the east, but between thirty and forty persons had remained behind. On them Captain Bull took his revenge. Nine men and one woman were tortured to death on the spot. The woman was roasted over a fire; red-hot hinges were inserted into the joints of her hands. "Several of the men had Awls thrust into their Eyes, and Spears, arrows, Pitchforks, &c sticking in their Bodies." The dead were scalped, and some of the houses burned; but the "immense quantity" of Indian corn which the settlers had planted was left undamaged. About twenty persons were led off into captivity. Only three or four of the population escaped death or capture.[36]

Captain Bull was taken prisoner by the whites later on during Pontiac's War. When he was asked why he had so savagely struck the English, he would make no answer. But he smiled.

Thomas Penn, in England, when he heard the story of what happened to the Connecticut settlers at Wyoming, expressed an opinion with which the historian may fairly agree. "I am concerned," he wrote, "for the fate of those deluded Connecticut people, tho the consequence of their own folly."[37]

*   *   *

The murder of Teedyuscung, and the consequent massacre of those who arranged for and profited from his death, provide a fitting climax to a story which is the epitome of the tragic relation of white man and red in America. The aggressiveness of the European and the industrial naïveté of the Indian made a real coöperation almost impossible, even though Indians like Teedyuscung tried to bridge the gap by imitating white culture patterns, and even though white men like Conrad Weiser the Indian agent, George Croghan the trader, and the Quakers tried to find a measure of common interest upon which to develop a healthy common society. On the whole, however, Teedyuscung, who could not read or write, and who was mercilessly ridden by the specter of his own inferiority, was somehow the only person able to sense the heart of the problem: to grasp the principle that while the "civilizing" of the Indian was inevitable, it had to be a process undergone peacefully, in security, on Indian land, in Indian communities, at the Indian's pace. The only other possible solution was ruthless dispersal and extermination: and from this even most white men recoiled.

But at Wyoming, extermination has been completed. Factories and slums sprawl blackly over the Great Meadows; mountains of coal throw their shadows on the river where the Indians cast their nets. The city of Wilkes-Barre, heart of the fabulously wealthy coal regions of Pennsylvania, looms over the ashes of Teedyuscung's Town. The fury of Captain Bull, who killed twenty-six white men[38] to avenge the death of his father, was a puny thing against the weight of the European leviathan. The victory of civilization at Wyoming was a foregone conclusion; and the Indians knew it even then.

In 1772 the last of the Susquehanna Delawares were forced out of their homes at Wyalusing by the endless encroachments of the Connecticut settlers, who had returned to the valley after Pontiac's War, and the Pennamites—rival settlers from Pennsylvania. These Wyalusing Indians had been converted by the assiduous David Zeisberger. But they still remembered Teedyuscung and his dream. As their boat floated slowly down the river past the infant town soon to be called Wilkes-Barre, they slowly tolled their chapel bell.[39] It was a requiem and a farewell to Teedyuscung, who had wanted to make Englishmen out of Indians, but had been killed by the English for refusing to allow white men to steal Indian lands.

Bibliographical References

The bibliographical references are intended primarily to document particular statements and quotations in the text, but the references can also be used as a partial bibliography of the major sources used in the preparation of the book. On the first occasion when a book, journal, or manuscript is cited, the full title and location data will be given; succeeding references will follow an abbreviated form. Reference numbers in the text follow the material to which they allude. Abbreviations frequently used in the citations are the following:

APS . . . Library of the American Philosophical Society, Philadelphia

CR . . . *Colonial Records* of Pennsylvania (Minutes of the Provincial Council of Pennsylvania)

GSP . . . Genealogical Society of Pennsylvania, Philadelphia. The library is located at the Historical Society of Pennsylvania.

HSP . . . Manuscripts Department, Historical Society of Pennsylvania, Philadelphia

LOC . . . Division of Manuscripts, Library of Congress, Washington, D. C.

MA . . . Moravian Archives, Bethlehem, Penna.

NYCD . . . *New York Colonial Documents*

PA . . . *Pennsylvania Archives*

PSA . . . Pennsylvania State Archives, Education Building, State Capitol, Harrisburg

RYM . . . Records of the Yearly Meeting of the Religious Society of Friends of Philadelphia and Vicinity (located at Friends' Book Store, Philadelphia)

CHAPTER I: THE DELAWARES

1. William C. Reichel (ed.), *Memorials of the Moravian Church* (Philadelphia: Lippincott, 1870), I, 217; *PA*, f.s., II, 724.
2. HSP, Board of Trade Papers, Proprieties, XXI-1, 243.
3. Reichel, *Memorials*, 217.
4. The foregoing account of the development of the fur trade

Chapter I: THE DELAWARES—*(Continued)*

and the early settlements along the Delaware River, and their effects on the Indians, is pieced together from scattered references in B. Fernow (ed.), *Documents Relating to the History of the Dutch and Swedish Settlements on the Delaware River* (Albany, 1867), and in Amandus Johnson (ed.), *Geographia Americae with an Account of the Delaware Indians Based on Surveys and Notes Made in 1654-1656 By Peter Lindestrom* (Philadelphia: Swedish Colonial Society, 1925).

5. The foregoing account of the land tenure and social organization of the Delaware Indians from 1600 to 1763 has been abridged from a separate article by the writer: "Woman, Land, and Society: Three Aspects of Aboriginal Delaware Life," *Pennsylvania Archaeologist,* XVII (1947), Nos. 1-4.

6. The aboriginal material culture of the Delawares is more fully described in M. R. Harrington, *Dickon Among the Lenape Indians* (Philadelphia: Winston, 1938).

7. A. B. Hulbert and W. N. Schwarze (eds.), *David Zeisberger's History of the Northern American Indians* (Ohio State Archaeological and Historical Society, 1910), p. 16.

8. John Heckewelder, *History, Manners, and Customs of the Indian Nations* . . . (Philadelphia: Historical Society of Pennsylvania, 1876), p. 115.

9. See A. I. Hallowell, "Some Psychological Characteristics of the Northeastern Indians," in Frederick Johnson (ed.), *Man in Northeastern North America* (Andover: Papers of the Robert S. Peabody Foundation for Archaeology, 1946), for a discussion of a type of personality structure, among the linguistically related Ojibwa, which seems to have been very similar to that of the Delawares.

10. Heckewelder, *History, Manners, and Customs,* p. 254.

Chapter II: THE WALKING PURCHASE

1. *PA,* f.s., III, 263; Julian P. Boyd (ed.), *Indian Treaties Printed by Benjamin Franklin, 1736-1762* (Philadelphia: Historical Society of Pennsylvania, 1938), p. 163.

2. Boyd, *Treaties,* 162.

3. Boyd, *Treaties,* 193.

4. Paul A. W. Wallace, *Conrad Weiser: Friend of Colonist and Mohawk* (Philadelphia: University of Pennsylvania Press, 1945), p. 441.

5. Fragmentary genealogical data on Teedyuscung's posterity

CHAPTER II: THE WALKING PURCHASE—*(Continued)*
are contained in Frank G. Speck, *The Celestial Bear Comes Down to Earth* (Reading: Reading Public Museum, 1945). The writer visited the Delaware community now living on the Six Nations Reserve in Ontario during the winter of 1946-1947.

6. HSP, Gratz Coll., Letters from Richard Peters to the Proprietors, p. 69.

7. *Ibid.,* p. 70.

8. James Sullivan (ed.), *The Papers of Sir William Johnson,* 9 vols. (Albany: University of the State of New York, 1921-1939), II, 788.

9. Wallace, *Weiser,* 441.

10. Reichel, *Memorials,* 217-218.

11. *Ibid.,* pp. 29, 219.

12. *Johnson Papers,* III, 779. Testimony by Teedyuscung in 1760.

13. HSP, Board of Trade Papers, Proprieties, XXI-1, 179. Copy of report of treaty made in 1734.

14. *Johnson Papers,* III, 779. Testimony of Teedyuscung in 1760.

15. HSP, Logan Papers, X, 64. Letter of James Logan to Conrad Weiser, Stenton, 18 October 1736.

16. HSP, Etting Coll., Misc. Mss, I, 94. "Moses Tattamie's Accot. of Indian Claims, taken from his mouth at Easton by I. P." No date; probably in 1757.

17. RYM, Papers Relating to the Friendly Association, etc., I, 406. A second, undated, manuscript giving Moses Tattamy's account of the Walking Purchase.

18. *Ibid.,* p. 407.

19. HSP, Logan Papers, X, 64. Logan to Weiser, 18 Oct. 1736.

20. *Johnson Papers,* III, 767. Testimony of Teedyuscung in 1760.

21. HSP, Logan Papers, X, 64. Logan to Weiser, 18 Oct. 1736.

22. Boyd, *Treaties,* xxvii.

23. The data concerning Logan's interest in, and the operating conditions of, Durham Furnace have been taken from Arthur C. Bining, *Pennsylvania Iron Manufacture in the Eighteenth Century* (Harrisburg: Pennsylvania Historical Commission, 1938).

24. *PA,* f.s., I, 540. Minutes of treaty made in 1737.

25. HSP, Board of Trade Papers, Proprieties, XXI-1, 199. This map is only a copy, undated, marked "copia vera." It is

CHAPTER II: THE WALKING PURCHASE—*(Continued)*

included with a series of copies of documents submitted to the Board of Trade by Sir William Johnson in 1762. Johnson at this time was trying to disprove charges of fraud in connection with the Walking Purchase, and had at his disposal primary sources from both Quaker and proprietary agents.

26. *PA,* f.s., I, 541-543.

27. *Ibid.;* PSA, Indian Deeds, 1679-1791, Room 220, Case 48B, Drawer IV.

28. RYM, Papers Relating to the Friendly Association, etc., I, 407. Moses Tattamy's account. Cf. fn. 16.

29. Wallace, *Weiser,* 97-99.

30. *Ibid.;* HSP, Etting Coll., Misc. Mss, I, 96. This and the following quotations and descriptions of the Walk are taken from affidavits, both pro- and anti-proprietary, made by eye-witnesses recalling the 1737 Walk twenty years later, in 1757. On the whole, the writer feels that the pro-Quaker documents do demonstrate that Nutimus and the Forks Indians were dissatisfied with the Walk as soon as it was performed; but they do not *prove* deliberate dishonesty in a technical sense by the proprietary agents (who were many of them, in 1737, Quakers themselves). The passage of years, and the probable political bias of all individuals concerned in 1757, would make sweeping judgments, based on these documents alone, rather uncertain.

31. *Ibid.*

32. HSP, Board of Trade Papers, Proprieties, XXI-1, 229.

33. *Ibid.,* p. 243.

34. Wallace, *Weiser,* 99.

35. HSP, Peters Mss, III, 4; Boyd, *Treaties,* xxviii.

36. HSP, Etting Coll., Misc. Mss, I, 97.

37. Wallace, *Weiser,* 98.

38. HSP, Etting Coll., Misc. Mss, I, 97.

39. *Ibid.*

40. *Ibid.,* p. 96.

41. HSP, Board of Trade Papers, Proprieties, XXI-1, 229. This testimony was made by Edward Marshall himself in 1757.

42. Wallace, *Weiser,* 99.

43. HSP, Gilpin Coll., Vb 321 (Vol. I, Supplement # 2, of privately edited copy of Thomson, *Alienation*).

44. Wallace, *Weiser,* 99.

CHAPTER III: "GIDEON"

1. HSP, Penn Mss, Indian Affairs, IV, 30.

CHAPTER III: "GIDEON"—*(Continued)*

2. *CR*, IV, 413.
3. Reichel, *Memorials,* 15, 26.
4. *Ibid.,* pp. 14-17.
5. Benjamin Franklin, *Autobiography,* winter of 1755.
6. Oscar J. Harvey, *A History of Wilkes-Barré,* 6 vols. (Wilkes-Barre, 1909-1930), I, 308.
7. Reichel, *Memorials,* 24-30.
8. Wallace, *Weiser,* 125.
9. Boyd, *Treaties,* 38.
10. *Ibid.,* pp. xxxi-xxxiv.
11. Boyd, *Treaties,* 35-36.
12. APS, Iroquois Traditional History and Constitution, 176.
13. *CR,* IV, 624-625.
14. Boyd, *Treaties,* xxxiv.
15. HSP, Penn Letter Books, II, 25.
16. A. F. Berlin, "Lehigh County Indian History," *The Pennsylvania-German,* XI (1910), 288-290.
17. PSA, Provincial Papers, XV, 57.
18. Wallace, *Weiser,* 277-285.
19. Frederick Johnson, "Count Zinzendorf and the Moravian and Indian Occupancy of the Wyoming Valley, 1742-1763," *Proceedings and Collections* of the Wyoming Historical and Geological Society, VIII (1902-1903), 172.
20. Boyd, *Treaties,* 237; HSP, Penn Letter Books, VI, 47.
21. Eugene Leibert, "Wechquetank," *Transactions* of the Moravian Historical Society, VII (1906), 60-63.
22. MA, Letter from Bishop Spangenberg to Conrad Weiser, Bethlehem, 10 May 1757.
23. Reichel, *Memorials,* 219.
24. George Henry Loskiel, *History of the Mission of the United Brethren among the Indians in North America,* tr. by C. I. La Trobe (London, 1794), II, 124.
25. Reichel, *Memorials,* 36; Leibert, "Wechquetank," 57-82.
26. Loskiel, *History,* II, 124; Reichel, *Memorials,* 36.
27. Reichel, *Memorials,* 220.
28. *Ibid.,* p. 265.
29. *Ibid.,* p. 252.
30. *Ibid.,* p. 34.
31. MA, Letter from Bishop Spangenberg to Conrad Weiser, Bethlehem, 10 May 1757.
32. Loskiel, *History,* II, 104-105; Reichel, *Memorials,* 34.
32a. APS, Horsfield Pp., II, 525.

CHAPTER III: "GIDEON"—*(Continued)*

33. Reichel, *Memorials*, 92.

34. The religious concepts, beliefs, and practices of the Delaware Indians have fortunately been thoroughly described by three ethnographers, who have taken pains not only to report their own researches, but to collate the fragmentary colonial sketches: M. R. Harrington, *Religion and Ceremonies of the Lenape* (New York: Museum of the American Indian, Heye Foundation, 1921); Vincenzo Petrullo, *The Diabolic Root, A Study of Peyotism, the New Indian Religion, Among the Delawares* (Philadelphia: University of Pennsylvania Press, 1934); Frank G. Speck, *A Study of the Delaware Indian Big House Ceremony* (Harrisburg: Pennsylvania Historical Commission, 1931); Frank G. Speck, *Oklahoma Delaware Ceremonies, Feasts and Dances* (Philadelphia: American Philosophical Society, 1937); Frank G. Speck, *The Celestial Bear Comes Down to Earth* (Reading: Reading Public Museum, 1945).

35. David Zeisberger, *History of the Northern American Indians*, ca. 1780, ed. by A. B. Hulbert and W. N. Schwarze (Ohio State Archaeological and Historical Society, 1910), pp. 132-133.

CHAPTER IV: FLIGHT FROM GRACE

1. Reichel, *Memorials*, 227.

2. Boyd, *Treaties.*

3. Harvey, *History of Wilkes-Barré*, I, 309.

4. Loskiel, *History*, II, 150.

5. *Ibid.*

6. Reichel, *Memorials*, 137.

7. Johnson, "Zinzendorf," 157.

8. *Ibid.*

9. HSP, Pennsylvania Archives 1758-1759, Frederick Post's Paper, Delivered with his Journal, 19th Jany 1759.

10. Johnson, "Zinzendorf," 119-182.

11. LOC, Archiv der Brüderunität, Herrnhut, Rep. 14. A., #18, p. 120.

12. Johnson, "Zinzendorf," 168-169; Loskiel, *History*, II, 144.

13. Charles Miner, *History of Wyoming* (Philadelphia: Crissy, 1845), p. 41.

14. HSP, Society Coll., Letter from Bishop Spangenberg to Conrad Weiser, Bethlehem, 30 July 1757.

15. MA, Letter from Bishop Spangenberg to Conrad Weiser, Bethlehem, 10 May 1757.

CHAPTER IV: FLIGHT FROM GRACE—*(Continued)*

16. Loskiel, *History,* II, 150.
17. MA, Letter from Bishop Spangenberg to Conrad Weiser, Bethlehem, 10 May 1757.
18. Julian P. Boyd (ed.), *The Susquehanna Company Papers,* 4 vols. (Wilkes-Barre: Wyoming Historical and Geological Society, 1930), I, 28-39.
19. *CR,* VI, 34-36; Boyd, *Susq. Co. Pp.,* I, 42-43, 288.
20. HSP, Penn-Physick Mss, Accounts, XI, 52.
21. LOC, Archiv der Brüderunität, Herrnhut, Rep. 14. A., #25, p. 28.
22. LOC, Archiv der Brüderunität, Herrnhut, Rep. 14. A., #27, pp. 119-120.
23. *CR,* VI, 24-25; PSA, Provincial Papers, XV, 57.
24. *CR,* VII, 432.
25. Reichel, *Memorials,* 220.
26. *Ibid.;* Loskiel, *History,* II, 150-151.
27. *Ibid.*
28. *CR,* VI, 34-36; PSA, Provincial Papers, XV, 57.
29. Johnson, "Zinzendorf," 170-171.
30. Boyd, *Susq. Co. Pp.,* I, 284-289.
31. Johnson, "Zinzendorf," 170-171.
32. Loskiel, *History,* II, 157; Miner, *History,* 43.
33. Loskiel, *History,* 158.

CHAPTER V: A HIGH WIND RISING

1. *CR,* VI, 128.
2. Loskiel, *History,* I, 136; Vernon Kinietz, *Delaware Culture Chronology* (Indianapolis: Indiana Historical Society, 1946), p. 124.
3. John Watson, *Annals of Philadelphia,* 3 vols. (Philadelphia: Stuart, 1898), II, 171.
4. *CR,* VII, 359-360.
5. *CR,* VI, 156.
6. HSP, Penn Letter Books, III, 291, 313.
7. HSP, Berks and Montgomery Counties, Misc. Mss, p. 55.
8. Wallace, *Weiser,* 350-363.
9. *CR,* VI, 119-123.
10. *Ibid.*
11. HSP, Correspondence of Conrad Weiser, I, 47.
12. *CR,* VI, 119.

CHAPTER V: A HIGH WIND RISING—(Continued)

13. *Johnson Papers, I*, 405.
14. Wallace, *Weiser*, 249.
15. Boyd, *Susq. Co. Pp.*, I, 47, 124, 128-129.
16. *PA*, f.s., II, 559.
17. HSP, Dreer Coll., Papers Rel. to French Refugees: French and Indian Affairs, p. 62.
18. Johnson, "Zinzendorf," 173.
19. *Ibid.*, pp. 173-179.
20. HSP, Correspondence of Conrad Weiser, I, 47.
21. *Ibid.;* HSP, Conrad Weiser's Account Book, p. 126.
22. LOC, Archiv der Brüderunität, Herrnhut, Rep. 14. A., #18, p. 378.
23. *Ibid.*
24. *CR*, VI, 215-217; HSP, Penn MSS, Indian Affairs, II, 22.
25. HSP, Penn-Physick Mss, Accounts, XI, 105.
26. *Ibid.*
27. *CR*, VI, 252-253.
28. *CR*, VI, 215-217.
29. "Daniel Claus' Narrative," *Society of Colonial Wars in the State of New York*, Vol. A, No. 9 (New York, 1907).
30. C. Z. Weiser, *The Life of Conrad Weiser* (Reading: Miller, 1876), pp. 188-189.
31. HSP, Penn-Physick Mss, Accounts, XI, 75.
32. *CR*, VI, 358.
33. *CR*, VI, 360-371.
34. *CR*, VII, 639.
35. *CR*, VI, 360-371.

CHAPTER VI: PETTICOATS, TOMAHAWKS, AND BLACK WAMPUM

1. *CR*, VI, 457-458.
2. Randolph C. Downes, *Council Fires on the Upper Ohio: A Narrative of Indian Affairs in the Upper Ohio Valley until 1795* (Pittsburgh: University of Pittsburgh Press, 1940), p. 76-78.
3. *CR*, VI, 443.
4. *Johnson Papers*, I, 633-641; *PA*, s.s., VI, 264-300.
5. *CR*, VI, 422-423; APS, Horsfield Papers, I, 97.
6. *CR*, VI, 588-591; PSA, Provincial Papers, XV, 57.
7. *CR*, VI, 615-616.
8. Theodore Thayer, *Israel Pemberton, King of the Quakers* (Philadelphia: Historical Society of Pennsylvania, 1943), p. 91.
9. *Johnson Papers*, II, 29.

CHAPTER VI: PETTICOATS, TOMAHAWKS, AND BLACK WAMPUM—*(Continued)*

10. *CR,* VI, 640-641.
11. HSP, Gratz Coll., Letters from Richard Peters to the Proprietors, p. 15.
12. *Historical Collections Relating to American Colonial History* (Hartford, 1871), p. 659; HSP, Richard Peters' Diary for December 1755.
13. HSP, Richard Peters' Diary for December 1755; *CR,* VI, 647.
14. HSP, Horsfield Letter Book, 1754, Am.083, Deposition of Schmick and Frey; Wallace, *Weiser,* 396-398.
15. *Ibid.;* Library Company of Philadelphia, Ridgway Branch, Du Simitiere Papers, Yi-966.
16. *CR,* VII, 47-51.
17. *CR,* VI, 656.
18. HSP, Penn Mss, Official Correspondence, VII, 147.
19. HSP, Richard Peters' Diary for December 1755.
20. Library Company of Philadelphia, Ridgway Branch, Du Simitiere Papers, Yi-966.
21. HSP, Horsfield Letter Book, 1754, Am.083, Deposition of Seidle and Zeisberger; PA, f.s., II, 459-461.
22. *CR,* VI, 690.
23. PSA, Provincial Papers, XV, 57.
24. *Ibid.; CR,* VI, 697.
25. HSP, Horsfield Letter Book, 1754, Am.083, Deposition of Schmick and Frey.
26. *Ibid.*
27. *Ibid.*
28. *Ibid.; Johnson Papers,* IX, 334-338; Charles Thomson, *An Enquiry into the Causes of the Alienation of the Delaware and Shawanese Indians from the British Interest* (London, 1759), pp. 82-83; Samuel Parrish, *Some Chapters in the History of the Friendly Association for Regaining and Preserving Peace with the Indians by Pacific Measures* (Philadelphia: Friends' Historical Association, 1877), p. 35.
29. APS, Horsfield Papers, II, 527.
30. *Johnson Papers,* IX, 335.
31. Boyd, *Treaties,* 158-159.
32. Loskiel, *History,* II, 165.
33. APS, Horsfield Papers, I, 61-63; HSP, Penn Mss, Indian Affairs, II, 51.
34. Reichel, *Memorials,* 211; APS, Horsfield Pp, I, 97.

CHAPTER VI: PETTICOATS, TOMAHAWKS, AND BLACK WAMPUM—(Continued)

35. *Johnson Papers,* IX, 335.
36. LOC, Archiv der Brüderunität, Herrnhut, Rep. 14. A., #18, p. 428.
37. Reichel, *Memorials,* 347-348.
38. *CR,* VI, 751-752.
39. *CR,* VI, 753-755; *Johnson Papers,* II, 368-371.
40. *CR,* VI, 756-764; HSP, Penn Mss, Indian Affairs, II, 50.
41. *CR,* VII, 12-14; HSP, Penn Mss, Indian Affairs, II, 101.
42. HSP, Penn Mss, Indian Affairs, II, 98.
43. *CR,* VII, 52.
44. Thomson, *Alienation,* 84; *CR,* VII, 66-67.
45. *Johnson Papers,* IX, 333-334; *CR,* VII, 67-68.
46. *CR,* VII, 66-67.
47. *CR,* VII, 49, 53.
48. *CR,* VII, 66.
49. Thomson, *Alienation,* 85-86; *CR,* VII, 46-55, 67-68.
50. *Johnson Papers,* IX, 334-338.
51. *NYCD,* VII, 456.
52. *CR,* VII, 12-14.
53. *PA,* f.s., III, 45.
54. *Ibid.*
55. *PA,* f.s., III, 45-46, 56-57.
56. *Ibid.*

CHAPTER VII: FEAR

1. HSP, Gratz Coll., Letters of Richard Peters to the Proprietors, p. 140.
2. Reichel, *Memorials,* 221; *PA,* s.s., VI, 376.
3. *PA,* s.s., VI (1890), 381.
4. *CR,* VII, 49
5. *Ibid.,* p. 53.
6. HSP, Penn Mss, Indian Affairs, II, 101.
7. HSP, Deposition of John Cox, 17 August 1756.
8. M. Pouchot, *Memoir upon the Late War in North America,* 2 vols., tr. by F. B. Hough (Roxbury, Mass., 1866), II, 149.
9. *CR,* VII, 51-55.
10. *Johnson Papers,* II, 439-440.
11. *Johnson Papers,* IX, 368.
12. *CR,* VII, 67-68.
13. Pouchot, *Memoir,* I, 59.

CHAPTER VII: FEAR—*(Continued)*

14. HSP, Penn Mss, Official Correspondence, VIII, 9.

15. *Johnson Papers,* IX, 347-394.

16. Boyd, *Treaties,* 178.

17. This account of the Otseningo conference has been compiled from several sources: Boyd, *Treaties,* 178, 227; *CR,* VII, 100; *Johnson Papers,* II, 444-445, IX, 424-425, 455-457, 477-478; Thomson, *Alienation,* 86-87.

18. *CR,* VII, 296-298; HSP, Gratz Coll., Letters from Richard Peters to Proprietors, p. 141.

19. Boyd, *Treaties,* lxxii-lxxiii; *PA,* f.s., II, 619.

20. *CR,* VII, 103.

21. Boyd, *Treaties,* 137-138; *Johnson Papers,* II, 452-454; LOC, Archiv der Brüderunität, Herrnhut, Rep. 14. A., #18, p. 348.

22. APS, Horsfield Papers, I, 115; LOC, Archiv der Brüderunität, Herrnhut, Rep. 14. A., #18, p. 348.

23. J. N. B. Hewitt and W. N. Fenton, "The Requickening Address of the Iroquois condolence council," *Journal of the Washington Academy of Sciences,* XXXIV (1944), 65-85; W. N. Fenton, "An Iroquois Condolence Council for installing Cayuga chiefs in 1945," *Journal of the Washington Academy of Sciences,* XXXVI (1946), 110-127.

24. APS, Horsfield Papers, I, 115-119.

25. *Archives of the State of New Jersey,* f.s., XX, 39-41.

26. HSP, Penn Mss, Indian Affairs, II, 89.

27. *Archives of the State of New Jersey,* f.s., XX, 42; *PA,* f.s., II, 670.

28. Boyd, *Treaties,* 139-141.

29. *CR,* VII, 175; APS, Horsfield Papers, I, 135; Thomson, *Alienation,* 90-91.

30. *PA,* f.s., III, 57.

31. *Johnson Papers,* IX, 456.

32. *PA,* f.s., II, 665-666.

33. *Johnson Papers,* II, 490.

34. Pouchot, *Memoir,* I, 80.

35. *Johnson Papers,* II, 510-513; Wallace, *Weiser,* 445; S. K. Stevens and D. H. Kent, *Wilderness Chronicles of Northwestern Pennsylvania* (Harrisburg: Pennsylvania Historical Commission, 1941), p. 95.

36. *Johnson Papers,* IX, 478.

37. *NYCD,* VII, 99-118.

CHAPTER VII: FEAR—(Continued)

38. *Ibid.*, pp. 141, 146.

39. *PA*, f.s., II, 683.

40. Thomson, *Alienation*, 91-94; *CR*, VII, 188; *NYCD*, VII, 149.

41. APS, Iroquois Traditional History and Constitution, pp. 176-177; Conrad Weiser, "A Memorial of the Six Nations, 1744," *The American Magazine*, December 1744.

42. The account of the treaty has been pieced together from several sources: Thomson, *Alienation*, 91-94; *Johnson Papers*, II, 499-500; *NYCD*, VII, 153 ff, 247-249.

43. *Johnson Papers*, II, 614.

44. HSP, Penn Mss, Indian Affairs, II, 101.

45. HSP, Gratz Coll., Letters of Richard Peters to the Proprietors, p. 69.

46. APS, Horsfield Papers, I, 177 ff.

47. HSP, Deposition of John Cox, 17 August 1756.

48. HSP, Gratz Coll., Edmonds, Case 1, Box 13; HSP, Northampton County, Misc. Mss, Bethlehem and Vicinity 1741-1849, p. 47.

49. HSP, Etting Coll., Pemberton Papers, II, 15; Reichel, *Memorials*, 232; Thomson, *Alienation*, 94-97.

50. Reichel, *Memorials*, 236.

51. *CR*, VII, 199.

52. *PA*, f.s., III, 210; *PA*, s.s., VI, 566.

53. *CR*, VII, 200.

CHAPTER VIII: HE WHO MAKES THE EARTH TREMBLE

1. The meaning of the name *Teedyuscung* is obscure. Not all Indian names were obviously descriptive titles like *Laughing Boy* and *Sitting Bull*. Like English names, Delaware names sometimes were a conventional pattern of meaningless syllables. Various translations of *Teedyscung* have, however, been suggested. John Pemberton, in the earliest recorded interpretation (1783), held for *one who makes the earth tremble* (HSP, B. S. Barton Mss Box, Commonplace Book). The Moravians called him *the war trumpet,* but this was probably only a nickname. G. P. Donehoo suggests *the healer* (*Handbook of American Indians North of Mexico,* Bureau of American Ethnology, Bulletin 30, Part 2, p. 714).

2. HSP, Gratz Coll., Letters from Richard Peters to the Proprietors, p. 69.

CHAPTER VIII: HE WHO MAKES THE EARTH TREMBLE—
(Continued)

3. Loskiel, *History*, II, 179; Reichel, *Memorials*, 348; Harvey, *Wilkes-Barre*, I, 327; Miner, *History*, 49-50. Loskiel gives the date July 1756; Reichel and Harvey agree on July 1757; and Miner asserts that 1758 was the year of the killing.

4. HSP, Gratz Coll., Letters from Richard Peters to the Proprietors, p. 69.

5. *PA*, f.s., II, 721-722.

6. HSP, Gratz Coll., Letters from Richard Peters to the Proprietors, p. 72.

7. This description of Teedyuscung's wardrobe and habitual style of living is a composite, culled from various sources ranging from 1756 to 1759. Reichel, *Memorials*, 229-366; HSP, Gratz Coll., Case 17, Box 7, An Account of Linnen, Thread, & Cambric . . . ; HSP, Account Book of Indian Commissioners at Shamokin, Ledger B, 2 June—15 December 1759; PSA, Provincial Papers, XXIV, 59; Pennsylvania Historical Commission, Journal of John Hayes, 1760.

8. Loskiel, *History*, II, 179.

9. C. Hale Sipe, *Indian Chiefs of Pennsylvania* (Butler, Pa., 1927), pp. 369-370.

10. MA, Observations, made on the Pamphlet, intituled, "an Inquiry into the Causes of the Alienation of the Delaware and Shawano-Indians from the British Intrest," by Conrad Weiser, Chiefly on Land Affairs, p. 2.

11. HSP, Pennsylvania Archives 1683-1749, List of Indian Delegates, 27 July 1756.

12. HSP, Gratz Coll., Letters from Richard Peters to the Proprietors, pp. 69-70.

13. Boyd, *Treaties*, lxxvii.

14. *Ibid.*

15. *CR*, VII, 205.

16. Parrish, *Some Chapters*, 18; Boyd, *Treaties*, 306.

17. Parrish, *Some Chapters*, 18-19.

18. Parrish, *Some Chapters*, 21.

19. Boyd, *Treaties*, 142.

20. *Ibid.*, pp. 144.

21. *Ibid.*, pp. 144-145, 148.

22. HSP, Pennsylvania Archives 1683-1749; Wallace, *Weiser*, 405.

23. Reichel, *Memorials*, 256; Wallace, *Weiser*, 447.

24. Wallace, *Weiser*, 447.

Chapter VIII: HE WHO MAKES THE EARTH TREMBLE—
(Continued)

25. Boyd, *Treaties*, 147.
26. Parrish, *Some Chapters*, 28.
27. Parrish, *Some Chapters*, 22.
28. HSP, Penn Letter Books, V, 17.
29. HSP, Gratz Coll., Letters from Richard Peters to Proprietors, pp. 69-70.

Chapter IX: THE MUTINY AT FORT ALLEN

1. *PA*, f.s., II, 748.
2. *PA*, f.s., III, 46.
3. APS, Horsfield Papers, II, 269.
4. The narrative of the intrigues of Lt. Miller and the mutiny at Fort Allen was compiled from Major Parsons' letter to the Governor of 14 August (*PA*, f.s., II, 745); Wetterholt's letters to Parsons of 6 August (*PA*, f.s., II, 754) and 11 August (APS, Horsfield Papers, II, 253); and Reynolds' letter of 11 August (HSP, Northampton County Misc. Mss, 1758-1767, p. 53).
5. APS, Horsfield Papers, II, 257.
6. APS, Horsfield Papers, II, 269.
7. *CR*, VII, 225; Reichel, *Memorials*, 263-264.
8. APS, Horsfield Papers, II, 285.
9. The account of Teedyuscung's conversations with Major Parsons is taken from: APS, Horsfield Papers, II, 285.
10. Wallace, *Weiser*, 473.
11. *Ibid.*, p. 454.

Chapter X: THIS LAND IS MY INHERITANCE

1. Reichel, *Memorials*, 264-265.
2. *Ibid.*
3. *CR*, VII, 224.
4. *Johnson Papers*, II, 555-556.
5. *PA*, s.s., VI, 523.
6. Reichel, *Memorials*, 261.
7. *CR*, VII, 244-245.
8. Wallace, *Weiser*, 457.
9. *CR*, VII, 270.
10. *CR*, VII, 431-433.
11. *CR*, VII, 342-343.
12. Howard H. Peckham, *Pontiac and the Indian Uprising* (Princeton: Princeton University Press, 1947), p. 31.
13. *CR*, VII, 431-433.

CHAPTER X: THIS LAND IS MY INHERITANCE—*(Continued)*

14. *PA*, f.s., III, 44-45; *CR*, VII, 286.
15. *PA*, f.s., III, 5-6; *CR*, VII, 267, 278, 285.
16. *CR*, VII, 286-288.
17. *CR*, VII, 281-282.
18. *CR*, VII, 267-268.
19. Wallace, *Weiser*, 458.
20. *Ibid.*
21. *CR*, VII, 305.
22. Wallace, *Weiser*, 458.
23. *CR*, VII, 308-310.
24. *Ibid.*
25. *PA*, f.s., III, 32-35.
26. Boyd, *Treaties*, 153.
27. *CR*, VII, 309-310.
28. Boyd, *Treaties*, 150.
29. Boyd, *Treaties*, 151.
30. *CR*, VII, 431-433.
31. *Ibid.*
32. Boyd, *Treaties*, 154.
33. MA, Weiser's Observations.
34. *Ibid.*
35. Boyd, *Treaties*, 157.
36. *Ibid.*
37. MA, Weiser's Observations.
38. Boyd, *Treaties*, 163.
39. Boyd, *Treaties*, 165.
40. Parrish, *Some Chapters,* 40.
41. Reichel, *Memorials,* 274.
42. *PA*, f.s., III, 66.

CHAPTER XI: QUAKER POLITICS AND PROPRIETARY HONOR

1. *PA*, f.s., III, 66-68.
2. *Ibid.*
3. *Ibid.*
4. *CR*, VII, 357-358.
5. *Johnson Papers*, II, 657.
6. This analysis of the diplomatic crisis precipitated by Teedyuscung's charges of fraud is based on Wallace, *Weiser,* and on Boyd's essay, "Indian Affairs in Pennsylvania 1736-1762," which serves as the introduction to the *Treaties.*
7. *Johnson Papers*, II, 776-777.

CHAPTER XI: QUAKER POLITICS AND PROPRIETARY
HONOR—*(Continued)*

8. Thayer, *Pemberton,* 159.

9. This analysis of the motives which impelled Pemberton
and his colleagues to support Teedyuscung's charges of fraud is
based on Thayer, *Pemberton.*

10. Parrish, *Some Chapters,* 97.

11. John Watson, *Annals of Philadelphia,* 3 vols. (Philadelphia: Stuart, 1898), II, 171.

12. Wallace, *Weiser,* 510.

13. HSP, Private Pennsylvania Mss, 6 boxes, 3rd floor, uncatalogued.

14. HSP, Board of Trade Papers, Proprieties, XXI-1, 263.

15. HSP, Board of Trade Papers, Proprieties, XXI-1, 279.

16. Harvey, *Wilkes-Barre,* I, 309.

17. *CR,* VI, 710.

18. Boyd, *Treaties,* 158.

19. The actual charges expressed by Teedyuscung varied considerably from time to time, depending on the situation in which
the Delaware chief was speaking. The abstract of the charges
given here has been pieced together out of his various statements
at the series of treaties and conferences from 1756 to 1762, as
printed in the *Colonial Records, Pennsylvania Archives,* f.s.,
and Boyd's *Treaties.*

20. The proprietary defense (as of 6 January 1758) is printed
in *CR,* VIII, 246-261.

21. *Johnson Papers,* III, 778.

22. Wallace, *Weiser,* 125-132.

23. *Johnson Papers,* III, 847.

24. MA, Weiser's Observations.

25. *Johnson Papers,* III, 778.

26. GSP, Bringhurst, Claypoole, Evans, Foulke, and Parker
Papers, pp. 489-490.

27. Wallace, *Weiser,* and Thayer, *Pemberton,* give careful
day-by-day accounts of these and succeeding treaties, paying
special attention to the methods of the Quaker lobbyists in
influencing Teedyuscung and the Delawares.

CHAPTER XII: THE LAND AFFAIR WHICH IS DIRT

1. *Johnson Papers,* IX, 618.

2. *Johnson Papers,* IX, 592.

3. *CR,* VII, 429.

CHAPTER XII: THE LAND AFFAIR WHICH IS DIRT—
(Continued)

4. *CR,* VII, 474-475.
5. *CR,* VII, 477-478.
6. Boyd, *Treaties,* 173.
7. Boyd, *Treaties,* 175.
8. Boyd, *Treaties,* 182.
9. *CR,* VII, 296-298.
10. *Wilderness Chronicles,* 106.
11. *Wilderness Chronicles,* 107-108.
12. *Ibid.*
13. *CR,* VII, 587-590.
14. Wallace, *Weiser,* 472.
15. The day-by-day events of the treaty are narrated in Wallace, *Weiser,* 472-487.
16. *CR,* VII, 651-652.
17. Boyd, *Treaties,* 200.
18. HSP, Correspondence of Conrad Weiser, II, 77; Wallace, *Weiser,* 479.
19. HSP, Gratz Coll., Case 14, Box 30, Thomson's Letters.
20. Boyd, *Treaties,* 196.
21. Boyd, *Treaties,* 203.
22. HSP, Pemberton Papers, XII, 55.
23. *PA,* f.s., III, 257.
24. Boyd, *Treaties,* 205.
25. Boyd, *Treaties,* 204.
26. Boyd, *Treaties,* 307.

CHAPTER XIII: PEACE IN THE WEST

1. APS, Horsfield Papers, I, 115-119.
2. *Johnson Papers,* II, 752.
3. *CR,* VII, 724.
4. Reichel, *Memorials,* 343.
5. *CR,* VII, 734-735.
6. *CR,* VII, 773.
7. PSA, Provincial Papers, XXIV, 59.
8. HSP, Col. James Burd's Journal at Fort Augusta, 14 October—21 November 1757, entries under 21-24 October.
9. *CR,* VII, 773.
10. APS, Indian and Military Affairs of Pennsylvania, 1737-1775, p. 583.
11. *Johnson Papers,* II, 770.

CHAPTER XIII: PEACE IN THE WEST—*(Continued)*

12. PSA, Provincial Papers, XXVI, 11-f.
13. *CR*, VII, 773.
14. HSP, Etting Coll., Pemberton Papers, II, 48.
15. *PA*, f.s., III, 433.
16. Reichel, *Memorials*, 365.
17. Reichel, *Memorials*, 326.
18. PSA, Provincial Papers, XXVI, 11-f.
19. *CR*, VII, 773-774.
20. Pouchot, *Memoir*, I, 77-80.
21. Pouchot, *Memoir*, I, 92-93.
22. *Johnson Papers*, II, 753-754.
23. *CR*, VII, 735-736.
24. *NYCD*, VII, 331.
25. *CR*, VII, 762-763.
26. *Johnson Papers*, II, 753-754.
27. Christopher Saur, *Pensylvanische Berichte*, 18 February 1758.
28. *PA*, f.s., III, 333-334.
29. *PA*, f.s., III, 350-351; *Johnson Papers*, II, 787.
30. LOC, Archiv der Brüderunität, Herrnhut, Rep. 14. A., #27, p. 160.
31. Christopher Saur, *Pensylvanische Berichte*, 18 March 1758.
32. *CR*, VIII, 29-31.
33. *CR*, VIII, 32; HSP, Correspondence of Conrad Weiser, II, 127.
34. Public Record Office (London), C.O.5, 50, p. 161.
35. *Ibid.*
36. *CR*, VIII, 32-57; *Johnson Papers*, II, 826.
37. *Johnson Papers*, II, 785.
38. Christopher Saur, *Pensylvanische Berichte*, 1 April 1758.
39. Francis-J. Audet, *Jean-Daniel Dumas, L'Hero du Monongahela* (Montreal, 1920), p. 91.
40. *CR*, VIII, 86-96.
41. *CR*, VIII, 84-85.
42. *CR*, VIII, 98-99.
43. *Ibid.*
44. HSP, Peters Mss, V, 42.
45. *Wilderness Chronicles*, 114.
46. *Ibid.*
47. Harvey, *Wilkes-Barre*, I, 370.

CHAPTER XIV: THE DREAM

1. Boyd, *Treaties,* 196.
2. Boyd, *Treaties,* 197-198.
3. Thomson, *Alienation,* frontispiece; *Johnson Papers,* II, 754.
4. *Ibid.*
5. APS, Correspondence of Thomas and Richard Penn, 609-612.
6. Reichel, *Memorials,* 346-348.
7. HSP, Bartram Papers, I, 44.
8. Parrish, *Some Chapters,* 36-37.
9. HSP, Penn Mss, Indian Affairs, III, 26; *Johnson Papers,* II, 752-753.
10. *Ibid.*
11. Boyd, *Treaties,* 307; HSP, Richard Peters' Journal to Easton in 1758, entry of 25 October.
12. *Johnson Papers,* II, 753.
13. Boyd, *Treaties,* 307; HSP, Penn Mss, Indian Affairs, III, 26.
14. *Johnson Papers,* II, 754.
15. *CR,* VII, 756.
16. Reichel, *Memorials,* 354.
17. PSA, Provincial Papers, XXVI, 11-f.
18. HSP, Hildeburn Indian Papers, Box, uncatalogued, 2nd floor.
19. *CR,* VII, 770-771; *PA,* f.s., III, 304-319.
20. *PA,* f.s., III, 385; *CR,* VIII, 101-102, 110-115.
21. *CR,* VIII, 110.
22. Irene Stewart (ed.), *Letters of General John Forbes relating to the expedition against Fort Duquesne in 1758* (Pittsburgh: Allegheny County Committee of the Pennsylvania Society of the Colonial Dames of America, 1927), p. 17.
23. Reichel, *Memorials,* 365.
24. The narrative of the building of Teedyuscung's town has been compiled from: *CR,* VIII, 134-135; John Watson, *Annals of Philadelphia,* II, 127; Joseph H. Coates, "Journal of Isaac Zane to Wyoming, 1758," *The Pennsylvania Magazine of History and Biography,* XXX (1906), 417-426.
25. *PA,* f.s., III, 415.
26. *CR,* VIII, 125-128.
27. *PA,* f.s., III, 414.
28. *CR,* VIII, 129-134.
29. *PA,* f.s., III, 420.

CHAPTER XIV: THE DREAM—(Continued)

30. *CR,* VIII, 138-139, 142-145; Randolph C. Downes, *Council Fires on the Upper Ohio* (Pittsburgh: University of Pittsburgh Press, 1940), pp. 84-85.

CHAPTER XV: A BIRD ON A BOUGH

1. *CR,* VIII, 151.

2. *Johnson Papers,* II, 749-750.

3. *Johnson Papers,* III, 4.

4. RYM, Papers Relating to the Friendly Association, etc., I (1756-1758), 407.

5. *PA,* f.s., III, 544.

6. APS, Iroquois Traditional History and Constitution, pp. 175-177.

7. *Ibid.*

8. See Anthony F. C. Wallace, "Woman, Land, and Society: Three Aspects of Aboriginal Delaware Life," Section II (The Status of the Delaware Indians in the Iroquois Confederacy), *Pennsylvania Archaeologist,* XVII (1947), Nos. 1-4, for a review of the Delawares-as-women question.

9. HSP, Richard Peters' Journal to Easton in 1758, entry of 29 September.

10. *Ibid.,* entry of 30 September.

11. MA, Weiser's Observations.

12. HSP, Richard Peters' Journal to Easton in 1758, entry of 9 October.

13. Boyd, *Treaties,* 315.

14. Samuel Smith, *The History of the Colony of Nova-Caesaria, or New Jersey,* Burlington, 1765 (Trenton: State of New Jersey, 1877), pp. 440-441.

15. HSP, Logan Papers, Blue Logan Letter Books, III, 203.

16. HSP, Richard Peters' Journal to Easton in 1758, entry of 12 October.

17. HSP, Pemberton Papers, XIII, 1.

18. HSP, B. S. Barton Mss, Box, Commonplace Bk., Journal of a Voyage from Gravesend to Philadelphia, 1789.

19. The foregoing account of the treaty proceedings is compiled from: Boyd, *Treaties,* 213-243, 312-318; Wallace, *Weiser,* 520-552, except where otherwise noted.

20. HSP, Correspondence of Conrad Weiser, II, 143.

21. RYM, Indian Records (Mss), 1502-1800, D1, pp. 279-280.

CHAPTER XVI: THE FORBIDDEN TRAIL

1. Peckham, *Pontiac,* 50.
2. HSP, Penn Letter Books, VI, 89.
3. HSP, Benjamin Lightfoot's Notes of a Survey of a Road from Fort Henry (Pottsville) to Shamokin, 1759, Am. 269.
4. *CR,* VIII, 353.
5. *Johnson Papers,* III, 33-36.
6. *Wilderness Chronicles,* 150-153; S. K. Stevens and D. H. Kent (eds.), *The Papers of Col. Henry Bouquet* (Harrisburg: Pennsylvania Historical Commission, 1943), Vol. XVI, Series 21655, p. 54.
7. *Wilderness Chronicles,* 126.
8. Nicholas B. Wainwright (ed.), "George Croghan's Journal, 1759-1763," *The Pennsylvania Magazine of History and Biography,* LXXI (1947), 305-444, p. 346.
9. John W. Jordan, "James Kenny's 'Journal to Ye Westward,' 1758-59," *The Pennsylvania Magazine of History and Biography,* XXXVII (1913), p. 438.
10. *CR,* VIII, 403-406.
11. HSP, Penn Mss, Official Correspondence, IX, 126.
12. *CR,* VIII, 401.
13. *CR,* VIII, 414-425.
14. *PA,* f.s., III, 698.
15. *CR,* VIII, 435-436.
15a. Diary of John Hays, May-June 1760. Ms copy prepared by the Pennsylvania Historical Commission.
15b. A. M. Gummere (ed.), *The Journal and Essays of John Woolman* (New York: Macmillan, 1922); Janet Whitney, *John Woolman: American Quaker* (Boston: Little, Brown, 1942).
16. *PA,* f.s., III, 717-718.
16a. The religious ceremonies at Assinisink are vividly described in two manuscript journals which I have seen through the courtesy of the Pennsylvania Historical Commission, who prepared copies; Journal of Christian Frederick Post, April 1-June 30, 1760; Diary of John Hays, May-June, 1760.
17. There are two journals, neither of them fully printed, which tell the story of Teedyuscung's trip up to Pasigachkunk with Post and Hays. Part of Hays's journal is printed: *PA,* f.s., III, 734-744; and a copy of the Ms original is in the custody of the Pennsylvania Historical Commission. Several copies of Post's own journal, with his barbaric English spelling corrected by the

CHAPTER XVI: THE FORBIDDEN TRAIL—*(Continued)*
eighteenth- or nineteenth-century transcriber, exist in manuscript. The copy used by the writer is located at: GSP, Bringhurst, Claypoole, Evans, Foulke, and Parker Papers, Part II, 477-495.

18. Croghan, "Journal," 380.
19. *CR*, VIII, 497-501.
20. HSP, Penn Letter Books, VI, 305, 311-314.
21. *PA*, f.s., IV, 40.
22. GSP, Post's Journal, entry of 4 June.
23. *Ibid.*, entry of 17 June.

CHAPTER XVII: POWDER FAMINE

1. *PA*, f.s., IV, 58.
2. *CR*, VIII, 500-501.
3. *CR*, VIII, 564-572.
4. HSP, Penn Mss, Wyoming Controversy, 1731-1775, p. 61.
5. *CR*, VIII, 595.
6. *CR*, VIII, 612-614.
7. *Johnson Papers*, III, 391-392.
8. *Ibid.*
9. *CR*, VIII, 594-601.
10. *PA*, f.s., IV, 67.
11. *Ibid.*, p. 66.
12. Boyd, *Treaties*, 247-262.
13. *Ibid.*
14. HSP, Penn Letter Books, VII, 61-62; APS, Correspondence of Thomas and Richard Penn.
15. *CR*, VIII, 659-661.
16. GSP, Post's Journal, entries of 19-20 May.
17. APS, Diaries, Fort Augusta, 17 February to 17 November 1760.
18. Albert T. Volwiler, *George Croghan and the Westward Movement, 1741-1782*. (Cleveland: Clark, 1926), p. 149.
19. *Bouquet Papers*, Series 21646, pp. 75-76.
20. Francis Parkman, *The Conspiracy of Pontiac and the Indian War after the Conquest of Canada*, sixth ed., 1870, 2 vols. (Boston: Little, Brown, 1898), I, 180-182.
21. The foregoing discussion of the Indian situation from 1758 to 1762 has been based to a considerable extent on Volwiler's biography of George Croghan. The inferences concerning the function of intoxication among the Indians have been stimu-

CHAPTER XVII: POWDER FAMINE—*(Continued)*

lated by A. I. Hallowell's article, "Some Psychological Characteristics of the Northeastern Indians" (cf. Ch. I, fn. 6).

22. Volwiler, *Croghan,* 146, 152.

23. *Wilderness Chronicles,* 215-216, 229.

24. Peckham, *Pontiac,* 98-101, 113-116; Parkman, *Conspiracy
of Pontiac,* I, 186-187.

25. APS, Horsfield Papers, II, 437.

26. APS, Horsfield Papers, II, 441-445.

27. Loskiel, *History,* II, 196-197.

28. *CR,* VIII, 663-664.

29. Boyd, *Susq. Co. Pp.,* II, 119.

30. Boyd, *Susq. Co. Pp.,* II, 130-134; HSP, Board of Trade
Papers, Proprieties, XXI-2, #28, Mr. Sayres' Account.

CHAPTER XVIII: ROYAL INVESTIGATION

1. *Johnson Papers,* III, 837.

2. *CR,* VIII, 507.

3. *PA,* f.s., VI, 611.

4. *CR,* VIII, 507-508.

5. Boyd, *Treaties,* 254.

6. Boyd, *Treaties,* 260.

7. *Johnson Papers,* III, 686.

8. *PA,* f.s., IV, 74-75; APS, Horsfield Papers, I, 450.

9. *Johnson Papers,* III, 689.

10. *PA,* f.s., IV, 78.

11. *CR,* VIII, 707-708.

12. *Johnson Papers,* III, 745-746.

13. *PA,* f.s., IV, 80-81.

14. *Johnson Papers,* III, 760.

15. *Ibid.; PA,* f.s., IV, 80.

16. *PA,* f.s., IV, 81-82.

17. Thayer, *Pemberton,* 178.

18. HSP, B. S. Barton Mss, Box, Commonplace Book, Journal
of a Voyage from Gravesend to Philadelphia, 1789.

19. Except as otherwise noted, the narrative of the proceedings of the treaty has been drawn entirely from the accounts in:
Johnson Papers, III, 760-818, 837-852.

20. *Johnson Papers,* III, 823.

21. See Theodore Thayer, "The Quaker Party of Pennsylvania,
1755-1765," *The Pennsylvania Magazine of History and Biography,* LXXI (1947), pp. 19-43, for a concise account of Quaker
political principles in Pennsylvania.

CHAPTER XIX: DEATH IN THE VALLEY

1. HSP, Ledger A (1762) of the Indian Commissioners at Fort Augusta, p. 118.

2. *CR*, VIII, 499.

3. Lebanon Valley College, Montgomery Transcripts, Beylage zum 31ten Stück des Philadelphisches Staatsboten, Monday 16 August and 11 November 1762.

4. HSP, Penn Mss, Official Correspondence, IX, 184.

5. Cf. Bronislaw Malinowski, *The Dynamics of Culture Change* (New Haven: Yale University Press, 1945), Ch. IX, "Reflections on Witchcraft"; John J. Honigman, "Witch-Fear in Post-Contact Kaska Society," *American Anthropologist*, n.s., IL (1947), 222-243.

6. Loskiel, *History*, II, 197-198.

7. The account of the treaty is taken from: Boyd, *Treaties*, 263-298, 318-421.

8. Boyd, *Susq. Co. Pp.*, II, 166-169; Miner, *History*, 53; Harvey, *Wilkes-Barre*, I, 402.

9. Boyd, *Susq. Co. Pp.*, II, 166-169.

10. *CR*, IX, 6-9.

11. Boyd, *Susq. Co. Pp.*, II, 326.

12. *CR*, IX, 6-9.

13. John W. Jordan, "James Kenny's 'Journal to Ye Westward,' 1758-59," *The Pennsylvania Magazine of History and Biography*, XXXVII (1913), p. 186.

14. Boyd, *Susq. Co. Pp.*, II, 122-123; *Johnson Papers*, IV, 74-75.

15. Loskiel, *History*, II, 203; Reichel, *Memorials*, 71; Johnson, "Zinzendorf," 147; Miner, *History*, 53; APS, Correspondence of Thomas and Richard Penn, 700. These sources give substantially concurrent accounts of the facts of the murder and the burning of the town, although Reichel sets the date at 19 April.

16. Boyd, *Susq. Co. Pp.*, II, 221; Harvey, *Wilkes-Barre*, I, 414, 425-426.

17. Miner, *History*, 53.

18. Heckewelder, *History, Manners, and Customs of the Indian Nations Who Once Inhabited Pennsylvania and the Neighbouring States*, 1819, p. 305.

19. Johnson, "Zinzendorf," 147.

20. Reuben Gold Thwaites (ed.), *Early Western Journals (1748-1765)*, Vol. I of *Early Western Travels* series (Cleveland: Clark, 1904), pp. 186-187, fns. 11-12.

CHAPTER XIX: DEATH IN THE VALLEY—*(Continued)*

21. C. S. Rafinesque, *The American Nations or Outlines of their General History* (Philadelphia, 1836), I, 143.

22. Johnson, "Zinzendorf," 147.

23. Miner, *History,* 49.

24. Boyd, *Susq. Co. Pp.,* II, 215.

25. Boyd, *Susq. Co. Pp.,* II, 236-241.

26. *CR,* IX, 27-30.

27. HSP, Shippen Family Papers, VI, 17.

28. HSP, Pemberton Papers, XVI, 109; A. M. Gummere (ed.), *The Journal and Essays of John Woolman* (New York; Macmillan, 1922), 156-159.

29. APS, Horsfield Papers, II, 455.

30. HSP, Pemberton Papers, XVI, 109.

31. *PA,* s.s., VII (1895), 461-462; HSP, Shippen Family Papers, VI, 29.

32. HSP, Peters Mss, VI, 10.

33. APS, Horsfield Papers, II, 483.

34. APS, Correspondence of Thomas and Richard Penn, 719.

35. *PA,* s.s., VII (1895), 475-476.

36. *PA,* f.s., IV, 125-127; Boyd, *Susq. Co. Pp.,* II, 277, 282; *PA,* s.s., VII, 475-476; Historical Society of Dauphin County, Parson Elder Papers, Elder to Governor Hamilton, 30 September 1763.

37. APS, Correspondence of Thomas and Richard Penn, 722.

38. *Johnson Papers,* IV, 369.

39. Johnson, "Zinzendorf," 181-182.

Index

INDEX

303

Tachgokanhelle, Teedyuscung's son, 41

Tagashata, Seneca chief, at Easton treaty of 1758, 196 f.; interrupted by Teedyuscung, 200-202

Tanacharison, Seneca chief, 58

Tapescawen, Teedyuscung's counselor, 66, 151, 155, 170, 253, 263

Tattamy, Bill, Delaware Indian, 156

Tattamy, Joseph, Delaware Indian, 131 f.

Tattamy, Moses, Delaware Indian, 20, 28, 34 f., 37 f., 129 f., 133, 150, 157, 170, 213 f., 219; opinion of Teedyuscung, 138

Taughhaughsey, Delaware Indian, 25

Tawa Indians, 171

Teedyuscung, birth, parents, and siblings, 2; early life in New Jersey, 2, 18 f.; removal to Forks of Delaware, 19 f.; at Durham treaty in 1734, 20; at Pennsbury treaty in 1735, 21; first hears Moravians preach, 34; converted by Moravians and lives at Gnadenhütten, 39-41; lets father starve to death, 42; motives in becoming a Christian, 42-44; influence of Moravians on, 45-47; leaves Gnadenhütten for Wyoming, 47-54; accompanies Paxinosa to Gnadenhütten in 1754, 54; at Albany Congress in 1754, 56-58; welcomes missionaries to Wyoming, 63; at treaty in Philadelphia in 1755, 66; undecided on his position in French and Indian War, 67-76; attacks white settlements, 80-86; tribal composition of his followers, 87; visits Canyase, 92; acts as speaker at Tioga conference,

94 f.; returns to Pasigachkunk to plant corn, 96; visits Niagara, 96 f.; visits daughter of French Margaret, 100; goes to Easton, 100-102; at first Easton treaty of 1756, 103-15; style of dress, 105; and mutiny at Fort Allen, 116-23; calls council at Tioga in 1756, 126; at second Easton treaty of 1756, 126-36; charges Pennsylvania with fraud in Walking Purchase, 133-35; puffed up by Quaker esteem, 143; motives behind his charges of fraud, 146-48; visits Niagara in 1757, 151-55; at Easton treaty of 1757, 155-60; accompanies Ohio messengers to Philadelphia, 167-72; demands tribal reservation, 176-78; talks with Spangenberg, 178-80; and building of houses at Wyoming, 184-89; his policy in 1758, 192; at Easton treaty of 1758, 192-207; visits Ohio country, 210 f.; fights with Croghan, 211; at treaty in Philadelphia in 1759, 212; trip to Pasigachkunk and the Ohio, 213-22; loss of influence with Indians, 222 f.; threatens Connecticut people in 1760, 223-28; at Easton treaty of 1761, 225-28; predicts war, 237; and final settlement of Walking Purchase charges, 240-51, 252 f.; charges whites with poison attempt, 254; resists Susquehanna Company in 1762, 255-58; murdered, 258-61

Theodora, niece of Teedyuscung, 120

Thirty Years' War, 32

Thomas, George, Governor of Pennsylvania, 38

Thomson, Charles, 195, 261; appointed clerk to Teedyuscung,

Weiser, Conrad, 23, 47, 51, 60, 62, 64, 86, 90, 93, 112, 114, 137, 143-45, 152, 157-59, 167, 170, 175, 196 f., 202, 265; at second Easton treaty of 1756, 128-36; opinion of Teedyuscung, 137 f.

Weiser, Sammy, 51, 54

Welagameka, Delaware settlement, 20, 23

White, John, 118

White, Robert, 225

Whitefield, George, 31 f.

Wilkes-Barre, 261, 265 f.

Wills Creek, murders at, 67

Windham, Conn., 50

Woodbridge, Timothy, 61, 258

Woolman, John, 262 f.

Wright, James, 72

Wyalusing, Delaware settlement, 222, 262, 265 f.

Wyandot (Huron) Indians, 241

Wycliffe, John, 32

Wyoming, removal of Gnadenhütten Indians to, 47-55; deserted, 84; repopulated and redeserted, 88; villages burned, 95; plan to build English fort there, 96; building houses, 184-90; Teedyuscung demands Six Nations give Delawares deed to, 206 f., 226-28; Susquehanna Company votes to settle, 238; invasion in 1762 by Susquehanna Company, 254-58; town burned in 1763, 258-61; deserted by Indians, 262 f.; massacre at, 264

Wyoming Indians, mixed bands of Delawares, Mahicans, Shawnees, et al., status before increment from Gnadenhütten, 48, 55; uneasy about Connecticut purchase, 64-66; maintain anxious neutrality, 67-69, 73-77; attack Pennsylvania, 78 f.; dietary, 215; reaction to Teedyuscung's assumption of authority, 215 f.; desert Wyoming after Teedyuscung's death, 262-63

Yeats, James, 28

Zander, Moravian missionary, 34

Zane, Isaac, 136, 187

Zeisberger, David, 12, 14, 44, 241, 262, 265

Zinzendorf, Count, 32-35, 38, 47-53, 180

4969　　　　　3292